ABOUT THE AUTHOR

Wendy James is an Australian-born journalist and writer, living in the UK since 1966. Since she retired, she is mostly known by her married name Wendy Dear.

Oh Mr Dunbar,
if only I'd known

A Life in Magazines

A MEMOIR

BY WENDY JAMES

John Dunbar, the Editorial Director of Odhams in the 1930s,
was a man with a strong social conscience, and he thought
Woman magazine should have one, too. As a result, its sales
dropped like a stone, and it was not until he had accepted the
facts of magazine life that the circulation began to rise. No
one working on women's magazines should ever forget this.

Back cover photographs

Top row, l to r: Woman magazine, © IPC 1987; Colin Thomas, ©IPC Magazines 1984; ©Whinfrey Strachan Ltd/Rigby International Ltd 1982; © Astra Press 1974

2nd row, l to r: © Choice Publications 1993; © 1973 Wendy James and Susan Kedgley, Abelard-Schuman Ltd; Dave Elliott, © 1980 Orbis Publishing Ltd; Roger Tuff, © September 1974 Astra Press Ltd;

3rd row, l to r: © IPC 1974; Bradford & Bingley 1991; © Choice Publications Ltd 1990

4th row, l to r: Art Kane, © 1988 Lear Publishing; © IPC Magazines 1974; Wendy James personal photo

5th row: Michael Leale, © BPC Publishing Ltd 1970; Laurie Purden personal photo 1991; Bryce Attwell, © National Magazine Co Ltd; © 1990 Choice Publications 1990

❀ Created with Vellum

For Ian, Dani, Sally and Chris who shared much of my working life, taking the rough with the smooth.

CONTENTS

INTRODUCTION

Magazines have been part of my life since I was about 12, growing up in an Australian country town. I loved reading *Girl*, which came all the way from the UK and gave me astonishing information that I doubt I would have come across in any other way. Much later, as a journalist, I discovered that this is what magazines are designed to do – provide inspiration and entertainment for many types of readers.

I earned my living in Britain working on several different types, though none was like any you can buy today. But the 20th Century was boom time for these publications and in their own way they reflected what was happening in society and how we lived. They are history. As I was part of it, just a tiny cog in a big wheel, I thought I'd write down what I remembered of my 40+ years of working on them.

And there was another reason. I realised I was keeping up with many former colleagues via death notices or obituaries. That wasn't good enough. They should be remembered as part of the amazing creativity behind a huge number of weekly and monthly magazines aimed to pleasure a wide range of ages and interests.

It's been quite a journey for me, finding links and opening windows into an industry that is fast-changing, possibly even disappearing, plagued by the vicissitudes of modern technology and communications as well as ways of living. From that small country town, I ended up working for many of the big names in publishing in the UK and Europe – some of whom, to my surprise, would be influential in magazines in Australia and New Zealand.

I thought it percipient of editor Pat Roberts-Cairns to mark Good Housekeeping's 75th birthday by saying: "There's no point in having a heritage if you can't turn it into a future." That was in 1997, just on the verge of the worldwide web and the effect it would have on everything in our lives. Now the future looks to be digital and publishing is changing dramatically. Che sera, sera.

I am grateful that several people from my past added their knowledge of the working life we shared. If there are errors, and in any publication the odds on this occurring are high, they will be mine (but I hope not!).

FROM BLACK AND WHITE TO COLOUR

L ondon really was *the* place to be in the Swinging Sixties. There were many terrific attractions – Carnaby Street, the pubs and music – but little was free. You needed money to enjoy them and I was in dire straits. I'd been a newspaper reporter in Australia and New Zealand and once I got here I thought I'd quickly find a job in Fleet Street, the home of 'all the news that matters', pinnacle for all ambitious journalists. It wasn't happening. My experience counted for naught.

Paying for a bedsit in Kensington was eating up what savings I had so, in desperation, I joined a secretarial agency and became a temp typist. Two fingered, but very fast, after months of copy typing the Saturday race results for the paper I worked on in Wellington. Not many of the jobs I was sent to were interesting, but I really liked the Swiss chemical company where we were given soup and sandwiches for lunch. Saved me having to buy a meal.

The law firms were best. I'd done quite a bit of court

reporting Down Under and the processes fascinated me. One firm had Bertrand Russell as a client – my CND and Committee of 100 hero – though, sadly, I never saw him. In these offices I gained a welcome insight into legal punctuation: if you use it, and place it wrongly, it could allow a different interpretation of the writer's intention (as Lynne Truss showed cleverly in her book *Eats, Shoots and Leaves*).

In spare moments I used the typewriter to apply for every job in daily and weekly publishing advertised in the Situations Vacant columns in the broadsheets (large-size newspapers that you had to fold to read properly, especially on the Tube or bus). There were no 'media' sections then (or Human Resources departments either, just Personnel), and *The Times* had only recently taken ads off the front page.

It infuriated me that male Aussies and Kiwis had no trouble finding jobs in Fleet Street, mostly working shifts on the dailies (a common way for those employed elsewhere to earn extra money, a practice that eventually would attract the interest of the taxman). I sent off many letters and I did get some interviews – at *The Guardian*, *The Observer* and *The Daily Mirror*, but condescension was ever present. "You haven't lived here so how can you know about Britain?" asked both Peter Preston (*Guardian*) and Derek Jameson (*Mirror*, but who went on to *The Daily Express* and *News of the World* later). "Try a provincial paper" was the suggestion. I said (in my huffiest voice) I'd worked on *Commonwealth* papers but that meant nothing. My face, and most probably my gender, didn't fit.

As I had been a general reporter, I hadn't thought to

apply for jobs on the women's pages. After a while I went for anything that seemed possible – and bingo, I was invited to an interview for a position on the subs' desk of one of the world's leading women's magazines, about which I knew little. There was a link to Fleet Street. Behind these publications were the huge circulation tabloids – at that time black and white and read all over.

For the newspaper owners, magazines were the way forward. It made financial sense. They provided colour pages for advertisers to present their wares and the huge, high-investment printing machines were kept employed. The new publications would be a treat, an escape from dull lives and exude glamour for their millions of buyers. Yes, millions.

Because of my interest in politics (had you guessed this already?) I'd applied for and was in the running for another job, at the Central Office of Information, a sort of PR arm of the government that provided facts and figures about the UK to journalists or officials from other countries. I'd had two interviews, with questions coming thick and fast from four besuited men: what did I know about Prime Minister Harold Wilson, the unions, the health service and other things pertinent to life in Britain in the 1960s? [This was when there was a Macfisheries on every high street that sold fruit and vegetables as well as 'wet' fish – with no explanation available I presumed that meant fresh. More mysteriously, Boots the chemist had a lending library.]

I had no problem with my answers as I was a long-time reader of the *New Statesman*, which reached Australasia by sea. While the information was four to five weeks out of date, the details were there to be absorbed. I told them I was looking forward to being in the UK as so much was going on. I shook their hands firmly, looked them in the eyes and smiled. It was what an Australian was taught to do.

My interviewer at *Woman's Own* – the letterhead called it 'The National Women's Weekly' – was also male: Ken Pickin, the chief sub, spruce in a dark, pin-striped three piece suit. This was not an outfit much seen in my experience, but it was everyday wear for him, as were my hippie-style dress, stockings and little white gloves.

There was no such thing as dressing down then – how you looked was *always* taken into account. With my very long red hair, freckled face and little makeup I was nothing like the Face of '66, 16-year-old Twiggy.

I'd bought and read a few issues of *Woman's Own* so I had some idea of content but questions about production required careful answers. The black and white newspapers of my training were not produced in the same way as colour magazines. My personal references from my previous editors, at *The Evening Post* in Wellington and *TV Times* in Sydney, indicated I was a willing worker, and a trier (I'd covered everything from courts to councils, to finance and theatre).

Ken had a newspaper background, too, and wanted to have trained journalists on the 12-strong subs' desk. Traditionally, many on the desk were secretaries, always women, promoted to it as a way of thanking them for loyal service. (Several famous editors started this way, as I was to learn much later.) But this was how females moved

upwards and onwards in a world where men were the
dominant force – though fewer in number.

As luck would have it, I received both job offers on the
same day. The COI letter confirmed me in the post of
assistant information officer. After a six-month trial I
would be a British civil servant, with good working
conditions and guaranteed pension.

[Nothing is forever, however. The COI closed for good
in March 2012 – I would have retired by then, presum-
ably with a good pension! Their work has been taken over
by the British Council, a PR arm of the UK.]

Ken's letter told me I'd have a paid trial period of three
months then I would reap the benefits of working for
George Newnes, part of the Mirror Group, one of the
biggest publishers in the world. With a weekly circulation
nearing 3m *Woman's Own* was not a publication to be
sneezed at. I reckoned working on it couldn't be that
different from a newspaper, so that's what I chose.
Months later a woman who'd gone from a women's magazine to employment in a government department told me
she'd discovered heaven after years of hell.

The first six months on the desk at *Woman's Own* were
a struggle. I frequently didn't understand what people
were saying, caught in a gulf between Antipodean English
and English English. It wasn't just the different accents
but the inflections, the way words were used. The sense of
humour often escaped me entirely.

IN TROUBLE FROM THE START
The working atmosphere felt really strange after the
newsrooms I was used to. I felt I had taken an

irrevocable step backwards and had become a 'women's writer' – female journalists who compiled the 'society gossip' and domestic pages in newspapers. Not that writing was even part of the job. Worse still was that a subeditor was up shit creek without a paddle.

Subs were the foot-soldiers, the pedants who made the 'creative' people on the staff wince. No one seemed to understand how essential we were. We were the original, intelligent, word processors, ensuring that every story had a start, middle and end, that names were spelled correctly, ages were right, facts were checked for accuracy, that nothing was published that could be misconstrued or libellous, that there were no unintended *double entendres*. Of course we knew that writers wouldn't make mistakes intentionally...but a sub was the fail-safe, the catcher behind the stumps.

We didn't have Google or Bing then – though you can't take anything you find on these search engines as the whole truth. Since the advent of 'post-truth' and 'fake news' and 'Surveillance Capitalism' these know more about us than we know ourselves. At *Woman's Own* our checks were done painstakingly by phone or by looking up reference books we had at hand or in public libraries (at least that got us out of the office).

Even a fiction sub had to be on the *qui-vive*, to make sure names of characters were not the same as any known living persons (in phone books or electoral rolls if a specific area was part of the plot, or *Who's Who*, or biographical encyclopedias). You couldn't risk imagined characters having similarities with actuality, particularly if the plot showed them in a doubtful light. It could result in a charge of libel.

* * *

I started work on the subs' desk at *Woman's Own* on September 26 1966. The offices were in Tower House, in Southampton Street, London WC2, at the lower end of which was the famous Savoy Hotel on the Strand. The one-way street led to the old Covent Garden flower, fruit and vegetable market made famous through the transformation of George Bernard Shaw's play *Pygmalion* into the all-singing and dancing *My Fair Lady*.

It was a dreadfully gloomy day in what was a "leaves of brown came tumbling down" autumn. After weeks of rain the streets were awash with crates, paper and detritus from the market. Wolf whistles from the porters accompanied every step, which made me blush in those early days, but I soon got used to them and the mess underfoot. Working on the desk was another matter.

Thinking back, I must have come to the UK with too many preconceptions, not enough real understanding of the four countries that were the United Kingdom. I didn't expect everything to feel so foreign, so very different from Australia and New Zealand. No 'Howyagoing mate' greetings, no overwhelming feeling of friendliness. The people I met seemed distant, tight lipped. But it was *Woman's Own* for better or worse. After all, I had come for the 1966 World Cup and was only going to be overseas for a year. The plan was to get some new skills, hear good music and move on.

I never took a sickie. Even when the autumn and winter weather was at its worst I managed to get to work. In rain, hail and snow, from Waterloo Station I walked across the Hungerford Bridge, often in the company of shy and very tall Graham Brock, a designer in the art department, who sadly was to die in his 50s of a spinal disease. But then we were young and together strode along the Strand and up Southampton Street to Tower House, a building that today houses a range of businesses but then was mostly about publishing.

Woman's Own was on the third floor, and behind the reception area were corridors and closed doors where a staff of about 120 (predominantly women) created the material that appeared on the pages every week. I wasn't surprised that the editor was a man; this was usual Down Under too. George Rogers – known as Rog though we minions called him Mr Rogers – was well built and red faced, and he was treated like God.

This was a tradition that went back to James (Jimmy) Drawbell who ran *Woman's Own* for many years. At the bigger-selling *Woman* a group of men, which included John Dunbar (though I didn't know about him then), held the power. These well-honed newspaper veterans knew just what the little woman at home should want.

LINES TO MAKE YOU LAUGH
Though *Woman's Own* was a 'colour' magazine it was printed on paper remarkably like a daily's, the wrapping of choice for a portion of fish and chips. One of its claims to journalistic fame was the catchy coverline '*Knit your own Dutch cap*'. It was funny (if you

knew about that type of contraception), but I laughed more at the headline in a Broken Hill newspaper of November 1947: *"Millions see Princess Elizabeth and Prince Philip consummate their marriage"*. (The page was displayed at the Journalists' Club in Sydney to remind all to get their facts, and verbs, right.)

The subs' desk was literally a long, wide table. When I first arrived I was at the end furthest from the chief sub – at the head, of course – but over time moved along until I was right beside him. I was surprised that so many people came and went. No sub saw the desk as permanent, all on the lookout for possible moves in or out of the company. And new publications often appeared.

Jose Northey, in the chair beside me, had seemed perfectly settled but suddenly she was gone, enticed away to *Intro*, an innovative music magazine, created by *Woman*'s editorial team. It was tabloid size combining pop entertainment with fashion, beauty, fiction and features about the time of 'flower power'. It cost 1s 6d and lasted six months. You'd have thought it would appeal to all the young who were attracted to the American 'hippy' culture. The peace and love movement spread around the world, offering great music and new ways of dressing.

Freedom was the new focus and it was right up the street of *Nova*, a maverick mag described as being for 'the new kind of woman'. I kept hoping a job would turn up there so I could apply. I loved the way it tackled subjects thought to be controversial, like the war in Vietnam, abortion and medical advances. There was shock value in pictures and words on strikingly designed pages with lots of white space. It too was edited by a man, Dennis Hackett, and it survived for some time.

We were a mixed lot on the desk. Ken didn't speak much and John was almost monosyllabic. In fact there wasn't a lot of talk. Near me sat Sally, who was a sky diver in her spare time. Opposite sat Rosemary, a cheerful Northerner who had become sole earner after her husband lost his job. He didn't tell her for six months. He left home each day as though going to work, and she never suspected anything. We swapped recipes: I still have hers for Beef Stroganoff and I know she enjoyed my lamingtons, a popular Aussie confection of luscious sponge coated in chocolate and desiccated coconut. I missed her when she and her husband felt they had no choice but to go back to their hometown.

Another redhead joined us, a New Zealander, and she spoke my language – or nearly (it's the sound of the vowels that are different: I said catch, she said cetch). Glenys was married to fellow Kiwi Les Gibbard, a cartoonist who joined *The Guardian* in 1969. For 25 years he made an impact with his fierce and sharp eye, and pen, for any political situation.

What was uncanny was that he emulated David Low, also from New Zealand, who had done the same on the same newspaper in the 1940s and 1950s. It was said his wartime art made him Churchill's favourite cartoonist.

Glenys and I had friends in common in Wellington and chatting about them and life out there made me feel less homesick for a country that wasn't my own but I loved with a passion and thought I would return to. [Tall and amiable Les, born in 1945, died in 2010.]

Subs joined the desk from other parts of the company. Doreen Wells was from the 'teen magazines' (*Honey, Petticoat, 19*), but after a while went to Australia with her husband and children as 'ten pound Poms', as immigrants were known. It was a gamble: you had to stay two years or pay that money back as well as your own fares to return to the UK. The whole family was willing to take a chance, a good Aussie trait. I wished her well and was surprised that I felt no urge to go with her. I was starting to enjoy being in the UK and could now mostly understand what people were saying (I was getting good at guessing).

On the subs' desk I found I had much to learn, and fast. On newspapers, where the printers were usually at the back of the building, I mastered having to read upside down the slugs of hot lead fed into the galley forms from the linotype machine. That skill wasn't needed at Tower House because all the typesetting was done at the Sun printers at Watford, to the north of London. Ken arranged for all of us to be inducted into this vast production centre. We saw the whole process in action, from the arrival of the copy and pictures through to the printing on the ginormous and noisy machines. And we had a good lunch in the canteen.

What was essential as a magazine sub was being good at proof-reading, spotting spelling mistakes (literals) and wrong fonts (characters in type that aren't like the rest). I flourished at using a depth rule, an unknown object to a subeditor today but then used to calculate type size and leading (the white space between lines). Computers do it all for you today.

I could quickly estimate lengths of copy, and was a demon at checking facts. I also cut whole books down to publishable parts. One of the biggest challenges was by Christiaan Barnard: choosing three lots of 4,000 words out of 70,000 to tell the story of the South African doctor's pioneering work in heart replacement surgery.

In putting the magazine together there is no process used then that is still used today. The way it looked, the paper, the printing methods were simply of another time. It was very labour intensive. You lived permanently in the future, the only way to deal with what were called 'lead times' – that is, how many weeks were needed to get text, photographs, art work and layouts finalised for the printer. It was a 12-week rollercoaster, from choice of content to finished issue. *Woman's Own* in those days, often 144 pages a week (very hefty by today's standards), was a huge production number.

The 'look' of *Woman's Own* and *Woman* was achieved by a four-colour printing process called photogravure which ate money at the creative stages but this outlay was acceptable when print runs were large and a profit resulted. No wonder the magazines fought to keep their readership high.

Both weeklies were created in the same way. The text from each department, marked up by art and subs in a specified type font and size, was sent to the typesetter. It came back as galleys – lengths of paper named after the metal trays which received the metal slugs spat out by the linotype machine (the ones I learnt to read upside down).

No one working in media today would recognise any of this. The art department created the layouts, pasting the galleys in columns, allowing space for illustrations, on to single or double pages called spreads.

After this, titles and sells (journalese for introduction, in newspapers called a standfirst) would be added, plus crossheads (which break up long lengths of type) and captions. All are simply words, usually displayed in bold or bigger type to catch the reader's attention. It was the subs' job at this time to choose the descriptive words that summed up the subject on the pages. Choosing them could be fraught with danger. Today we'd call it bullying but back then, when job security wasn't all that certain, those in charge held all the cards and you didn't dare step out of line. It wasn't worth arguing back.

My nemesis was the supervising editor, the one who had invited me to be interviewed. He was in overall charge of subs, art and production and was best described as mercurial, his persona noticeably affected by the time of day. Any contact involving pages was not considered wise too soon after lunch.

I was easy to tease, especially about my accent and hair colour, and he liked to see me blush. He liberally used the f-word. We were as children to him, to be rebuked and reminded. His big power play was to call us into his office, make us stand in a line against the wall and then sneer at our combined, wasted, efforts on sells, and jeer at our capacity as journalists. I can't believe we just stood there and took it, but we did. Back on the subs' desk we'd re-arrange phrases and compromise clichés until he accepted the words we produced. I dreaded rousing his sarcasm.

I remember feeling deeply sorry for the very reticent John. He'd done his National Service in the Korean War so was used to taking orders. But in civvy street should he really have to take this sort of treatment? He left a few months after I arrived, returning to newspapers which he said were less combative. I wasn't too sure about that. There I'd seen sheets of copy torn up and thrown on the floor by the chief reporter or chief sub, at which point whoever wrote the piece just returned to their typewriter and started again, probably fuming inside. But that's the way you learnt to write what the paper wanted.

* * *

Just as the smell of printer's ink and newsprint pervaded the newspapers I worked on, at *Woman's Own* it was the smell of the thick, muculent cow gum used in making the layouts. Much later this adhesive was considered a danger to health because of the fumes it emitted but it became a victim of modern production methods anyway. What we call 'cut and paste' on computers harks back to those times.

And cigarettes! Most of us smoked and had our ashtrays nearby. At first I had a dinky little pipe, North American Indian I think it was. I found puffing on it difficult while typing and the mouthpiece got a bit hot. I then changed to rolling my own because I had no money for tailor-mades, as cigs in packets were known.

I quite liked the way it made everyone around me embarrassed. Getting some reaction from people who I was beginning to think were bereft of feelings cheered me up! Once I could afford it, I moved to black tobacco – untipped Disque Bleu and Gauloises made me feel closer to Paris which I had loved from my first visit.

In survival mode, I developed a fail-safe approach to captions and crossheads that didn't bring wrath down on my head. I even received a £10 bonus from the editor in 1967, for my captions on a feature about Covent Garden. It all boiled down to me having sufficiently sorted out the subtle differences between English of the southern hemisphere and English English, difficult though they are to explain. I also suddenly tuned into the humour and laughed along with everyone else.

But I was living a double life. I couldn't understand how women could go on reading week after week the same 'make yourself perfect' features and not wonder why the real problems we all encountered in the real world were hardly touched on. But I was just a sub: what I thought mattered not a jot.

* * *

I wouldn't have known when I was growing up in a small country town in Australia that I was being drawn into a publishing web: start with the young and encourage them to move onto other publications as they get older. American comics like *Mad* fuelled my imagination and a British magazine called *Girl* was full of wondrous stuff like careers advice (I veered between being a dietician, physiotherapist, doctor, occupational therapist and journalist. And journalism won.).

Girl came by sea, along with *Woman's Weekly* which my

older sisters bought to read the love stories and every detail about the Royal Family in the 'Old Dart' as my Dad (who'd never left Australia) called it. All were weeks out of date, but it didn't matter.

We were willing captives of the Mirror Group, which in London produced one of the world's highest circulation newspapers *The Daily Mirror* (on which Australian campaigning journalist John Pilger would much later make his name).

FIRM FOCUS ON WOMEN

In the 1950s Mirror Group was on a roll: there was a huge surge in sales of *Woman's Own* (launched in 1932} and the younger *Woman* (born 1937). *Woman* in particular aimed to discuss any subject pertinent to the lives of domestic and career women. The opportunity for both was to reach out to all the adult females (over 21) who had been enfranchised in 1928. To put this in perspective, women won the vote in New Zealand in 1893 (the first in the world) and in Australia in 1901.

By the 1960s, both were selling about 3m copies a week, unheard of today unless you're talking about magazines produced for Chinese women in China. They must have been providing a service. *Woman's Own* had a great leap forward thanks to serialising the memoirs of 'Crawfie' – Marion Crawford – who had been governess to the young princesses, known by their affectionate nicknames Lilibet and Margaret Rose. Her 'indiscreet' revelations (which were not revolutionary by today's standards) upped the magazine's circulation, edging it closer to

Woman (subline: *National home-making weekly*). Not getting the serial rights was a bitter blow to the magazine's editor Mary Grieve who'd been authorised by Odham's editorial director John Dunbar to bid £10,000 (explained in her book *Millions made my story*, 1964). Drawbell paid £30,000.

Up to 1963 the Mirror Group had three publishing entities: George Newnes, Fleetway (formerly Amalgamated Press) and Odhams Press producing a range of publications. These were merged to form the International Publishing Corporation (IPC). The two big sellers aimed at women were in the same stable but remained rivals. The problem was their circulations were declining and would never be so high again. A plateau was reached in 1966 when I joined *Woman's Own* but I don't think it had anything to do with me.

* * *

Production was the hub of the whole enterprise. Those who worked here 'stamped' the magazine with its identity – giving the final, finished 'look' to the pages so readers were in no doubt it was *Woman's Own* they had in their hands. The combined skills ensured that the arrangement of pictures and text, week after week after week, was reassuringly familiar yet different enough from what went before to entice the reader in.

George Cannon, several years older than me, started here on the same day as I did. He had trained as a teacher after National Service but opted instead for a job dealing directly with the printers – probably one of the most important roles in publishing then – and ensuring all deadlines were met. He knew he had to keep the printers sweet: if they chose to stop work for any reason, the magazine would not come out.

The layouts themselves, when the departments and assistant editors had finished writing all over them, often looked appalling, a challenge for the typesetters who had to decipher it and make the changes before sending us finished – known as 'clean' – page proofs. I am full of admiration that they did it week in, week out.

The subs used a set of markings that hailed back to Johnson's *Typographia* (1824) so the instructions to the printer were clear and consistent. We made sure everything was done in pencil until the absolutely final changes made by interested parties were added – then we inked them in. At the end of a day's work, the desk was covered with fine paper-dust created by our ferocious use of rubbers. Perhaps I should use the word erasers, as rubbers have other connotations in English.

George's team chased everyone, no matter at what level, to ensure that copy and pix were delivered on time and that layouts, either completed or in the process of completion, were ready for the courier to collect twice a day for the printer at Watford. Late afternoons were very tense times, and getting the material organised was often soul-destroying, but he was remarkably unemotional. He couldn't take it personally. It was simply the job.

The subs had a set of rules to follow and their biggest hurdle was the feature writers who felt their precious words were endangered. "Pedantry" was a word that could be spat out in real anger. A subeditor had enough difficulties without being earnest, but I couldn't work out why they thought we were doing it deliberately.

There were traps for the unwary. Commercial enterprises had their own 'readers' who scanned publications to ensure their products were not unfairly targeted or not given due credit. "Chanel-like" was not acceptable, for instance, because there is only one Chanel. All proprietary names had to have a capital (Cellophane and Sellotape, for example). One of my early calamities was letting Aspro go through in a health feature, when I should have changed it to the generic aspirin. It was the chief sub who had to face the editor when a lawyer's letter pointing out the error of our ways was received. And we cringed in sympathy.

In newspapers I learnt very early that while facts are sacrosanct, words are not – and willingness to alter a story was essential. On *Woman's Own* the writers thought their words were gold dust. If I found a factual error I could point it out but the writer had to alter the text.

As a subeditor, it was not my place to change copy. We were not regarded as journalists, but as production mechanics. I might boil with indignation, but I couldn't let it show.

2

CREATING A PHENOMENON

Despite me thinking there couldn't be much difference between working on a newspaper and a magazine, I soon found I was wrong. The everyday practices at *Woman's Own* were nothing like what I'd been used to and my Aussie confidence took a bit of a bashing. I tried to explain to my English partner that it seemed to be a clash of cultures overlaid with a frosty disdain but he just said "What did you expect?". His family had actually emigrated to Australia in the 1950s because they were fed up with the UK. He was not likely to be sympathetic.

I had never been shy and retiring but in this new environment I felt I had to be introduced before I could speak to anyone. I'd never worked with so many people before and it took a long time to work out who was who and the departments they came from. There was no common area where the staff got together. And you were just expected to know who everyone was, by some magical osmosis. Those who ventured near our subs' desk, which seemed to be in some sort of Outer Mongolia, often only did so if something was wrong and they wanted to let us know. And naturally it was our fault.

All the women were dressed to the nines, always made up, and only in our production area – full of arty types, as you'd expect – was the clothing more relaxed. The truth was that my wardrobe was very limited: I was going through the 'only own what I can carry on my back' phase. I had neither time nor money for buying the latest clothes, and the only makeup I wore was lipstick and block mascara which came in a small mirrored case. It was applied to lashes and brows with a tiny brush – I used spit to moisten it which was hardly hygienic! (Cake mascara, as it is also known, has now had a renaissance).

I veered towards the men and women working around me as they were more likely to go to the pub after work. This was normal practice Down Under, and certainly regarded as an occupational hazard on newspapers. The watering holes on the edge of Covent Garden (some of which are still there) were good places to get to know a few of my workmates. Nothing too personal, and someone was always ready to tell jokes.

We rarely saw Rog who ruled over everything, yet our area was where he had worked as photo editor and played a part in launching a young Roger Moore's acting career. In the 1950s Rog hired Roger as a model for some knitting features and after one session he lent him a tie to smarten him up for an audition he was attending later. In 1972 after his successful TV series *The Saint*, Moore became the third 007 (following Sean Connery, who died in 2020, and George Lazenby). But he no longer needed to work as a model.

The editor's large office overlooked Southampton Street and was protected by an outer area controlled by two secretaries. When the senior one moved (either to the subs' desk or one of the departments), the junior one took her vacated desk. That's how things progressed. Some jobs were considered more superior, a step-up as it were.

Teenager Terry, the cheerful young runner in the production hub, made a classic remark when there was a change at the top: "Does that mean we all move up one level then?" I wonder if he stayed in publishing.

* * *

G radually I got to know the routine behind creating each issue. The people behind the closed doors along the various corridors came up with the ideas. But their planning had started months previously – this is what I mean by living in the future. Each department head drew up a list which was discussed with the assistant editors, then the topics were allocated to a publication date according to relevant factors like the seasons, national events, whether the magazine was being promoted (mostly on radio and in newspapers at this time, to increase circulation).

Royal birthdays or anniversaries were always noted and planned for simply because it was a known fact that any of the monarch's lot on the cover sold issues (as they continue to do, from the days of Princess Diana and now with the two daughters-in-law she never met).

None of this happened overnight: three months before the publication date, the content of an issue would be decided and colour pages allotted (the rest would be black and white), the aim being to get a good mix: a formula with an unspoken motto 'inform, entertain, educate'. The vital one was entertainment. The overall aim was to make the reader feel happy to turn the pages and enjoy what she was reading.

The black and white pages were for the 'regulars' – the well-known contributors who were in every issue, generally in the same place. Their articles were processed later than the colour. The poem of Patience Strong was a 'floater': filling a space that occurred anywhere – for example, if a feature fell short.

Patience was a legend – from 1935, her poems appeared daily in *The Daily Mirror*'s Quiet Corner, moving later to *The Sunday Mirror* and *Woman's Own*. Yet how many knew that behind the poetic words was Winifred Emma May who had an exceptional career in both poetry and music? By the age of 21, she had more than 100 published songs to her credit, including the lyrics of the wonderful *Jealousy* sung by tenor Richard Tauber in the 1930s. Today, Jacob Gade's music is heard mostly as a ballroom tango but I defy anyone not to bring Winifred's words to mind as the tune plays:

> *"Twas all over my jealousy,*
> *My crime was my blind jealousy. . ."*

Her autobiography, published in 1981, was called *A Poem In My Pocket*, and in 1985 her book *Fifty Golden Years* commemorated a half century penning poems. She died in 1990 aged 83. I only saw her once when she visited the office but how I wish I had known her.

* * *

W oman's Own's regular commentators were 'names' in the mid 1960s. One was familiar: the 'God slot' from the cricketing cleric capped for England, Reverend David Sheppard, who I saw play at the 'Gabba in Brisbane when I lived there in 1962-63.

A touch of controversy was part of the magazines' mix, too: to pen the tricky topics *Woman* had Godfrey Winn and *Woman's Own* had Beverley Nichols. Both seemed very old to me but their camp theatricality was much approved. I never saw Nichols but he wrote more than 60 books, including ghosting Dame Nellie Melba's 'autobiography' in 1925. He was multi talented (writing plays and poetry, was a gardener and cook), contributing to *Woman's Own* from 1946 to 1967. Canadian Barbara Kelly took his place; she was the wife of TV presenter/journalist Bernard Braden who focused on consumer matters on *Braden's Beat* (where Esther Rantzen, now a Dame and one of Britain's living treasures, was a researcher).

Percy Thrower was one of a group of venerated gardeners who wrote for many publications (in 1974 he created BBC TV's *Blue Peter* garden). He had extra space in *Woman's Own* at those times of the year when there's more to do outdoors and lawns were a favourite topic. It could have been a bore for a sub without a garden (but working on his copy stood me in good stead in the future). One of his acolytes was a young Alan Titchmarsh, who's made his name as a garden commentator, TV and radio presenter, and novelist.

When readers were asked via marketing surveys how they read the magazine, they frequently said from the back. Why? Because here were the popular Starscope, Gypsy Leon Petulengro's weekly prognostications (astrological forecasts were avidly absorbed), and the problem page with the byline "Mary Grant". Angela Willans joined the staff in 1963 and made up the page from readers' letters about broken hearts, jealousy, loneliness, despair, rejection, infidelity, feelings of inferiority, bullying, domestic violence, debt, unemployment, family break-up. Not many subjects were put in the 'too difficult' file. Problem pages and the agony aunts in magazines reveal the personal situations of the time.

Other 'regular' pages were pseudonymous. Doctor's Diary by "Dr Roderick Wimpole" tackled 'wimmin's ailments'; if full details of important subjects like menstruation or menopause couldn't be given (lack of space or not considered apt), readers could send for specially produced pamphlets containing pertinent information. I don't think men's problems were broached then.

Subjects like periods and the problems that go with them were not regarded as distasteful when advertisers bought space to bring their products (such as sanitary aids) to the readers' notice, discreetly. The "Jane Dunbar" page carried what are now accepted as 'advertorials' or 'paid content', a hundred or so well-chosen words that the advertiser paid for – in magazines today these can take up many pages.

"At Your Service" answered readers' queries on myriad subjects. It was the realm of Sylvia Duncan who'd had a formidable career in Fleet Street. She also wrote hard-hitting features on subjects close to a woman's heart – infidelity was special topic for her I seem to remember. 'Confessional' articles about real life situations (such as postnatal depression) used made-up names.

"Ruth Martin" wrote on mother and child subjects; when I joined the staff she was Claire Rayner, trained nurse and midwife, who would become one of the UK's leading agony aunts and health campaigners, and best-selling fiction writer. She was a tall, well-built woman with a big laugh and forthright approach. She'd have taken on any topic, if the magazine's policies hadn't restrained her. I liked being the sub in charge of her copy.

"Your Letters" offered prizes: for the star letter (£3 – in old money) or recipe (£2). Letters arrived at our offices in their hundreds every week and were read and answered by a roomful of women called letter writers. They sent out the special leaflets, in plain envelopes, on a range of female-related topics that women might be reluctant to talk to their doctors about. The remaining correspondence went to the Letters Page editor, At Your Service, Ruth Martin, Mary Grant and the 'practical departments' so they could choose what to follow up.

* * *

'Domestic subjects' were a huge part of *Woman's Own*, angled to be pertinent to readers' lives. The names of employees in the practical departments did not accompany their contributions, the tradition was to use a 'house' byline: cookery's was Jane Beaton (possibly a rip-off of the short-lived but long lasting Mrs Beeton of 19th century home management and cook-book fame), fashion's was Suzanne Grey, beauty's was Diana Day, home's was Anne Lennox; knitting, curiously, had no byline. Marguerite Patten, who'd advised the women of Britain on cooking matters during World War 2, was named on her features, all illustrated with black and white drawings.

The departments were to my eyes like Aladdin's caves, with rails of clothes, boxes of lotions and potions (breakthroughs in the world of beauty, like different coloured eyeshadows and mascara 'wands', were on the horizon), new foods to taste, equipment to try. Cookery had two kitchens where every recipe to be published was tested, tasted, and then photographed under the watchful gaze of the style editor Joan Page from the production hub. IPC had a department of (male) photographers in the building and they didn't get a credit then in the magazines.

Knitting was the calmest place of all, the only sound the click of needles as an extraordinary range of garments – popular with readers as everyone knitted then – were created in conjunction with the influential wool companies. Even planning a photo session was done in a whisper. No one wanted to disturb the person checking instructions – every single line of a pattern had to be gone over by the department as well as the sub on the desk who was handling the subject that week. Dropped stitches could lead to trouble.

It surprised me that those working in the practical departments, all of them female, were not trained journalists but were rated as merchandisers, providers of information for captions or recipes. It would be some time before the situation changed.

* * *

The 1960s was the era of the loggia (patio), the rumpus room (family room) and keeping up with the Joneses next door (who'd bought a new washing machine, vacuum cleaner, curtains, carpet etc) – the start of the age of materialism, a rejection of the dourness of the 1950s. Homes were changing with modern furnishings and equipment but saving money by reviving objects with paint or fabric or whatever was important. This craft element continued the war-time 'make do and mend'. (Years later, I would learn more about DIY Britain.)

Two women shared the byline Anne Lennox. One was feisty Kitty Grime, ready to fight her corner if her proposed project brought criticism from the higher-ups who were not at the coalface like she was. I have no idea why she joined *Woman's Own*. Her obituary in *The Guardian* (2007), revealed she had been a university graduate and teacher, and had a special place in the world of jazz, as a singer, pianist and lyric writer. In the 1950s she wrote concert programmes and notes for records' cardboard sleeves.

"In 1953," said Kitty's obituarist Val Wilmer, "she produced a state of the art brochure for (Johnny) Dankworth's first big band, while advising Cleo Laine, the band's young singer, on matters of fashion." In the 1980s Kitty sang in pubs, at lunchtimes entertained at the Royal

Festival Hall, and ran courses in voice production for women at London's Central YMCA. Such prodigious talents, and how sad that I didn't know of them. The trouble was that in our working life we were under pressure, wrapped up in our own jobs, and lives outside, so there wasn't time enough for each other's own stories.

Woman's Own made sure it was value for money by adding eight, 16 or 32 page supplements to issues to draw in the readers. There were few colour pages and illustrations were black and white. Even so, they were a bargain. You paid 4d (as pence were written, pre-decimal) for the magazine and got 16 free patterns to knit or crochet.

Cookery extras were always winners, especially if the focus was on chocolate, baking or dishes that saved time – not so different from today. Beauty produced readers' makeovers, with new looks for face and hair – illustrations showed how to apply make-up or style hair – with the latest clothes added for full effect. There was a distinct difference between what you wore for work or at home, for evening, at weekends, or change of seasons.

It was a time when readers lapped up prescriptive guides – to etiquette, deportment (words you rarely hear today), budgeting, table settings, spring cleaning, getting married. And the exertion involved in making them right for the magazine was breathtaking. Yet rejection was possible. Every Thursday the editor and assistant editors gathered round the conference room table to check the contents of the issue that would start having to be prepared for the printers in two weeks' time. The features and fiction departments brought forth the special star interviews, the triumph-over-tragedy stories (known as

TOTs), a lighthearted quiz (usually man-woman relationship dilemmas) and the big name short story or serial.
These were the 'meat' of the magazine, which spread
through the issue. The subjects for the regular contributors would be decided (to prevent overlapping between,
say, the doctor and the women's health page).

Material for the practical pages was scrutinised
closely. The beholders could be ruthless: the choice of a
plate or cloth, the look of the food, the clothes, the photos
– anything could be objected to. If a reshoot was ordered,
no extra time was given. No wonder Kitty got riled.

The fiction editor showed the planned illustrations for
the short stories – often several an issue, rarely in colour
– and a new or ongoing serial. This original art was
bought in or gave employment to imaginative artists
working on a bench in the art department. Fiction had its
own subs who made cuts and changes without losing the
plot or any characters. They ensured that "the story so far"
at the start of the serial helped readers catch up with what
had gone before.

Once the conference had chosen, the subs worked
with the departments to meet the deadlines. The long
features that were common in magazines then are rare
today (people don't have time to read them it seems) but
it was the subs' job to ensure they were easy to compre-
hend, and had the correct 'please turn to' and page
number. There was also an accepted tradition about not-
overlong paragraphs and making reading easier. Did
readers notice that the top and bottom of each column
had two or three full lines before a new paragraph
started? That no line had fewer than two words? Prob-

ably not, but the subs had to. One word at the top of a column was known as an orphan, at the end of a paragraph it was a widow, and a widow was unacceptable. I don't know why it couldn't it have been a widower, equally solitary.

Our 'bibles' were an English dictionary, thesaurus, gazetteer of the British Isles, *Brewer's Dictionary of Phrase and Fable* and a book of rules for compositors and editors. 'Compositors' are a relic of the past, when the setting of type (in hot metal), and putting words into print, had just one consideration: not to inconvenience the reader. How this was achieved was stated in *Hart's Rules*, an all-in-one guide for those involved with typesetting, first printed in 1893 for "compositors and readers" at the University Press, Oxford (today's Oxford University Press). "Readers" examined every line for literals (spelling mistakes) before they went to press.

Of all the departments, features was the most daunting. Subs, bearing page proofs or queries, could usually knock on any other department's closed door then open it and go in. Not so with features. You had to wait for an imperious "Enter!" or "Come!". Was it my feelings or imagination that made the room always look dark? At one end were writers Margaret Peters, James Leasor and Douglas Keay, all of whom had links to Fleet Street.

Margaret Peters was always kind to subs. She had an eye for tragedy stories, producing people and their terrible experiences to order. She also did an excellent series on Liverpool's Alder Hey Hospital and the life-saving treatment of children there. Television didn't have soaps like *Casualty* and *Holby City* then – *Woman's Own* took readers behind the scenes and gave an exclusive insight as *Hospital* and *24 Hours in A&E* do now.

James Leasor died in 2007, aged 83, and according to his obituary (*Daily Telegraph*) worked for three days a week at *Woman's Own*, writing under the name of Douglas Anderson, a psychiatrist who dispensed advice on such matters as why women are unfaithful (was there mention of the men too?). He also worked on *The Daily Express*, and wrote thrillers, historical novels mostly about World War 2, and biographies (including famous film actors Kenneth More and Jack Hawkins).

Douglas Keay was short and dapper (I think Twinkle-toes might have been his nickname), always dressed in a dark suit and tie, with a coloured handkerchief poking out of his breast pocket. He did many of the major interviews and keenly watched how his words were treated (once when I tried to shorten tarmacadam to tarmac it was thought reprehensible). He had a reputation as *the* Royal watcher, writing many books about the Queen, Queen Mother, Duke of Edinburgh, Prince Charles, and Princess Diana who died so tragically in 1997.

Douglas found a good buddy in Dennis Beaven, the picture editor, and they bonded over long lunches. Dennis's ears and eyes were always alert for exclusive picture stories which added cachet to *Woman's Own*. He was full of bonhomie, a smiler of the Cheshire cat variety. His deputy, Brian Mumford, couldn't have been more different, though his bark was worse than his bite. Dennis and Brian shared an office with style editor Joan Page who fought her corner with panache. It was not an area known for calmness.

* * *

This features room was a hothouse for talent, full of young bloomers who helped out with research and aimed to become top writers. Anthea Disney, an attractive young woman, moved on to a Fleet Street tabloid in the late 1960s. For one feature she 'blacked up' and lived as an Asian for some weeks to experience discrimination first-hand. It was a stunning exclusive. Over 40 years later she was Executive Vice President of Content at Rupert Murdoch's News Corp in the US. She was distantly related to the famous Walt.

Tall, blonde Iris Burton had a stellar career in magazines: she went from this room to be deputy to editor Peter Jackson on *TV Times* (a big seller then), after which she returned as editor of *Woman's Own*; in the 1980s the Germans enticed her to be launch editor of the huge-selling monthly *Prima* and weekly *Best*; eventually she was editorial director of IPC. Janet Horwood had a grounding in rewriting in this room which led her to *Woman*, *Woman's Weekly* and later to *Choice* (remaining part of my life), and a career writing self-help books.

The writer who intrigued me most was Betty Messenger. She typed wearing lace gloves and always had a fine square of chiffon perched on her bouffant hair and tied under her chin. She had a special understanding of Leon Petulengro, continuing the tradition of Gypsy Xavier Petulengro, the first star of prediction at *Woman's Own*. Betty rendered Leon's astrological forecasts into perfectly formed chunks to fit the allotted space each week. These were done months ahead of actual publication so prescience was essential. She was behind Leon's sun sign forecasts for the year ahead, his guides to fortune telling, and insight into the Romany Oracle which held his papa's secrets of life and happiness. As Elizabeth Messenger, she ghosted a raft of his books.

* * *

F iction was very important to the magazine and the department was quiet as you'd expect, as everyone was reading. Good romantic fiction, either bought in or commissioned, was one of the reasons *Woman's Own*, *Woman* and *Woman's Weekly* (then with a pink and blue cover – changing to full colour in the late 1960s increased circulation dramatically) – sold so well. The fiction guru at *Woman's Own*, before my time, was Robert Henry, who I was told wore nylon shirts and carried a small cane shopping basket wherever he went.

It was said he was a transvestite who eschewed the men's WCs at Tower House, preferring the privacy – even the glamour – of those at The Savoy Hotel down the street on The Strand. He was, gossip declared, a disinherited member of the Rothschild family who made money from buying and selling shares.

He gave 17-year-old Pat Pett, newly qualified from Pitmans shorthand and typing college (considered essential requisites for wannabe journalists), her start and her career would culminate, after a few meanderings, at *The Sunday Express*. Being a successful sub was instinctive to her. We had the same birth date (though she was younger) and I admired her efficiency in getting pages to the right people in production at the right time. Her long blonde hair fell over one eye, 1950s style, like Hollywood's Veronica Lake. Her cheerful, willing ways, enlivened by a penchant for flirting, put her in everyone's good books.

The glamorous Judith Burnley, who could have stepped straight from a romantic scene with her abundant black hair and scarlet lips, was in charge when I arrived but she left to write two quite well reviewed novels. In came the well-built and amiable Lesley Saxby from *Woman's Mirror*, a weekly magazine produced by *The Daily Mirror* which had closed. Even though it was selling 880,000 a week in 1967, this was not deemed enough. [To put this in perspective, that circulation is more than double any woman's weekly publication in the UK today.]

Magazine editors knew they'd reap the benefit of pre-book publication from big names like Agatha Christie, Nicholas Monsarrat, Catherine Cookson and Noel Coward. The cost was simply an investment as readers were waiting in line. A first instalment could be 6,000 words and the novel could be read over several issues. Abridged or condensed books were sought after at this time. You could buy whole sets of shortened tomes if you had a mind to and on a shelf in your sitting room, they looked impressive even if you didn't read them.

* * *

As subs, we didn't see much of the man in charge of features, Robert Bruce, but I remember him as a charmer. I now know he was also a published poet (in 1956 and 1969). We had most contact with his deputy,

Janice James, a blonde, flirtatious, assured and determined woman for whom the saying "sharp to the bottom of the glass" might have been composed. She'd been behind many of the scoop buys serialised in *Woman's Own*, obtained through keeping in close touch with agents and publishers who were most likely to have the books she was interested in.

In the 1960s magazines like *Woman's Own* and *Woman* were fodder for Fleet Street. It's hard to imagine now, when far too many newspapers are featurised and celebrity-mad, that in those days news was their main purpose. The jam of the weekly magazines were the exclusive interviews with the stars – the writers worked hard to set these up through theatrical agents in the UK and US – which the papers plundered for their own use.

It was the magazines' own fault. Their PRs sent out press releases with early copies hoping for publicity – and to their chagrin most of the time the papers didn't even attribute their source! While the magazines' circulations were doing all right, this was merely an irritation to the editors, but once they started to fall it became a real concern. How could they stop Fleet Street from stealing their thunder.

3

THE CHALLENGES OF 1968

L ooking back to this time it seems strange that
Woman's Own wasn't routinely tackling big issues
that affected women – like going out to work, childcare
and further education all of which were important to
their lives. But this aspect was added, according to
Cynthia White, author of Women's Magazines 1693–1968,
because of a report from psychologist Dr Ernest Dichter,
president of the Institute of Motivational Research in
New York.

In 1964 IPC employed Dr Dichter to examine Woman's
Own to "assess its performance in relation to the needs of
the present and possible requirements of the future, and
in relation to the other 'service' magazines, particularly
Woman". He "interviewed in depth" readers and non-
readers and interpreted the findings against what he knew
to be socio-psychological trends in the female population.

"He pointed to the changes occurring in the 'needs,
problems, goals, tastes and self images' of English women,

due to wider and better education, exposure to mass media such as TV, affluence and the growth of women's employment, particularly after marriage," wrote Cynthia White. [Americans often call Britain England.]

He concluded that a "new type of woman was emerging, a balanced woman who can combine, adjust and compromise femininity with independence, personal fulfilment with family responsibilities, and modesty with basic human values as she perceives them." He said classifying women by age wasn't meaningful and that they should be grouped according to their outlook, experience and activities. Feminism, which was appearing about this time, would not have fazed Dr Dichter.

But the sharp drops in circulation must have given pause for thought: in 1966 *Woman's Own* was selling just under 2.2million a week and by the end of 1968 it dropped to under 2million. *Woman,* the first colour magazine, had a similar loss. Why were these grand old ladies losing their buyers? What happened to loyalty? Had the women changed as Dr Dichter thought? Did they no longer need the information or advice that packed each issue or were they getting it elsewhere? Was something else tempting them away?

Television could be considered competition, but it wasn't occupying viewers 24/7 like it does today and in its limited broadcasting hours didn't offer information that magazines provided. But times were a'changing.

* * *

M y memories of those early days are vivid. I started in 1966 and Jane Reed, the new fashion editor, arrived not long after having been delayed by a health problem. She was short and jolly, in her 20s, a few months younger than me. She'd come from the teen magazine *Honey* and was remarkably buoyant.

In her department was writer Penny Vincenzi, soon to move to *Nova*, the newest monthly magazine, on a floor above ours. Diane Knight was a fashion assistant and her willowy model looks attracted the males on our corridor. Ken wasn't the only one to blush or stare at his feet when she was near.

Fashion as a subject was in the process of change; what was now available to buy was altering fast, as were people and attitudes. In 1966, Mary Quant was awarded an OBE for her distinctive contribution to fashion – the mini skirt. It received notoriety when some Continental countries banned the wearing of it, seeing it as "an invitation to rape" – an outrageous attitude that resonates with today's controversy over blaming the victim.

The skimpy garment, named after the designer's favourite car the Mini, was worn over what were known as stocking tights (their arrival consigned suspender belts to history or sexual fantasy). Checking your profile, front and rear, before you left home was essential if you were menstruating and wearing a pad.

When Mary Quant was interviewed about the 1960s, she said the erogenous zone of the time was the crutch (others might call it crotch) while the bust – commonly used to describe women's breasts or chest – was virtually abolished, at its best when flat as a pancake. The explanation, said Mary, was that the bosom was a symbol of motherhood and now the west had the contraceptive pill, motherhood wasn't in vogue. But the skinny girl/woman was, and Diane Knight was a perfect example.

Fashion, actually, was a dilemma. What did the word mean? After the austere post-war years the young and trendy preferred not to look like their mothers and secretly hoped the clothes would make them look like the models on the pages. How could 'fashion' in a magazine be right for all of them? 'Haute couture' designers created for the rich, the film stars and Royalty, but the garb for most people came from the shops on the high street, the department stores. And we couldn't always tell readers where to get the clothes shown as they had been selected months before shops and department stores had committed themselves to buying them in. It would be years before stockists were included.

The fashionable way forward was to make your own clothes – sewing patterns, printed on flimsy see-through paper, were sometimes given away but were easily available at a haberdashery (every high street had one). The *Woman's Own* experts showed the made-up garments and how best to accessorise them to develop individual style.

The magazine's own special offers were also very popular. Fleet Street was the inspiration for these: the Biba dress, a short shift designed by the owner of the headline-making store in Kensington High Street just for *Daily Mirror* readers to buy, was an extraordinary success. The magazines latched on to the idea of commissioned outfits delivered by Royal Mail so readers were up to date in the way they dressed no matter where they lived.

Queen of the fashion pack at *Woman's Own* was known by the subs as The Duchess. Phyllis Digby Morton appeared three days a week superbly clothed and coiffed, but I didn't know then that she had been the first editor of a magazine called *Woman & Beauty* (it closed in 1963). Her husband Henry Digby Morton, a fashion designer, in 1939 was responsible for the bottle-green uniform of the Women's Voluntary Service (which volunteers paid for).

The Duchess's word, in a most extraordinary accent (to an Australian's ear anyway), was law. And she loved having a go at the subs, relishing making Ken uncomfortable. "It needs a dog's dick," was a favourite demand, or "Who on earth put that dog's dick there?" Eventually I learnt to look at an exclamation mark without blushing.

AN EARLY INFLUENCER

Phyllis Digby Morton had a television career in the 1950s on a programme called *Can You Tell Me?* In 2005 Dek Hogan reviewed a snippet from it in his TV Diary: "incredibly up-itself look at etiquette and fashion...was obviously from a time where only those with plummy tones in the Home Counties were expected to own television sets." But I found out more than this.

In 1940, when Britain was under attack from German planes, she and her husband, as paying passengers, boarded *The City of Benares*, a four-year-old liner which left Liverpool in a convoy heading for Montreal. On board were 406 people – crew and passengers, including 90 children aged between four and 15 – being

evacuated to the safety of North America. The ship was mid-Atlantic on the night of September 17, in a fierce gale, when it was torpedoed by U Boat U48 and sank within 30 minutes. The death toll was 294. Phyllis and Henry were among the survivors along with only 13 of the children. The story of this tragedy is told in *Children of the Doomed Voyage* (2006) by Janet Menzies, a Fleet Street journalist.

My status as the only Aussie on the subs' desk went with the arrival in 1967 of Ita Buttrose who I should have known about but didn't as I never was part of 'women's journalism' in my reporting days. She was woman's editor of *The Daily Telegraph*, one of Sydney's two biggest news-papers (the other was *The Sydney Morning Herald*) when she won a trip to the UK with her architect husband Alas-dair Macdonald.

They'd decided to stay for a while so both could gain more experience in their chosen fields though why Ita should take such a lowly job still amazes me. She a couple of years younger than me, a fashion plate, always beauti-fully turned out, as they say, hair worn in a French pleat or chignon and make-up immaculate.

In those days only men wore trousers to an office, and women's everyday wear included stockings (or stocking tights) and gloves, the theory being that as a journalist you never knew who you might be called on to interview (in actuality, this didn't affect the deskbound subs whose only outing might be to the nearest public library to check facts in reference books we didn't have in the office).

It was good to have Ita with us on the desk. I bowed to

her instincts with fashion and beauty while I was more at home with crafty subjects and health, which I knew something about as I had been a trainee nurse for nearly two years before I left to start in journalism in 1959. Ita's confidence was something to behold. With her, cajoling was an art form and a closed door would not deter her. I don't remember her going at the pub with us but everyone knew her name (possibly because it was unusual).

Things were changing around us. In 1968 Robert Bruce, who was now editor after George Rogers moved upwards to become publisher of *Woman's Own* and *Nova*, brought in Dee Remmington as features editor. She, too, had been about to start on *Woman's Mirror* when it closed.

With years of Fleet Street experience behind her, she was charged with obtaining regular exclusives. Janice James was her deputy. Les Walton, ex *Woman's Mirror*, was managing editor, overseeing production, subbing and reader offers. Jane Reed was assistant editor in charge of practicals, art editor Peter Lawrence was associate editor, and the bullying supervising editor had left (to my relief).

I kept hoping a newspaper job would turn up. I still hadn't got used to working so far in the future, never living in the time you're in. On newspapers what you wrote was in print usually within 24 hours. On women's magazines it could take months.

In earlyish-1968 Nigel Lloyd, features editor of *The Observer* colour magazine where I had applied in the past, contacted me to say they were starting a children's section and would I be interested? This was the chance I'd been waiting for, but alas it was not to be. I had just discovered I was pregnant and starting afresh at this stage would have been too difficult. With too many unknowns ahead of me, I suggested sub Sally to him and she got the job.

To everyone's surprise – including her own, I seem to remember – Ita was also expecting. What else could we say but 'snap'! She and I went to the editor, separately, to break the news. There was no statutory maternity leave then (now there is maternity and paternity leave; in Australia it is called paid parental leave). It was traditional to finish work four to six weeks before the birth. We had no option but to resign though we were told we could return later should we want to.

A YEAR OF CHANGE

1968 was a dramatic year at IPC with the complete restructuring of magazine management, according to Cynthia White. Under the chairmanship of Arnold Quick, the separate houses – Newnes, Fleetway and Odhams – were phased out and their publications allocated to one of five newly-created groups, each with its own chief executive: women's weeklies, women's monthlies, young magazines, practical and juvenile magazines, and special interest and miscellaneous magazines. Administration of all these magazines had up till then been carried out in 37 different buildings! The basis of the changes, though, was to improve marketing and provide new services for advertisers including a collective rate card structure...offering volume and series discounts and special positions in the magazines. It was accepted that the new arrangement would naturally benefit readers.

* * *

A t *Woman's Own* it was a very productive time. As Ita and I blossomed, our pregnancies well encompassed by the then popular, voluminous, tent-like dresses, we were known as Tweedledum and Tweedledee (names given by production editor George Cannon or his sidekick Tony Scudder, I suspect) and I think we might have looked remarkably like the original Tenniel drawings in *Alice in Wonderland* and *Through the Looking Glass*.

Our energy was prodigious. We both got on well with Dee, who I regarded as a mate as well as a colleague. She was, as Iris Burton was to write in her obituary many years later (2001), "of the just-do-it school of journalism" – and we were on the same wavelength.

Gradually changing technology was helping *Woman's Own* to find new ways to look different. Lead times had lessened slightly, we were using more two-colour processes along with intricate layouts. These came from the imagination and fast-moving scalpel of the flamboyant art director Dennis Whelan, working mostly with The Duchess and her ally, beauty editor Caroline Richards. The pages benefited from his vivacious approach and the subs were under pressure to make the words fit tiny shapes and spaces.

Today, with computers, it is easy to cut-and-paste and kern (squeezing letters to fit a space). At that time, with bastard measures (that is, not standard column widths), every single character had to be worked out on a typewriter and counted to ensure the words fitted. Typewriters! I can recall the 'ping' as the end of a line was reached and you pushed the carriage return.

The real irritant was the carbon paper – the only way of keeping one or more copies of whatever it was you were typing. Sometimes three or four pieces were interspersed with A4 sheets. Any errors were whited out with Tippex, and you had to do the same on every page. No one could surely regret the passing of carbon paper or not bless the coming of the copier. [This, however, brought an unintended consequence – increased costs of production which had to be reckoned with eventually.]

I'd noticed very early on that the Brits say 'sorry' a lot, and the subs made apologising to the printers an art, to keep in their good books. I think we probably grovelled. We were made aware that confrontation might cause them to stop work. In Fleet Street, print-related unions were famous for bringing production to a sudden halt, usually over pay, but also conditions. One time, I remember, it was over the lack of teaspoons at the tea break.

The unions were well established at IPC, and working relationships were sometimes tricky. The secretaries and letter writers, for example, had to belong to the clerical branch of NATSOPA (the National Society of Operative Printers' Assistants) which merged at some point with SOGAT (the Society of Graphical and Allied Trades), and their approach to working practices – such as morning and afternoon stops for tea, and ending work on the dot of 5 or 5.30 – could irritatethe editors. The union had the final say in secretarial appointments and who could work where, which wasn't always appreciated. On the subs' desk there was no such thing as overtime.

During my pregnancy I was elected deputy father of the chapel (a traditional title that had nothing to do with gender). My appointment letter from the editor said I was required to be a member of the National Union of Journalists (which I was, a transfer from Australia) and I received my press card when I paid my subscription. This was like a mini passport and recognised by the police.

People in the art department belonged to either SLADE (Society of Lithographic Artists, Designers and Engravers) or NGA (National Graphical Association), the unions most associated with Fleet Street.

It was an important time as changes were on the horizon. Up until 1968, when the International Publishing Corporation set up IPC Magazines Ltd, merit rises were a standard way of increasing annual pay, but it was divisive as only some were rewarded. A new structure was sought so that journalists' and artists' grades, based on responsibility, could be established across all titles in the new groups. Once salaries for the grades were agreed, annual increases could be negotiated across the board.

So what exactly was responsibility? Many things were involved: whether you administered a budget, how many staff you oversaw, the importance of the role you played in preparing the magazine. The structure had to be right for the whole company. The negotiations were mostly done by the Father of the Chapel.

It made sense to me that subs were given a decent grading, though others simply did not understand why or appreciate just how necessary they were in producing the magazine to the expected standard. What was innovative was that each job had to have a job description. This, it was hoped, would prevent responsibilities overlapping. This often caused problems, particularly in relation to accountability and budgets.

I wasn't living in the UK in the early 1960s when a television series called *Compact*, about a woman's magazine, was shown – and had been the inspiration for many wanting to work on one. One of the surprises at *Woman's Own* was looking up from your work to find yourself being watched by a group of strangers who were visiting as part of a 'tour'.

It was good marketing: readers came to Tower House and were shown round the various departments where each head was expected to give a short explanation about their contribution to the magazine. Under the eye of Jean the receptionist, those on the tours did not witness sights such as senior male staff playing cricket with a tennis ball in the corridors after extended lunches.

What went on at IPC during the years I was at *Woman's Own* would have provided material for any television programme. On the lighter side, one of the subs, bearded Ken Ellis, set up as a clown to entertain at children's parties, and Harold from the art department became a transvestite. The rest was gritty drama.

One assistant editor, in charge of the letter writers' department, developed liver cancer and resigned, dying some time later at home. Another assistant editor ran off to the US with the publisher of *Woman* magazine. Patsy Kumm, a gifted assistant editor at *Woman* who had just published a cookery book (her husband worked with my partner at the BBC), died on an overseas press trip. Sylvia Duncan contracted a spinal disease that eventually killed her. The beautiful Diane, Twiggy-like in her willowiness but a heavy drinker, died after a tragic accident.

It was one of the perks of magazines that those higher up on the staff would be given one or two weeks' holiday organised by the travel editor in conjunction with PRs handling holiday companies and their non-judgmental reports would appear during January and February, grey-clouded months best for selling summer vacations.

George Cannon, as he rose through the ranks at *Woman's Own* and later *Woman*, when negotiating his salary always included – as quid pro quo for working whatever number of hours the editor demanded – a two-week, all expenses paid holiday for his family. And he got it, for production efficiency. Editor-designate Robert Bruce, always very approachable to subs, took his wife and two children to Malta on an arranged trips. He was unwell on his return with what was thought to be a gastric upset, but he was diagnosed with Malta fever (also called Undulant fever), a disease of cattle which is contracted via unsterilized milk or infected meat.

Tragically ironical, its other name is brucellosis (after Dr David Bruce, no relation, who found the link in 1887) and at this time there was an outbreak in Britain that was causing much concern. It turned out that Robert also had carcinomatosis, cancer in many parts of the body, and his illness brought his editorship to an end. He died in March 1971, aged only 35, causing a rearrangement of the hierarchy. I can't remember if Terry, the runner, was there then and moved up a level.

* * *

Ita gave birth to her daughter, Kate, around Christmas 1968, and my red-headed daughter, Danielle, was delivered by forceps in the middle of January 1969. It was a very cold winter and the snow, in my memory, lay on the ground for weeks. Ita, who'd moved to a rented house in deepest Kent sometime before the baby arrived – "We want to experience English country life," she explained – invited us down for a night in the February gloom.

Alasdair, known as Mac, was commuting daily to London by train and the house, typical at the time, had little heating. My little Dani had colic, I was still very hormonal and often on the verge of tears. Ita was a picture, not a hair out of place and make-up perfect, even at breakfast. Her little girl didn't even seem to cry.

Ita could have been the model for the *Woman's Own* woman whose every action we prescribed in the last issues we'd worked on. They covered the run-up to the festive season with a day-by-day plan for the reader's life including a timetable of what to buy and when, and what could be done in advance. Every minute was accounted for in executing a perfect Christmas Day, everything prepared and ready on time.

The men of the household were probably down at the pub having a drink, as tradition dictated. The *Woman's Own* woman went into action, pinny in place. She'd add the finishing touches to the meal and the table. She'd change into her special dress, do her hair and put her compact somewhere handy. It would be needed to dab over any shiny spots that might appear on her face while draining the vegetables or just generally slaving over a hot stove. I'd be taking my cook's tipple by this stage I suspect. [It was an editorial principle to give women well-meaning advice but making them feel they have to be perfect was a handicap that women's lib sought to eliminate – but that was a while away.]

It's funny how some things niggle in your memory. Over dinner, the subject of ambition came up – 'being ambitious' is not seen as a derogatory description for a woman in either Australia or the United States. Ita had a very keen sense of it, having been born into a journalist's family (her father had edited *The Daily Mirror* in Sydney and went on to run the Australian Broadcasting Commission's bureau in the US).

Ita was 15 when she started as a copy girl (a newspaper term for a runner, the stage before acceptance on the journalist training scheme). By 1965 she was woman's editor of one of Sydney's biggest dailies – the job she gave up for the big OE (overseas experience) as the Aussies call it. Her supreme confidence in dealing with others was understandable. The irony was that she won the trip, offered by a rival newspaper, for being chosen as the best dressed woman at the Royal Randwick races in Sydney which she was covering for her own paper. That's how luck works!

Even as we sat there with our new babes in arms, I could see the difference: I was the daughter of a country bootmaker with ambition but no journalistic connections while she already had 'form' in the field and aimed to be editor of the *Australian Women's Weekly*, the biggest women's magazine Down Under. It was nothing like the

UK's *Woman's Weekly* which started in 1911 – though both had big circulations.

[She would be involved later in making it a monthly (confusingly keeping the same title), after taking up an offer from Sir Frank Packer and his son Kerry, owners of Australian Consolidated Press, that she couldn't refuse. A magazine she started would be a game changer.]

With my whole body almost in the Aga, a farmhouse-style cooker using solid fuel – and the only heating in the room – I admit I felt a stab of envy listening to her set her course for the future. But I was so miserable I would have been envious of anyone who wasn't.

"Why aren't you ambitious like her?" asked my partner, adding to my anguish. What could I say? Ambition? I was only concerned to survive as a mother and for my darling baby to sleep more. I thumbed constantly through Claire Rayner's paperback *101 Things You Didn't Know About Pregnancy* (a signed copy she'd given me when my bump became noticeable) and was learning Dr Spock by heart. And the stitches I'd been given after my perineum was cut during the birth (called an episiotomy) were taking an uncomfortably long time to heal.

After a busy working life, I didn't find it easy being at home all the time with a small baby. I had no family to call on and the only friends I had made were those I knew from *Woman's Own*. My sanity was saved by phone chats with Maggie Daykin who had moved successfully from her secretarial role in the editor's office to the subs' desk and was enjoying the challenge. The word got round that I needed to earn money (I had shared responsibility for a mortgage on a terraced house in

Wimbledon) and Jane Reed, now associate editor, rescued me.

When Dani was about three months old, I started handling the 24 and 32 page supplements that helped boost sales of the magazine, working between the morning and evening rush hours. I drove my little green Renault 4 – it had an unusual gear-stick on the dashboard – to Covent Garden and parked among the rubbish (no parking meters then), and wheeled Dani in her pram to Tower House. My 'desk' was the floor of Jane's office, the layouts spread out around me, my daughter beside me in the carrycot. She was, by now, a joy and fortunately taking bottles as I wouldn't have been confidant breastfeeding in that environment. I worked this way, on and off, for months, but when Dani was nine months old, I found I was pregnant again which was certainly not planned. My financial situation was precarious and Jane was my saviour again. She was now editor designate and another restructure was on the way.

The subs had desks in the departments and there was no longer a central table. Ken Pickin remained the final conduit for all pages and I was asked to work with him. I was to train the subs in relation to their newly designated level of responsibility. I found Dani a childminder close to home and worked until three weeks before the birth, leaving each day at five o'clock to pick her up.

There was no lack of talented women on the staff. Gillian Allan, who went on to become chief sub of *Woman's Own* in the 1990s, told me that she knew nothing about any of the practical subjects we discussed. I must have felt instinctively that she had the right attitude to facts and communication. She'd come from the comics sector (where she met and married the talented Angus Allan, a Scottish cartoonist and saxophone player; he died in 2007), and I put her in the cookery department.

Lorry Spooner was 21 and newly married when she joined the subs' desk, relocating to the beauty department when the new scheme was introduced then a little later to the features department. Thirty years on, after spells as chief sub at *Marie Claire* and deputy editor at *Woman's Journal*, she returned to *Woman's Own* as associate editor. She loved being a sub, didn't want to be a writer, she said, and was good at her job, moving with ease from the old ways to the new when, years later, computers transformed magazine production methods.

Also in features was Angela Antrobus who'd joined as a subeditor from *Petticoat,* another teen mag. Angela, not long married to Paul, a keen sailor, would eventually have a career writing about conferences and incentive travel and the places, people, politics and practices involved.

The system worked well. The subs in each department took over the pursuit and editing of copy and oversaw layouts, after which Ken Pickin would see them through the next stage – the most difficult one – getting them signed by the relevant assistant or associate editor. It would be a rare day when changes were not asked for (it is an unwritten rule that the person above you always wants to rewrite something, usually captions). Even so, when I left to have my second daughter Sally in April 1970, everything looked hunky dory.

Because of antibodies in my blood, Sally was born with rhesus disease and her blood had to be replaced within 24 hours, a traumatic experience for her and for me as I watched. She seemed so tiny lying there with her old blood draining out one side and the new entering from the other. She was kept in a special ward for 10 days but I wasn't allowed to stay with her – hospitals were rigid then. Jan and Rennie Barrett, good friends visiting from New Zealand, looked after Dani at my home while I drove four times a day to breastfeed my new daughter and express milk which she'd be given during the night. I was exhausted by the time I brought her home.

The next few months were difficult. Poor little Sally had to have her heel pricked each week by the GP to test whether her new Type O blood was providing all that it should. She didn't like it at all and her cries were heart-rending. I breastfed for two months but my milk was drying up and the health visitor suggested that she be weaned. That worked well but even so it was tough.

My partner was overwhelmed by the whole situation. He was working late shifts at the BBC covering parliament (*Today at Westminster*) and often didn't come home at night at all. It became obvious that he had someone else and that we would part. I was in an awful state, emotional about the breakup and at a loss to know how I would survive with two daughters under two, with no money coming in and no family backup.

I'd kept in touch with Dee (by now assistant editor in charge of features) who invited me to come for a meal at her flat in Surrey on Boxing Day and to bring the girls. One look at my face told her all was not well, and after I'd explained the situation through tears she asked me if I would be interested in working for her, as her assistant. I could hardly believe my ears. I hadn't foreseen such a possibility and I was stunned.

Much later I heard that Dee had wanted Ita for the position, but she had taken up the offer from Sir Frank Packer and was back in Australia. I was feeling so desperate, it didn't matter that I was an also ran.

Dee made it clear that I had to have reliable childcare in place and that it wouldn't interfere with doing my job properly. I was going to have to learn how to be a single mother and full-time employee on one of the world's biggest magazines. There were going to be a lot of things to sort out – but at least I was no longer a subeditor.

4

NEW DIRECTIONS IN THE 70S

I n 1971 the two leading women's magazines now had female editors. At *Woman's Own*, because of his serious illness and prognosis, Robert Bruce had resigned and Jane Reed was appointed editor. At *Woman* women had been in charge from the start, first Miss Stuart Macrae followed by Mary Grieve who was there for 22 years, then Barbara Buss who took over in 1964. John Dunbar was Odham's editorial director and thus linked to *Woman*. I would find out more about him later.

Jane organised her new team. She found a new deputy with practicals' experience: Joan Chapman ex *Brighton Argus*, who commuted to London from Hove. She worked closely with Peter Lawrence, associate editor, responsible for the visual look of the magazine. Les Walton remained managing editor; Janice James was promoted to assistant editor fiction, with a new deputy Kati Nicholl; Dee, as assistant editor features, was backed by Diana Hutchinson as regular features editor (she would later be editor of Femail, at *The Daily Mail*).

The subs returned to the central desk, under a new chief sub Deidre Sanders (this clever woman would eventually be one of the UK's top agony aunts on Murdoch's daily *The Sun*) while Ken Pickin moved upwards to work on special projects, mostly with Les Walton. Subs no longer had charge of sells and headings – the words that draw readers into the story. These now came from the weekly conference, writ in stone (as it were) from above.

My new life and job began in earnest in January 1971, and I was full of trepidation. As Dee's assistant, I had to answer readers' letters, 'copy taste' ideas (ie, were they right or wrong for the magazine?), keep tabs on publishers and their forthcoming book lists, and prepare material for the conference. Jane's letter appointing me, at £2,400 per annum, wished me luck.

We never discussed it, but she possibly suspected that some of the writers might have difficulty accepting a former sub in this responsible role of assistant features editor. From their point of view I had no past other than *Woman's Own*. Fortunately Dee was in there like Flynn with full support.

The department she oversaw was packed with talent. Writers Iris Burton and Janet Horwood were there, along with Sue Pilkington, a beauty writer who had moved to features. Newcomers included another Australian, Jillie Collings, who had a deep interest in astrology which led her, after a while, to have her own star page.

Jill Guyte, Sheila Fullarton and Lori Miles would all be enticed to great heights in newspapers. Lori, in fact, became Fleet Street's first female editor, of *The Evening News* which was resurrected for a short time in 1987 (it had closed in 1980) to protect *The Evening Standard* from an assault on London's evening dailies by the black-browed Robert Maxwell – of whom, more to come.

Brenda Polan, a new sub on the desk, had a local newspaper background and a big future: she would make her way to *Woman*, to *The Guardian* on Farringdon Road (near Fleet Street) and later The London College of Fashion (as Director of Programmes, Media).

Dee nurtured her excellent contacts and was often closeted with them in her office, the only time the door was shut. She expertly sensed what was right for the magazine and found many goodies through literary agents (also known as authors' agents). The most memorable was the glamorous Pat Kavanagh, stunningly stylish, often in matching picture hat and gloves, from A D Peters.

[Her author husband Julian Barnes brought her to life in his poignant book about their time together and her death from a brain tumour in 2008. *Levels of Life* was published in 2013.]

Another frequent visitor was Carol Smith, a real go-getter starting out as a literary agent but also a to-be, very successful, novelist herself. Other visitors were Heather Jeeves from London Management, Ray Wergan from Transworld, an agency offering material worldwide, Doreen Montgomery and Shirley Russell from the Rupert Crew Agency, and Felicity Bryan from Curtis Brown.

[How sad I was to read her *Financial Times Weekend* obituary in 2020, of her death at aged 74 from an inherited cancer. She ran her own successful agency in Oxford for many years. One of her clients, author David Pilling, wrote: "Two days before she died, she received an MBE in a special ceremony...lockdown rules limited visitors to six. In spirit, hundreds attended."]

* * *

Dee was a nifty negotiator and skilful at commissioning. She had at the ready established pros like Royal specialists Graham and Heather Fisher and intrepid Irish newspaperman Alan Bestic who produced wow-factor features at her beckoning. Joyce Robins, a shy and introverted woman, found real-life stories about women in despair that made you weep (though names were changed to protect their identities).

Photographers generally went to Dennis Beaven, but some – like Tom Blau from an agency called Camera Press – would go to Dee. She welcomed, too, photo-journalism packages, with enticing words and pictures, from husband and wife team David Steen and Shirley Flack. He had worked on *Picture Post* in its heyday, apprenticed, aged 15, to renowned photographer Bert Hardy. Both had been on the ill-fated *Woman's Mirror* and Shirley had written the 'autobiography' of the teenaged model Twiggy.

Editor Jane was a dynamo, quite unlike Rog who had rarely been sighted by most of the staff. She toured the corridors frequently, calling into any of the departments without warning and firing ideas into the air. Dee decided it was my job to make sure I caught hold of her thought processes and her feature suggestions when she appeared in our office. We never knew which of them she would remember and have expected us to follow up. Dee liked to be well prepared and hated being asked by Jane in conference "And have you got such and such..." and find she hadn't. From my scribbles we'd decide which ideas to pursue, keeping our fingers crossed that her other ones would be forgotten. Much of the time the plan worked.

The downside was that we had a three-drawer steel filing cabinet filling up with finished, and unused, features which would have to be written off in the annual stocktake. There were several reasons for this. The issues were getting smaller. Jane was presiding over a plummeting circulation. And nobody knew what could be done about it. Indecision reigned. It was a tense time.

Why weren't millions buying *Woman's Own* as they used to? There was no doubt each issue was good value (6p in 1973). But as more and more women were going out to work perhaps they lacked time to sit down and read. If magazines were a treat, a reward, something to lose themselves in for a while, was there no longer any need, or even time, for that escapism?

Articles were rewritten over and over again, searching for some magic formula. TOTs – triumph-over-tragedy – stories were a mainstay. But Jane also added a lot more newsworthiness: *At Your Service* focused on what was going wrong in the community, or was doing well. One of her earliest concerns was that children in pushchairs were at the same level on footpaths as exhaust fumes from passing vehicles, problematical still in the 21st century and regarded as an environmental and health hazard needing world-wide attention.

She started the annual Children of Courage, which

continues to this day, gaining a useful Royal link as Princess Anne agreed to hand out the awards to the winners, which ensured press coverage. The stories of girls and boys who find ways of living with adversity reveal a concerning side of the UK (even today there is no real solution to many of their problems, eg, being a sole carer for a parent). The awards have the power to make the most hard-hearted count their blessings.

Jane was determined to give space to difficult subjects, usually involving families, and began campaigns that the readers could support. It wasn't until 1974 that I remember reading the word incest in a woman's magazine. Coverlined 'the family secret no-one talks about', Ruth Martin – Claire Rayner – chose her words carefully under the heading 'an intimate conversation with the friend you can trust'. I had left *Woman's Own* by then, but I kept that issue so I must have been impressed. There was another reason too: for the coverline "How to enjoy good health – ill, well, fat or thin, you are what you eat".

* * *

Food and its effects on our mind and body was a popular topic in all magazines Jane was involved in. Editors have to have their own antenna, their own instinct for what will make their magazines survive and grow. Jane latched on to what has become a phenomenal trend by promoting dieting as a way of life to those who bought and prepared the food and served it to their families.

A one-off she created, *Successful Slimming*, went on sale under the *Woman's Own* banner, and in 1974 became a bi-monthly. It did well in the 10 years it existed, particularly with its classes aimed at women (not unlike those of Weight Watchers and Slimming World today which have their own magazines). They were run nationally by a woman called Rosemary Conley.

Oddly, at a time when skinny Twiggy was in demand as a photographic model, excess weight and how to lose it had become a national preoccupation. The subject was surveyed in 1967 by the then 10-year-old Consumers' Association which asked members about exercise patterns, weight history, and slimming methods. Which? (as the CA is now known) explained that its readers were 'unlikely to be typical of the whole country' (and the numbers considerably smaller than *Woman's Own* readership), but that questionnaire was pertinent: Was the source of the slimming method a woman's magazine? Was the diet 'nutritionally adequate' or medically supervised?

[In the 1960s 'diets' generally related to illness and were the realm of qualified dieticians based in hospitals who created eating plans to restore the patient's health. The word 'nutrition' covered elements in foods that nourished the body; the word nutritionist didn't exist. Magazines were the main promoters of ways to lose weight.]

A NEW FOCUS ON FOOD

In 1969 a husband and wife team had amazing foresight. Tom and Audrey Eyton, seeing the need for information about food and its relationship to weight, started *Slimming and Family Nutrition*, a magazine in which they refused to run any ads that went against editorial standards. This would have been very unusual

then, and certainly now, as advertising remains the
prime source of solvency for magazines and
newspapers, and jobs depend on it. Audrey Eyton, once
a beauty editor at *Woman*, and Rosemary Conley
became the two most important dieting proponents in
Britain and in many parts of the world.
It was an incredible change: diet had become a regime
of eating aimed to help you lose weight. At *Woman's
Own* the cookery and beauty departments were
constantly asked to find new ways to get across the idea
of weight loss while offering enticing recipes. It was a
difficult double standard. And remains so today.

* * *

One strategy to get and hold readers *Woman's Own*
was to secure first rights of publication – for
fiction especially, which meant paying big money. At the
end of the 1960s two successes were *Jonathan Livingston
Seagull* and *Love Story* which became equally popular
movies. By the early 1970s the blockbuster era had
started, with books by Arthur Hailey, Pearl S Buck, R F
Delderfield and Harold Robbins selling millions of copies.

About this time I got to know Melbourne-born
Carmen Callil who had been a publicity manager at
publishing houses like Hutchinson, Panther, Granada,
Anthony Blond and Andre Deutsch. She was sharp, good
fun and a great story teller. I remember having a drink
with her to talk about a fellow Aussie, Thomas Keneally.

It might have been about the time she started her book
publicity business which she ran to boost the funds of

Virago, her own company, formed to publish books celebrating women and women's lives. It was an astounding success and Carmen went on to make her mark as a publisher, businesswoman, writer and critic; she was made a Dame in the 2017 Queen's birthday honours. And Keneally, multi-prizewinning author and playwright, is an AO (Order of Australia) and an Australian Living Treasure. The wonders of Down Under!

Woman's Own itself produced an amazing array of successful authors. Long before my time, Barbara Taylor Bradford – credited as the one who penned the first bonkbuster, a book describing liberal sexual encounters – had been fashion editor there. Not far behind was Penny Vincenzi who was a junior in the same department and was there when Jane Reed was fashion editor; her family sagas topped preferred holiday reading lists for years (she died in 2017).

Sarah Harrison was a university graduate who was accepted on the IPC training scheme and worked on everything from readers' letters to promotions. But she always believed that her future lay in fiction writing – and so it proved.

Her first book was *The Flowers of the Field*, inspired by her own family history and set in World War 1. It became a trilogy: *A Flower That's Free* was next, then *The Wildflower Path*. All particularly apt for re-release in 2014 and 2019, 100 years after the event. She has written many more (see www.sarah-harrison.net) including a textbook for novelists *How to Write a Blockbuster*.

CLAIRE RAYNER'S WRITING SUCCESS

At *Woman's Own* Claire Rayner did more than contribute articles on health and relationships. It was a great day when she and husband Des came to the office to tell Jane Reed and Dee Remmington that she'd secured a mega-bucks deal to produce three books of historical romance. Always larger than life, with this news she was exuberant. It was only the beginning. By the time she died in October 2010 one of her obituarists, Suzie Hayman, a fellow agony aunt, credited her with 90 published books – yes 90! That original three became a 12-volume family sequence called *The Performers*, published from 1973 to 1986. Mostly I remember her excitement at being able to afford a car large enough for the family, all of whom were tall and well built. Her son, Jay Rayner, is a highly-regarded food journalist, critic and musician. Claire started her working life as a nurse and midwife with a lifelong commitment to the NHS. When she was dying (according to one obituary) she told relatives: "Tell David Cameron that if he screws up my beloved NHS I'll come back and bloody haunt him." As so much has happened to it since 2010, I wonder if her ghost has been seen having hysterics in the corridors of power.

* * *

Janice James was excellent at picking what was right for *Woman's Own* and it was she who enticed Maeve Binchy, London editor of the *Irish Times*, to be a 'stringer' for the magazine. It was a necessary move because of the controversial subject matter now being included which might catch the eye of the ever-vigilant Irish censor. His job was to prevent distribution of publications which contained information about birth control, for instance, the most common topic kept from Irish readers, or abortion or divorce.

The answer was to produce an Irish edition in which troublesome pages were replaced with articles having a local slant. And that's how I knew Maeve, as a lilting voice on the phone (I love the sound of an Irish accent), when I'd ask her for something for a particular issue.

Her death, aged 72 in August 2012, brought universal tributes, with obituaries telling of her generous spirit, compassion and humour. The first of her 16 novels, *Light a Penny Candle*, came out in 1982, followed by several collections of short stories, but in the last 30 years of her life she suffered terribly from arthritis. She remains in the top 10 of Britain's most popular writers.

My first experience of securing a book extract made me aware of the importance of negotiating skills. I'd seen and heard Dee in action with the agents, and she was good at getting her way. My predecessor Janice James had a superb reputation, too, and had made many good buys. She had forged a link with Angus & Robertson, an Australian publisher, buying British magazine rights in various books, one on Dyslexia (only then being revealed as a major problem in education), another about American anthropologist Margaret Mead and her work with the islanders in the South Pacific, and one by science-minded Aussie GP Claire Weekes MBE on agoraphobia, a difficult health problem. *Woman's Own* was doing its best to widen the readers' horizons and knowledge base.

Having met A&R's new editorial director Ian Dear, I was offered *Dove*, about a 16-year-old boy who sailed alone across the Pacific. Film rights had been sold and Hollywood star Gregory Peck was cast as the father. Ian wanted a payment that had an awful lot of noughts in it. I talked it over with Dee then we both went to see Jane.

Even she was not authorised to spend that amount, she said, so she and I went to see Rog, the publisher. I think my blush matched his face colour as I explained why it would be perfect for *Woman's Own* and I was convinced he'd say no but he didn't! We paid the money and *Dove* appeared in three parts and went down well. (And, dear reader, much later I married Ian.)

* * *

Working full time with two very small children had many challenges but I knew that I had to cope with any problems that occurred; taking time off was never an option. My daughters and mortgage depended on me having this job and balancing it with home life was hard work. Sometimes the trade-off was not getting enough shuteye – I often nodded off as I read to the girls (supposedly to put them to sleep).

I don't think any exhaustion showed when I ended up in one of the beauty department's make-over features. Jenny Irvine (another Aussie) asked me to take part – and thus it was that my longish, bushy red hair (I could sit on it when my first daughter was born) was given a new shape and my face was made up professionally. My lipstick and block mascara might not be enough now that I was over 30 and looking my best was was essential.

Part of my job was meeting people who might have something to contribute. A young American woman called Leslie Kenton, dressed in flowing black from top to toe, a very large picture hat perched on long blonde hair, swept into the office full of ideas for lifestyle features, of natural ways of enhancing health and beauty. I took her to meet Jane, but nothing came of it.

A single mother in her mid-20s, with two small children at that time, Leslie was just beginning to carve a future for herself that would influence men and women around the world, just like her father Stan Kenton's big-band jazz. I will tell you more about her later.

Another meeting was with Sir Ranulph Fiennes and his wife, Virginia (Ginny), who'd called at Tower House without an appointment. They were a nice-looking couple, in their mid-20s, and had just returned from an adventure in Saudi Arabia. He was a charmer, talking eagerly about what they'd done, she was silent, but they impressed me. We never did their story, which was a pity.

His achievements went on to amaze the world and owed much to the shy, determined Ginny working in the background on his behalf. She died in 2004, aged 56, and he raised millions for cancer research in her memory. He remarried, had a child at a late age (for first fatherhood), and at 65 was the oldest Briton to climb Everest, at the third attempt. A Boys' Own hero, but not *Woman's Own*'s.

I became friends with Carole Blake, who started out as secretary to one of Britain's youngest and gifted publishers Edmund Fisher and moved, with him, as rights manager at Michael Joseph, W H Allen and Sphere books. We'd moan to each other over lunch about our personal problems and generally plan how we'd run the world (when one of us was made Queen).

It would have been her, I'm sure, as she went on to be one of the UK's most powerful literary agents allied to husband Julian Friedmann (who she later divorced, though they remained partners in the Blake Friedmann literary agency). It was a strange coincidence, as Julian had worked at Angus & Robertson with Ian Dear who became my husband in 1975. [Sadly Carole died unexpectedly, aged 70, in 2016. One of her books, *From Pitch to Publication,* is a reliable guide for wannabe writers.]

* * *

I enjoyed 'copy tasting'. It meant I could I follow up ideas sent in. In 1972 in the mail was a letter from a woman in Portsmouth called Hazel Inglis, writing on behalf of a group of men who had compiled their memories of World War 2 around a bitch called Judy, the recipient of the animal VC, the Dickin Medal. Writing came back into my life! Dee commissioned me to do a two-part feature for the magazine and this led to my first book (edited from the men's words) called *The Judy Story,* published by Souvenir Press.

Ernest Hecht, the owner of Souvenir, was a mate of Dee's, which is how I got to meet him. He was an ardent Arsenal fan, as I was – this is how luck works. [Ernest was singularly different as a publisher, as the obituaries after his death in 2017 revealed.]

Later that same year I met Klaus Flugge, from publishers Abelard-Schuman, who was seeking someone to write a book about mistresses, not historical ones but those living in our time when the women's liberation movement was growing. It was a great opportunity for me (though I knew little about the subject) and, serendipitously, a friend in New Zealand told me about Susan Kedgley who was in the UK for a short stay. Sue – feminist, writer and broadcaster who had expressed strong views about female/male relationships in a book called *Sexist Society* – agreed to co-author *The Mistress*.

What surprised us both was that we had no difficulty finding real examples: friends and friends of friends gave us many names. Of these, 35 women and 10 men agreed to be interviewed but not to be identified in the book. We drew up a questionnaire which asked the same questions of them all. It involved months of interviews and research. For me, it meant working day and night.

* * *

The 1970s was a very long decade. The dockers' and miners' strike of 1972 had a widespread effect on the whole of Britain and the Central Electricity Generating Board restricted the number of hours electricity could be supplied to different areas.

These power cuts were fun for my daughters who were bathed and fed by candlelight (fortunately I had a gas cooker, so meals weren't a problem) and we sat and read stories in the sitting room by the light of the coal fire and the methylated spirit lamps that I'd bought from a street market when I first arrived in the UK.

With their tall glass funnels and adjustable wicks they were so quaint, I thought, and now very useful. Some streets around Covent Garden still had gas lamps, whooshed into illumination by the lamplighters covering the area on foot, but the electric ones remained dark.

I wasn't doing well financially; a mortgage and child-care costs drained me. But how could I earn more money? The advances for the two books I was writing helped a little, but things were looking precarious in Britain and I wondered whether I should return to live in Australia, where at least I had family and friends. When I heard that my father was ill, I felt it was a sign. I needed to see him.

After a chat with my bank manager – in those days you knew who they were, and mine at the old Midland Bank was the very nice Mr Tilly – and his agreement to loan me money, I went to Dee and Jane. They generously allowed me to take two weeks' paid leave and four weeks' unpaid from December 18 1972 to February 6 1973. I booked return flights to Sydney.

Almost on landing, I realised why I had left Australia to go abroad in 1963: the heat overwhelmed me. For 10 days in a row the temperature was over 100deg (in the old measure) and because of the high humidity (about 80%) I just dripped sweat. Not perspiration, sweat. I hated it.

But there was a real air of excitement around. In November Gough Whitlam's Labor Government had surged in, replacing the Liberal-Country Party coalition that had run the country non-stop for as long as anyone could remember and changes were desperately needed. There were great hopes of putting right a lot of the wrongs in the country. It would end in tears, sadly, involving the Queen's representative in Australia (and therefore the Queen herself) who dismissed Whitlam controversially during a constitutional crisis in 1975.

I'd written to Ita Buttrose to tell her I was returning for a visit and she invited me to call her and we'd have lunch. Her new magazine was making waves: *Cleo* was sexy and funny with a full-colour centrefold that opened out to show a male whose state of undress was concealed by carefully arranged props. The rugged Aussie actor Jack Thompson (known for the film *Gallipoli*) looked delightful in a camp Grecian setting in the first issue – and others were happy to follow. [The making of *Cleo* became an Australian TV drama series in 2011, with Ita as a consultant, long after Kerry Packer, its publisher, died.]

Miss Buttrose – nobody called her Ita, I noticed – in 1973's summer heat was, naturally, as cool as a cucumber, extremely elegant and noticeably pregnant. It was good to see her and she seemed interested when I explained my situation. She (and others) pointed out that childcare options were almost non-existent in Sydney.

I'd need somewhere to live and help with the children and the price of both of those would be greater than she could offer me as a journalist. I didn't think I was earning well in London but I was better off there as I had a house, albeit mortgaged with an excellent fixed-rate deal obtained through my employers IPC, and the girls were content being looked after by Marianne Wright who lived directly across the road.

Checking out other possibilities, I caught up with Doreen Wells, now a happy New Australian (as incomers were known) working at *Woman's Day*, a weekly with a harder edge than the more mumsy but bigger selling *Australian Women's Weekly*. She secured me an interview which brought an offer of a features job. I really liked the magazine but I couldn't make the finances add up.

[In Cynthia White's *Women's Magazines 1693-1968* I learnt that there had been a *Woman's Day* in the UK, between 1858 and 1961 when it was merged, would you believe it, with *Woman's Own*.]

When I was growing up and wanted to be a journalist, magazines never crossed my mind. But *Australian Women's Weekly* had always been big business and there was new impetus with *Cleo*, as I learnt from Jenny Irvine who'd returned to live in Sydney and was working on *Dolly*, a very popular young women's magazine. It wouldn't be long before Australian versions of many British monthly magazines would be on the newsagents' shelves as well. But I had no insight into that.

In a way I was disappointed not to be staying, but enjoyed showing Dani and Sally off to their grandparents and my sisters and brothers living in various parts of New South Wales. I caught up with old journalist friends too, but after a party too far, in unremitting heat at a place called Windsor just outside Sydney, where everyone except me was smashed out of their minds on marijuana, I was eager to board the Qantas flight for London. That journey was a nightmare.

The weather at the end of January/early February of 1973 caused London and Manchester airports to close because of fog and snow. Our plane made an unscheduled stop at Athens, where we disembarked and were given freezer-cold sandwiches to eat while waiting for news. Back on board the captain announced that we might be able to go to Manchester but after an hour circling he was told to go to Prestwick. "Where on earth's that?" shouted one of the passengers. "Scotland," another replied. I didn't think things could get worse.

I had a child on either side of me fast asleep when we arrived about 10 o'clock that night. I appealed to members of the cabin crew for help but they said they were already over their shift limit and were no longer responsible for the passengers. Seeing me near to tears with frustration two other passengers, both men, offered to carry the girls while I coped with our luggage. We went by coach to a railway station and boarded a train that had no heating or food. At this point I realised how foolish I had been.

Because of the luggage allowance and because I had to carry the suitcase (no wheel-alongs then), I had only packed summer clothes. As Marianne's husband Mick was to meet us at Heathrow bringing winter things, the only extras I had were cardigans and tights for the girls and woollen beanies my mother had crocheted for them.

I was shaking with cold, as were the children. We snuggled up together and our combined warmth helped. Little Sally took off her beanie during the night and wrapped it around my hands. The tears I shed warmed me too. We arrived at London's Kings Cross station at eight in the morning, bedraggled and exhausted.

The immigration policy in 1973 was stern, and I knew that there might be problems at Customs. We had to go through the 'other passports' as both British-born daughters were on my Australian passport (children didn't have their own passports then) and while I had a stamp that showed I had right of abode in the UK – my mother was born in Chester, my grandfather in Liverpool – I was quizzed about what I was doing here. Fortunately I had had the foresight to get a letter from Dee identifying me and my role at *Woman's Own* so they allowed us to enter.

Since then, I've always travelled with documentation, including a copy of my naturalization certificate. Many years later, not having the right documents did irreparable harm to men, women and children of what was called the Windrush generation who came from British Caribbean countries to find jobs and settle here after World War 2.

I carried the luggage while the girls tottered alongside, their dolls in their arms, their beanies on their heads. I think they saw Mick first, his arms holding our overcoats. By listening to the news on the radio and making phone calls to Qantas he'd been able to track our route – he was the only one who knew where we were. What a hero. The whole journey had taken 48 hours.

A welcome home card awaited me from Dee. "Please come back soon!" she wrote, double underlining 'please'.

5

CRISES, SEX AND AUSTERITY

A day later I was at my desk. There was no time to be jetlagged: I had to deal with the correspondence that awaited me. The largest pile was readers' letters containing poems. While I was away, a poem – probably short and humorous, possibly a limerick – must have made it onto the letters' page. This always resulted in a deluge. *'Hey! Woman's Own is publishing poetry'* seemed to be the message that sped round the country. But we weren't, and I could only devise a "thank you but no thank you" letter to handle it.

I was only technically the poetry editor, for it was a passive post. Sometimes I had to pick a poem for Patience Strong's regular weekly offering, from a vast collection she supplied. Unless it had a pertinent theme for the time, the choice was likely to be because of its length as it usually filled a gap somewhere in a serial or long feature.

Art editor Martin Richardson, having placed the poet's galleyed words in a space on the relevant proof, always enquired mischievously whether we could cut a few lines. At least it made us laugh. Patience Strong was a phenomenon. Her "thoughts for every day", according to Wiki, were "usually short, simple and imbued with sentimentality and the beauty of nature and inner strength" which, even in a small space, contained an appealing message such as "Time is the friend of the breaking heart". You could call them early sound bites.

I was soon back in the swing by day, literally as it happened, as Jane had planned a special offer: 'Star Choice Singalong', a pack of two LPs (long playing records). The features department matched 40 catchy – but out of copyright – songs to agreeable stars of stage and screen (among them Anna Neagle, Frank Ifield, Kenneth More, Diana Dors, Harry Secombe, Des O'Connor and Barbara Windsor) and then found a record producer with links to reasonably priced musicians and session singers (who did the ooh-ahh-ahh in the background).

The record was made on a Saturday (my daughters and neighbours came along to join in the singing as well, all unpaid, but it was a fun outing) and Joan Page later set up a photograph in Tower House for the cover. Some of the staff stood around three brightly coloured pianos, the very latest style – at one sat astrologer Leon Petulengro, gold earring in place, who actually was a whizz on the keys – along with two stars, Tony Britton (actor, and father of TV presenter and novelist Fern Britton, died 2019) and Julie Ege (actor, and former Miss Norway who died in 2008). The lyrics were included in the magazine of December 1, 1973, so readers could sing along with the record they'd bought. It was phenomenally successful!

* * *

To complete the two books I'd been commissioned to do (they would be published later that year) I had to work at night after I had read the children to sleep. A lot of research was necessary for *The Mistress*. Co-author Sue Kedgley and I drew up a questionnaire to fill in when interviewing our co-operative, and fascinating, women and men (all of whose names were changed, as were any identifying characteristics, a tradition of women's magazines that I was used to). We decided on chapter titles (Free agent, Sex object, Male indulgence, Predators, Marriage maker or breaker?) and inserted pertinent particulars from the interviews to back up the themes.

I couldn't believe how these people juggled their lives in order to have long-term parallel relationships based on sex with someone they weren't married to. They were neither prostitutes nor kept women, but completely susceptible to the love of married men. And few married their lovers (interestingly, most didn't want to anyway).

For three of them, completing the questionnaire was cathartic – they brought their liaisons to an end after the book was published. One woman, who'd had a child by her lover and had him adopted, was, years later, contacted by this now adult offspring. She wasn't happy to be reminded of the years she felt she had wasted on the lover, so a rewarding relationship with the product of that time was never on the cards.

The Judy Story came together more easily. The idea for the book began in 1970, at a reunion of the Yangtse Gunboatmen's Association in Portsmouth. On the wall was a life-size painting of a liver-and-white pointer, its head framed in a ship's cowl – this was Judy RN.

She was well known to four men present. Vic Oliver, Bill Wilson, George White and Les Searle served on the British gunboats patrolling the Yangtse in China at the end of the 1930s and it was their anecdotes about where and when they had known the bitch that made the story. It ranged from the back streets of Shanghai to the fall of Singapore to Japanese prisoner-of-war camps.

Judy was listed as a POW and given a rice ration (hence the RN designation). She attached herself to a prisoner, Frank Williams, who, with the help of others, saved her life on many occasions. Just having her with them was an inspiration to the men and they nominated her for the PDSA Dickin Medal – the animal VC – which she was awarded in 1946. Edwin Varley, a friend of the four men, had completed a manuscript (*The dog with six lives*) that I set about editing on the night shift.

The men's agent Hazel Inglis was Australian – a lovely granny-like figure – and I drove down to Portsmouth a few times at weekends with Dani and Sally when I needed more information or to deliver proofs. *The Judy Story* was published as both hardcover and paperback and while quite well received it was never going to make my fortune – one royalty statement shows I earnt 10s 9d (about 53p). But it was obviously rewarding for someone else.

The story was retold in 2014 by Damien Lewis. Published by Quercus, the jacket proclaims his *Judy* as "A Sunday Times bestseller". Lewis, an award-winning journalist, author and film maker, is a dog-lover with a background that includes covering war zones so his credentials for writing such a book ticks all the boxes. *The Judy Story* is listed in the bibliography and Varley's tale is a good blueprint for the animal's early years.

The Mistress, published at the end of November 1973, did well for the co-authors! Joyce Hopkirk, deputy editor of *The Daily Mirror* and a friend of Jane Reed, heard about the book and bought pre-publication serial rights. Joyce had moved to Fleet Street after a fantastic year as launch editor of the British *Cosmopolitan*.

Sue and I shared this bonanza, and the publishers took a cut too, but it was more money than I could remember having. (In today's terms it was a pittance, dear reader.) I wrote to my bank manager Mr Tilly and told him that I could soon pay off my loan. He wrote back to say he was glad he had been sitting down when he read my letter. But I had other news for him too.

Everyone working at IPC was kept informed about ongoing projects within the company via the house news-paper which also carried ads seeking staff. After I returned from Australia I saw one for a new weekly for women, called *First Lady*, that would begin in October and applied for the job of assistant editor/features. I was now 33 and I felt I had to chase every opportunity. Bill Williamson, the editor, was a cheerful and dapper Scot, and one of the bright young men of magazines. After several meetings he offered me the post – described as a Senior Executive appointment – at £3,905 a year, a princely sum to my eyes.

When I broke the news to Dee and Jane I don't think either of them thought I was making the right decision, but they wished me well. It pleased them less that Renee, my secretary at *Woman's Own*, went with me. With hindsight, Dee and Jane's reaction could have had something to do with the very short life of another IPC weekly in 1972. Unfortunately, the name chosen for it – *Candida* – medically speaking is a form of thrush, an exceedingly uncomfortable affliction for women.

[According to *The Business of Women's Magazines* (by Brian Braithwaite and Joan Barrell, published in 1979), *Candida* was the brainchild of Jean Twiddy, editor turned publisher who was behind *Woman's Weekly's* change to full colour and resultant increase in circulation. Tragically, she died of cancer during the magazine's development and Angela Wyatt, editor of *Woman & Home*, was put in charge of what was to be an 'upmarket weekly'. She admitted later that she had no idea what the magazine was about. *Candida* lasted eight weeks.]

In publishing terms, 1972 was a year of mixed news. *Looking Good*, devoted to beauty, was launched privately by Penny Vincenzi (not yet started on her fiction-writing career) and her ad-man husband. Originally it was to be sold only in chemists – like the food-based *Family Circle*, published by Thomson, in supermarkets – but the high-street chain Boots wanted sole rights of sale, cutting out independent shops. "It started well but the magazine wasn't supported with good displays and distribution," said Braithwaite and Barrell.

British *Cosmopolitan* was an outstanding success for The National Magazine Company, but it was the death knell for the struggling *Vanity Fair*. When editor Audrey Slaughter saw her magazine sold to IPC to be merged with *Honey*, which she had started and edited in 1961, she set up a company to launch *Over 21* – the cover of its first issue declared *'Produced by the former staff of Vanity Fair'*. *Cosmo's* success also killed off *Flair* and *Modern Woman*, both of which had been popular in the 1950s.

One of the notable births was a young (for teenagers) magazine, *Look Now*, published by IPC. Behind its creation was Terry Hornett, who had left IPC to set up Carlton Publishing, a group providing editorial packages for publishers, quite an innovation. Some very famous names in women's magazines were to come from this group, but much later on.

Two other starts were ground-breaking: Gloria Steinem's *Ms magazine* (co-founded with Dorothy Pitman Hughes who, I read recently, has been largely airbrushed out of history) in the US, and the feminist magazine *Spare Rib* in Britain. Rosie Boycott – now a Baroness and a member of the House of Lords – and Marsha Rowe were the founders, and were also directors of Carmen Callil's publishing house Virago. All 239 issues of *Spare Rib* (1972-1993) have been digitised by the British Library, a sign of its importance in women's magazine history.

* * *

I t would not be the same with *First Lady* which I joined in October 1973 – with an intended launch in February 1974. Its prime aim was to widen the weekly market. The four top sellers were *Woman*, *Woman's Own*,

Woman's Weekly and *Woman's Realm* – the youngest, started in 1958, to take up the advertising that *Woman*, with its large circulation, had no space for.

First Lady, wrote Bill in my letter of appointment, would be "a topical weekly, generating excitement and surprise in the overall mix". It was to be sexier, funnier, and more outspoken than other magazines with no ban on any subject. It was going to be a challenge and not just because of the name (I never knew who chose it).

It was goodbye to Tower House for me. *First Lady* was set up on one floor in an old Odhams or Fleetway building in Long Acre, on the other side of Covent Garden, close to Charing Cross Road and Leicester Square – London's theatre world. The staff was small and each of the department heads – Judith Hall, fiction, Pat Roberts, fashion, Val Jackson, home – would be one-person bands with secretarial support. I told Bill about Leslie Kenton and to our delight she agreed to write beauty and health features, but as a freelance.

Bill and I set out to find the dramatic but different elements that would make the magazine lively and perti-nent. And I had to find some 'regulars' who could produce the right mix of words to touch the funny bone.

The 'stars' – astrology – was a must. The previous summer I had met Patric Walker, astrologer extraordi-naire, who thanks to a recommendation from Helene Hoskins – the legendary queen of the stars, Celeste, of *Harpers & Queen* – made his name at *Nova*. He was one of the first I rang to tell about the new magazine.

Would he be interested in doing weekly forecasts, incorporating an angle that might amuse the readers? He decided he would do it, but when we came to negotiating a fee he insisted that the contract only be for three months, and we'd talk in February when we launched.

Next I had to find a sex expert. Sex, in the 1970s, was all the rage. "We need a tantalising amount," said Bill. Behind us were the permissive Swinging Sixties and the 'love-ins' of flower power. Now, to relieve the gloom of this dark decade, we needed emphasis on getting more from the mingling of bodies, women taking charge of contraception and seeking new attitudes to relationships.

Alex Comfort's *The Joy of Sex* (subline *a gourmet guide to lovemaking)* was selling like hot cakes – a funny old book with caricatures of hippie-like people offering suggested techniques for starters, main courses, desserts etc.

Another book *4's Company*, by Donald Carroll, "a startling expose of group sex in England', was eye-wateringly graphic in its descriptions about sexual experiments and possibilities. The tabloids revealed that OMO, a boxed washing powder, took on new meaning in northern England – placed prominently in a front window it indicated to possible lovers that her indoors was "on my own".

From America came the idea of 'open marriage', when husband and wife are in agreement with alternative sexual arrangements while staying together. As a counterpoint to the power strikes, cheering up the bedroom with flickering candles and slippery satin sheets seemed very exciting. There was no limit to imagination.

Ita Buttrose's magazine *Cleo* with its nude male centrefold was going great guns in Australia. In the US a cheeky but earnest magazine called *Playgirl* (subline: *the entertainment magazine for women*) had articles with titles such as

"Masturbation as healer" and "Love on a trampoline". Each issue had a poster-size picture of a good-looking guy, usually with long hair (as was the fashion) and genitalia on display – always flaccid, never erect for that would rate the magazine as pornography (which had to be displayed on the top shelves at newsagents, for men only, and supposedly too high for young people, and short women, to reach). [*Playgirl* was relaunched in 2020, with a naked actress Chloe Sevigny, aged 45 and nine months pregnant, on the cover.]

Another, heftier, American magazine was *Viva*, edited by Bob Guccione, intended to be a female *Penthouse*. A reader's letter summed up the new attitude: "I bought *Viva* (because) I want to exploit men! I want to see men naked and think – God! What a man!" The fashion spread in one issue was great fun: "strippy-strappy superheel slings and sandals" showed footwear on women unclothed and entwined with heads out of shot.

The main feature was on tantric love, featuring naked, touching bodies in full colour photographs. This was something completely new to me, and I imagine a revelation to most who read it then. (This 'sexual yoga' has had a resurgence of interest in the 21st century with an exhibition at the British Museum.)

Serendipity struck at a press do when I met one of the *Viva* contributors, Robert Chartham, whose subject was 'The Sexual Fantasy'. Tall and distinguished looking, he had been editorial consultant to *Forum*, a pocket-sized monthly magazine that helped readers sort out their sexual problems. Anna Raeburn (eventually one of

Britain's top agony aunts though she preferred to call herself a sexual adviser) also worked here.

He gave me a copy of his latest book *The Sensuous Couple* in which he wrote: "To Wendy James, Good Fucking! Robert Chartham 1973". Needless to say, that word was never used at that time in women's magazines. Would we, could we, use it in *First Lady*? As it happened, no. And not just because editorially we'd decided that crudities would only be found in cookery articles.

After a decade of marriage counselling, Chartham had written several books: *What children need to know about sex*; *Sex Manners for Men*; and *Sex and the Over-Fifties*. On each he was described as the "world's best-selling sexologist". He was always provocative – it was impossible to have an ordinary, sex-free discussion with him. Every phrase, every word seemed to have another meaning. He had expansive ideas for keeping people sexually content and stress free: "There should be a room at workplaces where you can spend half an hour getting sexually in tune with your body, during a coffee break, or lunch time." A massage here, a massage there – he thought could do a lot of good. [Today, in more enlightened UK and US tech-based businesses, staff are offered ways to increase wellbeing in their employment package.]

Years after he died (in 1985, aged 73), I've found that he was two people, each extraordinary (I'm sure Patric would have said "What else could you expect? He was a Gemini."). His real name was Ronald Sydney Seth which he used for his travel and espionage books. In *A Spy Has No Friends* he told how, in 1941, he'd been commissioned into the RAF and the following year joined SOE (Special Operations Executive, British secret service undertaking subversive warfare in enemy-occupied places, states *The Oxford Companion to the Second World War*).

Then, according to him, he was parachuted into Estonia and captured by the Germans, spending most of the war in Oflag 79, before, in April 1945, being sent by Himmler to London, via Switzerland, with a message of peace. Wow. What a story. He never mentioned any of this to me, I might add. The web revealed it years later.

And there was more: in 2005 *The Guy Liddell Diaries (Volume 11 – 1942-1945)* were published. As MI5's director of counter espionage, Liddell had raised doubts about Seth's wartime experiences, noting in his diary: "....rang to say he was rather worried about the case of Ronald Seth. We thought that possibly some expert ought to interrogate him on his peace mission." And later: "Seth had with him a medical certificate stating that he was subject to paranoic tendencies. From the sensational nature of his story this indeed seems likely."

It was a very complicated story. *A Spy Has No Friends*, written in 1952, is still available. It was republished in 2008 by Barbara McAdam Seth, his second wife and an accomplished painter. The Robert Chartham I met was the pseudonym of the counsellor who ran sex education classes for UK teenagers. He called himself Dr Chartham – yet it was Ronald Seth who held the PhD in social science. A sort of portable doctorate. As a journalist you should never take anything for granted but he certainly surprised me. He never spared my blushes.

* * *

Getting a magazine together from scratch was exciting and Bill was an inspiring coordinator. Because of the lead times, we worked out a plan for six issues, the idea being that when the first – printed and looking great – received board approval a couple of weeks before it went on sale in early February, the others would be on their way through the production system.

We saw the readers as being much like the staff: in their 20s and early 30s, modern, full of curiosity, not prudish, interested in a wide range of subjects and people, and not afraid of learning more. The tone would be cheerful and uplifting with humour spread throughout.

A fine example in the first issue was 'No sex please, we're sailing' about husband and wife team Paul and Angela Antrobus taking part in a Trans Atlantic yacht race. Angela had done a 'me' in reverse, leaving *Woman's Own* in 1973 to go to Australia and New Zealand.

In *First Lady*, elements of fun and fantasy lay alongside topics of concern, women's sexual health for example, but the overall feeling we strived for in each issue was of joy of reading, of new horizons and attitudes. I was drawn to American writers like Erma Bombeck (*I Lost Everything in the Post-natal Depression*) who made family life sound irreverent and hilarious, and Linda Grimsley (*Guerrilla in the Kitchen*) whose humour focused on Women's Lib and domesticity – still the lot of most women. Our search was for anything to relieve the grimness and give us something to chuckle about.

A VERY DARK DECADE

Anyone who lived through the 1970s will remember what a disastrous decade it was! Industrially, politically and financially, those early years strained everyone's patience and optimism. Poor *First Lady* was overwhelmed by continual strikes, three-day and four-day working weeks and power cuts, all related to a worldwide oil crisis that seemed unsolvable.

We became convinced our building was haunted. Above us, on the top floor, was another magazine in development, *Duo*, for first-time homemakers, and they too suffered. Ann Lamarcraft, who had been Jane Reed's secretary, was working there and we often met on the stairs. We chose these as we were concerned about the lift – it would go up and down by itself, with no one in it. Or it wouldn't work at all, even when there wasn't a power cut. We wouldn't use it if we felt we were alone in the building; we had enough problems without becoming victims of its temperamental urges. I carried a torch in my handbag, along with cigarettes, lighter and matches, just in case.

The pub on the corner became our second office where we worked, often by candlelight, wrapped in coats and scarves, somehow coping with the chaos we were living through. The lights on the jukebox were out and Cat Stephens, whose melancholic songs reflected the strangeness of this time, was now silenced. It was a very long, cold and dark January.

Prime Minister Ted Heath, in desperation with the country's on-going problems, went to the polls in February and survived – just. We didn't. Bill came back from the vital IPC board meeting where he had presented *First Lady*, issue 1, and proofs of the second with the news that it was all over. IPC was not prepared to go ahead. The time wasn't right for a magazine that was promoting humour when there was nothing to laugh about.

We couldn't have known, either, that the health subject of our first issue, breasts, and the second, excessive drinking, struck personal notes with directors who had family members battling with breast cancer and alcoholism. Bill said they didn't write the whole idea off altogether, but it would all be put away somewhere until better times and looked at again. It never was.

Here's how the situation was summed up in *The Business of Women's Magazines*: "1974 was a singularly damp year." Braithwaite and Barrell mentioned three launches of magazines that were "intended to be innovative". In February, there was to be a new weekly ("rather appallingly titled") *First Lady* ("Hindsight shows us it was not a particularly exciting or original recipe."). In March, *Duo*, a young homemaker's monthly, was to appear ("painlessly withdrawn before birth") and *Woman's World*, for which an expensive launch had been planned, "was aborted, but resurrected in 1977". Their final verdict: "This must have been the biggest flopperoo spring in post-war publishing for a single company."

I cringed at their words. I felt truly sad for all who

worked on the three to-be publications. All that effort to create something new wasted. I think I cried for two days, unable to explain the tears to my little daughters who hugged me and patted my back to comfort me as they knew I did to them when they were unhappy.

* * *

At *First Lady* everyone was devastated, except Patric, that is, whose contract was to be renegotiated the day we closed. He said he couldn't see the magazine's future which is why he hadn't fully committed himself. I just thought he didn't want the job, but perhaps there could be something to astrology after all.

Patric turned out to be a godsend. He took me under his wing and drew me into a world that was surreal with its mixture of camp homosexuality and stars of stage and screen. He'd studied accountancy after National Service and in the 1950s was an entrepreneur, running his own 'gentlemen's' club in London and dabbling in property development. He was getting out of his depth when he was placed next to Helene Hoskins at a dinner party.

He didn't know she was the astrologer called 'Celeste' and was taken aback when she warned him of the imminent demise of a project that would leave him completely broke. Astounded by this stranger's foresight, he went to see her after the event (which happened, as she said) – and so began a new and lucrative career. As her pupil in the predictive art, she made him work hard which was what he needed in his perilous financial and mental state.

Patric was an absolute charmer, his voice burred by

Yorkshire, where he was brought up from the age of four, though he was born in the US, in the wonderfully named Hackensack, New Jersey. Name dropping came easily to him – his world of homosexuality encompassed many, including a famous Russian ballet dancer and an American TV heart-throb, neither of whom I met.

We got on well and I spent a lot of time at his enchanting flat in Mayfair where he lived above famous 1930s actors Jack Hulbert and his Australian-born wife Cicely Courtneidge, owners of the house. I could listen to him talk for hours.

Marjorie, Patric's housekeeper, guarded his time like a sentry and would not let anyone in without an appointment. But she was also very kind, and once when I had a meeting with Patric, she took my daughters off to see *Chitty Chitty Bang Bang* which starred Sally Ann Howes, a dear friend of her employer. She was, like the character she played, truly scrumptious, said Patric.

At this time Patric was offering private consultations, using a combination of ESP (extra sensory perception) and his astrological charts, to help troubled souls. He could only do this once a week, he said, because it drained him – and I saw that for myself after he had spent an hour with man of many parts Peter Sellers. Britt Ekland, his former wife, many years after his death, revealed the actor's difficult problems and suggested it was possibly because he was bi-polar. Another time I was at the house, struggling to absorb the charts, when Patric met actress Diana Rigg whose personal life was at a major turning point. [She died, aged 82, in 2020.]

Mike Molloy, who had just become editor of the *Daily Mirror*, was a friend and great fan of Patric's. He enticed him to provide daily forecasts for the world's once biggest selling newspaper and his fame took off. Mike was often at the Mayfair house as well, usually around six o'clock, calling in on his way to work.

This was drinks time, when the champagne or Chablis would be waiting in the ice bucket on the gleaming table in the elegant sitting room which was dominated by huge Chinese lamps. This was a room of Taste, much aspired to in the glossy monthlies, sumptuous, comfortable and welcoming. I wonder whether Patric ever told Mike that he would one day be a successful fiction writer.

[In his memoir *The Happy Hack* (John Blake Books, 2016) Mike has a chapter about Patric in which he reveals the source of the astrologer's mysterious private income. I can almost hear Patric talking about his liaison with an older man from one of Europe's wealthiest families, how he taught him about music and painting. When the old lover died, Patric inherited everything – or would have if the man's family had not threatened to contest the will. The settlement of an income for life and a supply of vintage wine would certainly explain Patric's lavish style, his urbanity, his theatrical generosity.]

Patric, a September Libran (which made him different from an October Libran, he said, though anyone who has encountered the vacillating qualities of those in that star sign might not agree), called me an Upside Down Scorpio. This, in effect, is Taurus – I was born in Australia in

November. He told me I had a gift for astrology that he felt could be developed. I always thought of myself as a rationalist but I liked the idea of second sight. For me at this time life was turbulent, and I was flattered. He divided his day into dedicated areas of work (in the mornings he did his forecasts for his daily and weekly syndicated column, followed by any monthly commissions) but he found time to introduce me to the charts. Or tried to; a lot of it was very bewildering.

Why was he so successful? He had a gentle tone and always stressed that the individual's free will is paramount whatever was happening with the planets, that any possible interpretations of their influence depended on self knowledge. He gave me a set of long-playing records he made in 1970 covering each sign which he wanted parents to buy so that they would know what to expect of their child born in 1971. His voice is fascinating still.

Several publishers had tried to get him to write about astrology but he was always reluctant. Then W H Allen made an offer he couldn't refuse. He asked me to work with him on a book they commissioned – *Patric Walker's Book of Astrology* – and I would get an 'Edited by' credit. We were going to share the sizeable advance, but so much was going on in his personal life at the time that I don't think his heart was in it. He returned the money. Librans, as he said, have difficulty making up their minds. [He changed it again later, in the 1980s, and the book was written but not with me.]

* * *

Whentch a magazine folds, as *First Lady* did before it was born, it was the job of the personnel department to inform staff about redundancy and what was due to them. For me it wasn't straightforward: I had to apply for any jobs within IPC that might be of a similar grade to the one I was on. Only if I didn't find one, or be accepted for one, would I get redundancy pay. Though I had only left *Woman's Own* five months before, much had changed in the weeklies.

Woman magazine, which was in Holborn, had a new editor after Barbara Buss retired and the choice was a man: Peter Lawrence from *Woman's Own*. He had brought George Cannon and Dee Remmington with him as associate editors to oversee production and features. There was a vacancy, however, because Jill Churchill, who had been an associate editor for some years, had been headhunted to start a new magazine called *Home & Freezer Digest*. I had to apply for her job.

There was no way I could be another Jill – she really was quite something. A tiny, glamorous woman who always wore the highest of heels, she went from being a fiction sub at *Woman* (in 1958), to becoming beauty editor, then promotions editor with the task of bringing the magazine into the Swinging Sixties.

I was interviewed by Peter, but as he didn't catch my eye throughout I knew I was on a losing wicket. I'd worked with him for some time at *Woman's Own* and I didn't find him easy. I got on much better with his successors Martin Richardson and Dennis Whelan – though one was rarely sober and the other often acted like a prima donna – than I did with him.

If Patsy Kumm had not died, she might have been the natural successor to Barbie Buss, even Jill Churchill would have been in line, but the new magazine came along before the vacancy. Peter had an art, not editorial, background but he convinced IPC management he was the right one. It wasn't to last. He died unexpectedly and a new editor, Jo Sandilands, who had been his deputy, was appointed. But that lay ahead.

With no job offered me at IPC, I could take redundancy, my first, and it was depressing. I was grieving as I would for a lost child. The redundancy money paid off debts and covered essential work on the house, including a new kitchen. Then I got a call from someone looking for a beauty editor and I recommended Leslie Kenton.

The job was at The National Magazine Company and Marcus Morris, the managing director and ordained reverend, fell for her in a big way. Now dressed entirely in white, she was most engaging with her beautiful skin and blonde hair. She returned the favour by putting my name forward as editor of *Womancraft*, the first and only do-it-yourself magazine for women.

6

CRAFT AND DIY TAKE OVER

W omancraft was a monthly magazine modelled on those designed for handy men at home: 'anything you can do, we can too' sort of thing. I'd never heard of it. It had been acquired by *Good Housekeeping* publisher Jack Blanche and he had put GH editor-in-chief Laurie Purden in charge with the aim of relaunching it.

Laurie had not long received her MBE for services to women's journalism when I met her. My immediate thought was that I'd found another Ita Buttrose, the perfect woman with whom the reader would want to identify. She was always immaculately dressed and groomed, well made-up, lips and nails brightly coloured. She had a passion for turbans which made her look taller, though she was already tall, and wherever she went she carried her menthol cigarettes and lighter. Her gravelly voice and accent, and laugh, were fascinating.

It is useful to remember what life was like in 1974. France was declared to be in recession and in Britain things were tough and politically chaotic. The February general election had resulted in a hung parliament which affected the nation as well as the future of all the political parties. Money was a problem. For years you could only take £50 with you if you went abroad; when you collected it at the bank, your passport had to be stamped. Even when the allowance went up to £300 leaving the country was expensive. In fact, many activities were curtailed by a lack of cash and the increasing cost of living.

With all this going on, surely a magazine that helped you get more out of life would be a runaway success?

Laurie had ideas about 'softening' the approach to the 'hard' subjects (those involving concrete, mortar and pipework, for instance) while applying many crafts to home situations – a wonderfully huge canvas. I was (and still am) sure that there is little women cannot do (especially if they have to through necessity) and being multitaskers enjoy new challenges that add to their skills.

It was an unusual interview. I couldn't produce anything to say I was good at DIY, which I had done in my own home simply because I had little money, that home decorating and cooking were more than hobbies. But having heard about my career to date she decided I was resourceful. I took away a few issues of the magazine – it first appeared in 1972 – to write a review that included my thoughts on what worked and what didn't, what might be changed, and how I would change it. I think I sweated blood over it.

With times tough, an upsurge of interest in domestic subjects and crafts seemed logical. Instead of moving house, people might be better off expanding the space they had, even doing the work themselves. Articles (about tiling, wallpapering, painting etc) could all do with clear step-by-step instructions to ensure success.

You should remember that this was before the huge DIY supermarket chains like B&Q, Homebase and Wickes existed, and only hardware shops on the high street sold what you might, or might not, need. Professionals kept the tricks of the trades to themselves – could we reveal them? Even if you didn't feel up to doing it yourself and had to employ a qualified person, it was useful to know what they were doing and to understand technical terms.

As part of joining Europe, decimalisation was on its way and we needed to understand how this would affect us in our everyday lives and the impact it would have on all types of measurements. How would Britain get on without its imperial ways!

Ever idealistic, it appealed to me that a magazine like *Womancraft* could encourage its readers to know exactly what was involved in keeping a home in good order. Traditionally it was left to the men, but as a single mother I had to take responsibility for the house I was paying the mortgage on, and the car I was buying on HP (hire purchase plans were usually called 'the never never'). I had learnt that knowledge is power.

Just changing a household plug, for instance, was considered a man's job – the colours of wires, amps and fuses being too much for the little woman. Nonsense. Instructions for how to do it were on an Irish linen tea towel that had been sent to *Woman's Own* by a women's electrical education group. It hung on my wall for years.

(It is no longer needed today as all electrical products are sold with plugs molded on.)

Facing me now though was the reality of magazine publishing. The real consideration for making *Womancraft* successful was who would advertise in it. Publishers do not produce magazines out of the goodness of their hearts – they want to reap profits. National Magazines had a stable of earners and there would be no support for *Womancraft* if it didn't bring in the bickies. Jack's ace was aligning *Womancraft* with *Good Housekeeping*, the monthly magazine that had established a prime position over many years. Laurie dramatically increased its circulation when she was editor between 1967 and 1972, hence her MBE.

Its prize core was the GH Institute which had its own section in the middle each month, featuring what had been tried and tested. Cookery was its *pièce de résistance* but the Institute would tackle any domestic subject that readers had a vested interest in. Now people working there would add their expertise and authority to *Womancraft*, and this (fingers crossed) would attract advertisers.

Laurie and Jack were a good team and had worked together for many years at Hulton Press – publishers of *Picture Post*, a magazine renowned for its photo journalism (it died before I arrived in the UK). Keith Kotch, who Laurie married in 1957, worked there as did Marcus Morris who was the originator (along with the artist Frank Hampson) of the famous boys' comic *Eagle*.

When Marcus moved to NatMags he enticed Laurie to join the company in 1963 and, following spells at *Vanity Fair* and *House Beautiful*, she was appointed editor of GH which became as much a household name in Britain as it was in the US (and remains so today).

Laurie started her career in her teens (she was born in 1928) at George Newnes, as a junior secretary on *Woman's Own* in the 1940s in the office of James Drawbell (the one they called God). She then moved to a pocket-size magazine called *Home Notes*, eventually becoming its fiction editor. She was allowed £5 a week expenses to entertain writers and agents at restaurants within walking distance of Tower House...the Savoy Grill on the Strand and Rules in Maiden Lane were the most favoured (£5 wouldn't go far in either today). I have no difficulty imagining her coaxing the best out of her guests.

Her forte was anglicising bought-in American short stories for *Home Notes*, but she wrote her own as well, in her lunch hour, for *Woman's Own* to 'fit' the themes of art work bought from the US. She rose to be assistant editor at *Woman's Own* and was involved with the very popular *Girl* – the magazine of my early teens which in 1958 had a circulation of 650,000 – and edited *Housewife*.

DOMESTICATING WOMEN OF TASTE
Housewife was a glossy monthly whose direct rival was *Good Housekeeping*. Laurie's staff and their specialities are now synonymous with the history of British women's magazines, indeed of women's interests in the 1950s and 60s: Constance Spry (of flower-arranging fame) was in charge of home; Rosemary Hume (founder of the London Cordon Bleu Cookery School) was responsible for cookery; beauty was shared by Phyllis Digby Morton (who I'd known as The Duchess

at *Woman's Own*) and Anne Scott-James (a Fleet Street pioneer who died aged 96 in 2009; her son Sir Max Hastings is a former *Daily Telegraph* editor and highly regarded historian).

I liked Laurie from our first meeting. With two young daughters (a few years older than mine), she knew what was involved in juggling working life with marriage and parenthood. I don't even remember if there were other applicants for the job, but I thought it might be a gamble for Laurie and Jack to appoint me, a single mother.

My experience in journalism was wide but I had no track record in the home/fashion/craft area and, as editor, I would have to manage staff as well as creating a magazine with deadlines. Would I be able to handle these new responsibilities? I didn't know but I was ready for the challenge – and it came. Thanks to Marianne and Mick, who were happy to continue with care arrangements for my children, I was able to accept the job, my first as a magazine editor.

After National Magazines bought Astra Press (which owned *Womancraft*), Laurie had overseen several issues. GH was in Chestergate House, just a hop, skip and jump (or a fast run if you were late) from Victoria Station, and *Womancraft* had one large, open-plan office on the top floor near the GH Institute where all the testing was done.

The inherited staff, editor Marilyn Berry and Fran, her deputy, left to join a new London weekly magazine called *City Limits* – an innovative publication run along co-operative lines and set up by former staff of *Time Out*, the leading listings magazine. [*City Limits* closed in 1993;

Deborah Orr whose memoir *Motherwell* was published posthumously in 2020, also worked there.]

A freelance writer, Carol Sarler, who began in journalism on the IPC training scheme, was working on articles that had been commissioned, rewriting them with a more feminine angle or at least lessening the masculine. It took some doing. *Womancraft* included traditional male topics such as home brewing and woodworking on the grounds that they should not be beyond women. We often found copy on these subjects a challenge and came to accept that the sexes approach practical things differently.

[Carol went on to become editor of the teen magazine *Honey* (1980) and later a successful Fleet Street columnist and broadcaster, offering her often-controversial views in *The Times* and *The Spectator*. According to her obituary in *The Guardian* (she died, aged 70, in 2020) she was an enemy of what she regarded as soppiness and her generation's feminism was "all about what women could do" – my sentiments entirely.]

* * *

What I hadn't known when I joined *Womancraft* was how longstanding the interest in do-it-yourself was in the UK and how many publications focused on it in the 1950s. The internet, and eBay in particular, transported me back to the past. 'Practical' was the keyword. *Practical Television* was the most astonishing: one cover showed a man taking a TV apart, not a wise idea at all! *Practical Wireless* was equally adventurous. *Man About the House* (subline *The leading do-it-yourself magazine*) was popular, as was *Houseproud* (*for those who take practical pride in their homes*).

George Newnes, publisher of *Woman's Own*, had *Practical Householder* and also *John Bull*, an odd name for a magazine that seemed to cover everything from plumbing to home decorating (at one stage it was selling nearly a million copies!). All of these cost 1s 3d an issue; *Do It Yourself* (*for the practical man about the house*) was just 1s.

The covers were illustrations (full colour photography for these was still to come) of men and women companionably working on a home project. In 1957 one showed a man installing a new fitted kitchen while the wife is alongside tiling the wall – both dressed as though going to a party, and with no protective covering at all. It would indeed be an ideal home if you didn't get messy while working on it.

In 1974 one DIY magazine enticed women in: *Homemaker* (*the practical how-to-do-it monthly*). It started in 1959, price 1s 3d, with coverlines such as: "A gay idea for hiding away a fold-up table", and incorporated *Easy* (*his and her do it yourself magazine*) in the 1960s. By the 1970s, the editor Bob Tattersall, who would later marry the homes editor of *Good Housekeeping* Diana Austin, put the focus mostly on home decorating.

Home & Freezer Digest, powered by the dynamic Jill Churchill, was doing well. This small format magazine – about the same size as *Reader's Digest*, *Home Notes* and *Home Chat* (a sister magazine of *Woman*) – was designed to fit in a handbag. Jill made it different from anything else around, with articles on a wide range of home-related subjects that were short but to the point.

The universal interest in crafts and DIY was possibly a reponse to lack of choice on the high street though Terence Conran's Habitat in Chelsea had been making a difference to home furnishings for a decade. [Conran died in 2020, aged 88, and obituaries noted his strong influence on modernising everyday living, introducing continental quilts (duvets) and chicken bricks among myriad other household items.]

The November 1972 issue of *Womancraft* revealed that people made their own rugs, roller blinds, candles and wine. Then the cheap tipple of choice was Hirondelle – red and white, from France, blended from various sources and bottled in the UK – and wine industries in Australia and New Zealand were a glint in the eyes of some entrepreneurs. Making your own was a popular pursuit but tastings of offerings like Chateau Willow or Domaine Kings Road made you wonder if the effort was worth it.

There were modern takes on ancient arts like macramé (tying knots in string), batik (creating designs by differential dyeing) and cold enamelling (striking examples were seen at the Tutankhamun exhibition at the British Library; people queued round the clock, and block, to get in).

Knitting machines were a 'must have'. With one of these and a set of punchcards you could create an unlimited variety of patterns for clothes and soft furnishings. A bit like the old pianola, on which you played wonderful music by pressing pedals which turned the punched rolls inside. We had one in my childhood home in Australia.

* * *

By the time I started work, on April 1, 1974 (April Fools' Day, but I naturally hoped it was an auspicious date for new beginnings!), Laurie had brought in Gabi Tubbs, formerly a junior in GH's fashion and beauty department. Gabi's job was to add features with a softer touch. She had a young son, Oliver, and worked three days a week, commissioning original patterns for knitting, crocheting, sewing and gift-making, overseeing photography and organising copy. Her husband Pierre was well known in the music business.

Our art editor Valerie Hobson and her assistants Flick Ekins and Val Pountney had space in a corner of the GH art department, on the floor below. Carol McCartney, head of the Institute, gave her support and some of the staff (Cassandra Kent and Gill Smedley in particular) became regular contributors. Rosemary Milner was in charge of promotions and offers for both magazines.

We gained new staff: Sue Ross was assistant editor; Jane Sheard, Roma Trundle and Christine Hart (later Parsons) were editorial assistants (in reality, the writers); Ros Washington was office manager/secretary, and Patricia Pett, a former colleague at *Woman's Own*, came in as a freelance sub and frequent contributor. She had left her fulltime job to have her son and daughter. The Aussie contingent doubled when Sandra Funnell (later Harris) joined as a freelance sub.

Later on, there was another helper, too: Christina Berlin, an American whom we 'inherited', was in some way related to the Hearst family, American owners of National Magazines. She was a Mikhail Baryshnikov 'groupie' and (according to Wikipedia, and I understand this may be unreliable) had been instrumental in helping the Russian ballet star to defect in 1974 during a tour of Canada. Perhaps she was sent to the UK as a penance! But she fitted in well with our team.

Womancraft, overlined 'Good Housekeeping's do-it-yourself magazine for women', was relaunched to the trade – advertisers, distributors and newsagents – on a Thames riverboat. It was orchestrated by the fast-growing advertising wizards Saatchi and Saatchi, then headed by the charismatic charmer Tim (later Lord) Bell, helped by the PR firm Brian Begg and Associates. This was the same formidable coupling that launched *Cosmopolitan,* but instead of sex and orgasms they now had to arouse interest in the delights of DIY.

Tim, arch supporter of Margaret Thatcher, died in 2019 and I read in the obituaries that he "could sell condoms to a cardinal" and although this wasn't strictly necessary in *Womancraft's* case their tactics must have worked. The Audit Bureau of Circulation figures published in March 1975 tell the amazing story: in July-Dec '73, *Womancraft's* circulation had been 28,260. A year later, July-Dec '74, it was 78,223 – a massive leap. We must have been doing something right. We hoped it was because we made ourselves indispensable.

We included central pull-outs, A-Z style supplements, that readers were encouraged to keep. *Handbook for Harassed Cooks,* for instance, a four-parter, covered all the words in all languages that appeared in cookbooks and on menus. *An A-Z of Adhesives* was not something to sniff at (it explained all the different types and what they contained as the serious social problems of glue sniffing were on the horizon).

Bugs and Beasties pinpointed the scourges afflicting house and garden and gave remedies. A six-parter, called *How to Cope,* solved tricky problems around the house, from rejuvenating burnt saucepans to replacing damaged tiles. An element of saving money was always built in as well as encouraging new skills.

We sold binders so readers had their issues ready to hand when needed, providing an index of all articles published, and when. Yearly sets could be completed by buying back numbers that might have been missed. Advertisers had an index plus a freepost service so enquiries could be passed on – this was quite original at the time. In the digital age, it seems antiquated.

It was the same with printing, then stuck in a time warp. Because of the cost of production, colour pages were mostly allocated to ads, or a promotion. That left editorial with black and white which really does look very dreary, page after page after page. Spot colour helped the designers to make some difference to the appearance of the 'hard' subjects – and did we go to town on those!

How to keep your car in good order, insulate your home, build a brick wall, lay a concrete path, the ins and outs of building an extension, a buying guide to parquet flooring, changing a tap washer – and, of course, understanding electricity and rewiring (with the help of the Electrical Association for Women, now sadly defunct). Jack Smith, token male in the GH Institute, was our able supporter and willing guide to interpreting subjects generally considered for men only.

A WASTE-CONSCIOUS TIME

Two of the watchwords of the 1970s were self-sufficiency and recycling, both of which were pertinent to *Womancraft*. Ways of reusing materials were invariably welcomed and sometimes could be profitable. The recycling of waste paper in particular was a boon for charities whose volunteers went from door to door collecting old newspapers. In 1973, the Scouts made more than £160,000 from the business, said a newspaper report. On the home front, you could buy a device to turn old newspapers into brick or log shapes for the fire – and it has re-emerged today in our, at last, waste-conscious world.

Crafts were a Pandora's box waiting to be opened. We'd find the specialists – for macramé or decoupage, stencilling or marbling, patchwork or upholstering, for example – and Gabi and Val would devise ways of using them to best effect around the home. Then we made the processes involved as easy to follow as possible. Sometimes, getting the instructions right, and able to be understood by a 14 year old – in my training as a journalist, this was the age to be aimed at (though the tabloids prefer 12) – was like translating from a foreign language. The only successful way was to learn the craft, so the 'how to do it' was clear – and were there some furrowed brows at times!

Step by step pictures or commissioned art work showed each stage clearly. We had to be careful not to fall foul of *Reader's Digest* which had originated the 'bible' of DIY (continually updated and still on sale today). It covered all the hard stuff – plumbing, building, electricity

– and we were alerted early to their excessive interest. A lawyer's letter implied that one of our step-by-steps appeared to have a remarkable similarity to one of theirs. Ours showed a woman's hands! But we had been warned and from then on took extra care with our illustrations.

* * *

Our biggest stumbling blocks were the production processes and the cost of having enough pictures to explain the subject. *Womancraft* really needed to be like a Victorian card machine where you turned a handle and the cards quickly flipped over – giving the viewer a story.

That's what we have today, of course: watching a DVD or YouTube videos which brilliantly show techniques. And you can stop and start and repeat any part you want. A craft is learnt more easily by watching someone else.

We made much of 1970s fashion in knits, crochet and dressmaking, which most women did then, having learnt the methods from their mothers or at school. Dear Gabi, with her wonderful sense of style, came up with superb designs worked out with the influential and thriving wool companies. This was the time when every high street had at least one wool shop and a haberdasher's as well. If you could handle a sewing machine, there was one sure way to have designer outfits – make them yourself.

In 1974 Gabi presented a wardrobe of clothes to make from patterns. It was described as "a mix and match collection to give you haute couture at a fraction of the price". 'Haute couture' – yesterday's way of talking about creations from rarified couturiers – indeed! For that's

what the big companies like Simplicity, Style and Butt-
erick filled their hefty tomes with.

These had their own shelf in shops so you could look
through and find anything from a baby's bonnet to a ball
dress. With pattern in hand all you needed then was the
right fabric, confidence and time.

Womancraft also ran gardening features. One contributor was Leslie Johns; he and his wife Violet Stevenson
had just completed a book on fruit growing and cooking
(published by Angus & Robertson). Later we had Sheila
Howarth who was a proponent of 'grow to eat' – a style of
living that has made Hugh Fearnley-Whittingstall a
household name today. [Producing food from home
gardens was a rewarding bonus of the virus lockdown.]

Cookery, including vegetarian, was offered in all sorts
of ways so that skills – like cake making and icing, for
example – could be developed. There was also straightforward advice on making the best use of a freezer and
microwave oven, innovations of the 1970s, with time
saving in mind. This help was needed now that more
women were going out to work.

* * *

On the V&A website, the museum that ensures that
the past is not forgotten, I discovered that *Womancraft* had made its mark. Among fashion and jewellery
features, an entry called 'Knit a work of art from a free
pattern' said: "If art is supposed to challenge our percep-
tions and make us look at the world in a different way,
then Freddie Robins succeeds on both counts. Her career

began . . .when she won the *Womancraft* magazine knitting competition, with a knitted interpretation of a tuxedo in mohair. This set the tone for the subversive sweaters she is known for today." Imagine that – subversive sweaters! Freddie, an artist and senior tutor and reader in textiles at the Royal College of Art, was 16 when she won the 1981 competition, but I wasn't on the magazine then.

I hoped I'd come across the reader who covered an armchair in herringbone pattern with interwoven brown tights (previously washed, she assured us), an unusual upholstery idea that was dramatically inventive at the time. We were always careful not to veer towards the kitsch. Jane Sheard, who went on to have a successful career in the UK as well as *Australian Good Housekeeping*, told me she kept a special folder of readers' ideas that were beyond the pale.

On the *Good Housekeeping* website here, I found a response to a question posed by the deputy homes editor: how crafty are you? 'Rosies' wrote: "I have...a half-made patchwork quilt in my project box which started in the 70s and unfinished Clothkits outfits, half-made corduroy trousers for a toddler who has grown up and left home, and two years worth of *Womancraft* magazines which I am sure must be worth something now as Seventies fashion has come round again."Amazingly, Clothkits continued as a mail order company. And 'Rosies' would be pleased to know that she's not alone. I have a half-finished bargello cushion cover – in bright primaries – I started for the September 1974 issue showing a stunning array of patterns in this quick-to-stitch, attractive tapestry.

Packed away in boxes are the folders filled with the

magazines I collected. I'm sure one day my grandchildren will look at them, for they are a type of history. They do look old fashioned but some content remains pertinent today. And they have a presence online: the library of the University of Southampton holds the complete *Womancraft* collection, from 1974 to 1977.

* * *

The National Magazine Company was very different from the working world of IPC. It was a much smaller organisation for a start, and the atmosphere was less pushy. Everyone was always well dressed; no female employees yet wore trousers/slacks/jeans. I don't remember hearing shouting or swearing, there were no prima donnas or show offs – though the well-proportioned Jack Blanche with his bushy, wide moustache, twinkly eyes and bald head liked to be mischievous and enjoyed being surrounded by young women.

Charlotte Lessing, editor of *Good Housekeeping*, was always polite and appeared on occasion to be interested in what was happening to *Womancraft*, usually during her wine tasting sessions at the Institute (when she retired she specialised in wine writing and travel. She died in 2017). Anne Gregg, her deputy, was warmer and oozed sympathy (she became a household name with a TV travel series and died far too young of cancer in 2006).

Willie Landels at *Harpers & Queen* was exactly as I imagined an artist to be, physically flamboyant and charming. When *Womancraft* relaunched he sent a card wishing us well. He had employed Leslie Kenton and her natural beauty and health approach was receiving a lot of publicity, boosting the magazine's sales.

I caught up with Sally Adams who was deputy editor at *She*. I'd known her from the National Union of Journalists at IPC (she and Pamela Carmichael had worked at *Woman's Mirror*, I learnt from Anthony Peagam who was a sub there in its early days; he went on to edit *TV Times*, run AA Publications, and contributes to the web's Gentleman Ranters).

THE REAL SUCCESS OF *SHE*

A very popular monthly magazine, *She* was run by the formidable duo Pamela Carmichael and her husband, art director Michael Griffiths. Pamela had taken over after the founding editor Joan Werner Laurie died with her lover Nancy Spain (a regular on BBC radio shows) in a 1964 plane crash on their way to the Grand National at Aintree. It was a lovely magazine, funny, mischief-making and about real people. The secret of the duo's success (it was said) was that they made a point of never meeting writers or readers. They commissioned everything by mail, an extraordinary feat. *She* started in 1955 and came to an end in 2011 ('*She's come undone*' said the headline in *The Economist*). A circulation of nearly 145,000 was not enough to save it.

The most daunting person I met at NatMags was Deirdre McSharry at *Cosmopolitan*. She succeeded to the editorship after Joyce Hopkirk returned to Fleet Street. She was the one, when fashion editor of *The Daily Express*, who had spotted the young teenaged Twiggy and set her on the path to fame.

I think she saw *Womancraft* as a lost cause though I never thought that women interested in DIY were unlikely to read a magazine that promoted self expression or self fulfilment. Much more approachable was David Coombs, editor of *Antique Collector* and father of the NUJ chapel, responsible for the annual request to management for improved salaries for journalists.

The editors were invited to take sherry with Marcus Morris a couple of times a year (I don't know whether this type of activity ever happened at IPC). It was better when Laurie was there for she was never out of her depth in business or small talk. I didn't want to find myself alone with Marcus. Probably because I remembered awkward silences when he had taken me out to lunch not long after I arrived at Chestergate House.

With all that had gone before – the end of my relationship, redundancy, being a single mother – I was feeling very women's lib-ish, very independent. He liked that; he even remarked "I hope you're not going to get married again" to which I replied, "Of course not." I was taken aback. At least I didn't say never.

What I didn't know was that ten months later my personal life would change, and that I would accept Ian Dear's proposal of marriage. We went together to the new year party Marcus and his wife always held at their Thames-side home at Limehouse, now an exceedingly fashionable part of London but then a nightmare to get to from southwest London where I lived.

The guests were people from Marcus's present and

past companies as well as friends and neighbours: literary agent Deborah Owen (who was married to Liberal MP Dr David (later Lord) Owen), and Edmund Fisher from publisher Michael Joseph. Tom Rosenthal wrote his 1995 obituary (*The Independent*): "Fisher, in a trade not short of larger-than-life characters, was one of the most endearingly flamboyant."

Many of the *Womancraft* staff came to our wedding reception in July 1975, held in a marquee erected at the old New Zealand rugby ground called Aorangi Park at Wimbledon. Today it is part of the All England Lawn Tennis Club and is covered by tennis courts and lawns kept green by automatic sprinklers.

My family from Australia couldn't be there but I was delighted to have my good friends Laurie and her husband Keith and their daughters Emma and Sophie, Carol McCartney from the GH Institute, Dee Remmington who was associate editor at *Woman*, and Patric Walker. My astrological friend said he thought we'd chosen an auspicious date and as Ian and I are still married all these years later, his percipience was spot on.

Marcus sent his best wishes with a gift: a cocktail strainer which was an *objet d'art*, but the thought was appreciated. Carol's gift was apt: decorations for the top of two cakes. One had wedding bells entwined, the other a baby in a crib. Within weeks of deciding to marry, I was pregnant and there was no hiding that at the church though the full, maxi-length fashion of the time helped.

I'd chosen silk voile with appealing red and white flowery swirls (the dress was made by Brenda Evans, a dressmaking neighbour, from a Vogue pattern) and similarly patterned cotton for short dresses for my daughters, the flower girls. They looked gorgeous, in colours complementing the scarlatina rash (a less acute form of scarlet fever, rampant at the time) on their face, legs and arms. Fortunately they'd passed the contagious stage.

We had a wonderful trad jazz band outside on the grass, an invitation to everyone, including the waitresses, to twirl and twist in the sunshine. It was a great day.

* * *

Gabi lent me a couple of maternity dresses which saw me fashionably through the next few months during which my pregnancy was closely monitored. Because of antibodies in my blood, I had frequent blood tests and several amniocentesis tests (though I know now these can be dangerous to the baby, I don't remember knowing it then) and the doctors advised that I be induced at 38 weeks. On October 10 I started three months' leave at a very reduced salary.

I left Chestergate House on the Friday and went into hospital early the following Monday, October 13. My waters were broken surgically, the spinal injection was put in place and Ian and I played Scrabble. I was holding the winning letters (including a z) at 2.20pm when Christopher arrived, his birthdate shared with formidable politicians Margaret Thatcher and Edwina Currie.

In her congratulations card, Laurie included an introduction for a possible feature: "If you want to try something that's creative, satisfying and almost always fun, try Mothercraft. The editor, who should know, explains the ins and outs of a technique that's guaranteed to produce results in nine months flat."

Hmm. With what is known about giving birth today, her idea sounds very old fashioned, and I'm not sure about the 'fun' bit. Christopher was an unusual shade of yellow, caused by my antibodies, and was whisked away to Charing Cross Hospital to be 'cooked' under special lights until his haemoglobin count improved and his jaundice disappeared. Ian drove to the hospital twice a day with my expressed breast milk so his son could be fed.

We brought our baby home after two days. The girls adored their new brother and the family time we had together was rare. I had been a working mother since 1971 and our lives revolved around the time restraints imposed by the jobs. Fortunately I think my children were very resilient and we enjoyed this unusual togetherness.

Too soon it was time to return to the office and the first step was to give up breast feeding at Christmas. It isn't advisable to stop, without any medical help, at a celebratory time! No liquid of any sort must pass your lips for 24 hours. Ian took over bottle feeding for a couple of days so my breasts could dry out without any stimulus from Christopher's hunger cries.

I was back at my desk at *Womancraft* in the second week of January 1976 and Gabi's second child, Nadine, was born in the spring. It was to be a year of hard work, but it was glorious – sunshine all the way. In fact, it was one of the driest years on record which was to bring about subsidence nationwide, a pertinent subject for us. We were first to publish an article about how trees growing near a house could endanger the foundations.

Womancraft was holding the readers gained since the relaunch but the circulation seemed stuck. We needed to move ahead – like Jill Churchill's *Home & Freezer Digest* which was outselling the prime contender in the market *Good Housekeeping*, an extraordinary achievement.

I was beginning to suspect something wasn't right, but I couldn't work out what was holding us back. I realised how little I knew about big business. It seemed a good idea when Michael Bird, NatMags' head of reader research (he later became MD of Thomson Magazines), carried out a survey of *Womancraft* readers: a mixture of subscribers, those who'd made an inquiry as a result of an ad, and those who'd responded to an offer.

Under scrutiny was the August issue of 1975, a year after the relaunch. During that year there'd been a double dip recession in the economy and inflation reached a postwar high of over 25%.

The response rate was a very healthy 56% and, overall, those surveyed generally approved the eclectic mix with cookery, crafts and hobbies (screen printing, pottery, embroidery etc) scoring highest. And their replies revealed that not only were they a very bright lot but also presented a fine snapshot of British women.

A SURPRISING LOT OF READERS

The survey's biggest revelation was just how unusual *Womancraft* readers were: 30% were under 25, and 36% between 25 and 34. A whopping 27% finished their full-time education aged between 21 and 23 – a footnote said that the national average for all adults terminating their education at 21+ was 4%, for women it was only

3.2%. Yet 8.3% of *Womancraft*'s main readership finished their education at 21+. We learnt that 65% were married, 69% had children under 15, and 48% worked fulltime – a footnote drew attention to the national average of 23.6%, and 24.8% in the 25-34 age group.

Our readers were intelligent, educated, hardworking married women with children. Wasn't that great? Wouldn't these results be ammunition to support investment in more promotion? No. There were no whoops of joy from the survey's instigators (MD Allan Boddy, publisher Jack Blanche and advertisement/marketing manager Ian Harkness). It's taken me years to conclude that National Magazines bought Astra Press as a tax loss, to offset the profits from the hugely successful *Cosmopolitan* and *Good Housekeeping*.

I thought the company saw *Womancraft* as a magazine that fitted in well with the others it published. Naivety is a sad quality in a journalist. Michael Bird's findings probably ended up in a filing cabinet. Lost in the mists of time.

Despite it all, Laurie urged us on. We continued to produce issues packed with helpful features like how to do your own divorce, write a will, build a car port, and make your own flies for trout fishing – almost the same article appeared in *Financial Times Weekend Magazine*, over 30 years later. *Womancraft* went further, however, setting the finished flies in clear resin to become an unusual *objet d'art* (naturally we explained how to do that, too). I still have the one we featured.

* * *

The last year was 'hairy', as Laurie described it in a letter to me later. We were always searching for some magic that would boost our circulation – if we could get it over 100,000 we'd be fine. But the ABC figure for the six months Jul-Dec 1976 was only 87,000. In 'niche market' terms now that wouldn't be beyond the pale. Then, it was.

I have clear memories of the sense of dread that hung over all our actions. Brian Braithwaite and Joan Barrell wrote in *The Business of Women's Magazines*: "National Magazine Company, much more used to success than failure nevertheless found themselves with the latter in 1977." [At that time Brian was publisher of *Cosmopolitan*, and Joan associate publisher.]

They said *Womancraft* was aimed at "the woman reader with time on her hands who could be persuaded to take up a hobby or two". How twee that sounds now! And I disagree with them completely. It was a do-it-yourself magazine for women, it was educational and innovative, and I think different from what were called 'service magazines', a description hinting of subservience. Importantly, *Womancraft* was utterly bewildering to those who were selling advertising space.

When Val Hobson, the art editor, decided to move house beyond commuting distance, Jack and Laurie handed design to an outside group called Bryan Austin Associates. Designer Françoise Trainaud, formerly of *Home & Freezer Digest* and also *Woman's Mirror*, aimed to improve the look of the issues.

Deputy editor Peter McHoy left to write gardening

books and he wasn't replaced. But we now had a chief sub, bearded Jeff Boyle, a crafts editor Caroline MacDonald-Haig, and a Girl Friday called Kelly. We made much more of 'home' subjects, features considered more main stream, more likely to attract advertisers. Freelance writer Sylvia Madden explained the tricks of colour scheming, for instance, and showed readers how to create a kitchen that's right for the way you live. [Looking at them now, I can see they could almost be a blueprint for the planning sections of B&Q and Homebase which set up out-of-town warehouses years later.]

THE TRICK IS TO SMILE AS YOU CLEAN
Womancraft made much of artist Malcolm Bird's gently humorous illustrations. They brought joy to _How to clean up and stay smiling_, special pullouts in the May and June 1977 issues – yes, we accepted that women were likely to do most of this domestic stuff. And these features could almost have been the prototype for the popular Channel 4 series _How Clean Is Your House_ over 25 years later. It starred the talented Aggie MacKenzie who'd worked at _Good Housekeeping_ for many years.

In 1977, our guest cook for six issues was Michael Barry. His philosophy, explained in his book _Crafty Cooking_, was: "Crafty cooks use short cuts if they get you to the same place quicker and with less work – not if they show up in the final dish."

Michael Barry was in fact Michael Bukht, who started his career as a BBC trainee. It was Michael Barry who read out his recipes on Michael Aspel's morning programme on Capital Radio (he was one of the directors). He did demonstrations in major stores like Debenhams and for 17 years in the 1980s and 1990s was one of the four presenters on BBC TV's *Food and Drink*.

He was a founder of the radio station Classic FM which must have helped make him his fortune. Michael, who was also awarded an OBE, died far too young at 69, in 2011, and the obituarists were full of praise for him as a person and originator. He had impressive resilience and was always a go-getter, full of ideas.

I treasure the memory of a dinner party Ian and I went to at his house in Wandsworth (before he and his family moved to Kent). Other guests were Laurie Purden and husband Keith Kotch, and Tom Mangold, the BBC Panorama reporter who'd worked with Michael when he was editor of current affairs.

With such a mix, the conversation never flagged though we were lost for words as the food appeared: the first course green, the second orange, and the third pink, or was it purple? Eventually we learnt that Michael had done a demo at Debenhams on brightening up food, and rather than throw out the dishes he'd prepared we were eating them! I can see his face now, reflected in that bright green jellied avocado.

* * *

At the end of March 1977, almost three years from the day I started, National Magazines announced that *Womancraft* was to cease publication. Laurie had told me the news a couple of weeks before but I was asked not to tell the staff. It was a horrible time. In the trade weekly *Newsagent and Bookshop*, the headline about the closure summed up the puzzle: '*Womancraft merger – can 90,000 women be wrong?*'. Peter Arnott-Job wrote: "To the retailers and the readers of the do-it-yourself magazine for women, Womancraft seemed to be doing fine; newsagents could have pointed to many other publications they found more difficult to sell."

Jack Blanche was quoted, saying the decision was taken by head office in America. "It must be remembered that everything we have done with the magazine since we acquired it in 1973 has taken a great deal of time and effort. This represents a substantial investment. Costs are increasing all the time, especially of print and paper and there comes a time when a decision has to be made whether to carry on or call a halt," he said.

"It looks as if you have to sell 150,000 copies of a magazine with a cover price of 60p to do well. Our cover price was 20p not long ago and then it went up to 25p but the upward trend in circulation continued. The price will go up to 30p with the May issue."

In the next issue of the paper, Marcus Morris refuted Jack's statement in a letter to the editor: "It was a decision taken here, for which I accept full responsibility. Our American parent company did agree with our decision. There were powerful reasons why Womancraft had to cease publication." He didn't elaborate.

I'd like to have been a fly on the wall when Jack tackled Marcus about this – if he ever did. It made Jack, the publisher, sound as though he didn't know what he was talking about. And Marcus was not going to admit that the whole exercise could be put down to accounting.

I was beside myself with despair. I just couldn't believe that we'd worked so hard and it was all going to be taken away from us. Dee Remmington, still at *Woman*, immediately got in touch to offer commiserations and I rashly said I wished I could find the money to buy it myself.

"Leave it with me," said Dee. She'd just interviewed an heiress who was on the lookout for good causes to invest in. I even – cheek, really – went to my own bank to try and raise the money. Some hope. Neither was on the cards, probably just as well as in real terms I had none of the expertise or chutzpah needed for such an enterprise.

Then Marcus received an offer from Jane Reed, now a publisher at IPC, and George Rogers, a board member, to buy the magazine. Our fate was sealed. The June issue would be the last we produced, and would include ads for *Sewing & Knitting*, the IPC magazine with which *Womancraft* would be merged.

IPC provided an explanation of the magazine's changeover and within this the outgoing editorial team was allowed a small space. I suspect the words were a mix of mine and Laurie's.

"Womancraft has never been a run-of- the-mill magazine, never believed in escapism, always preferred the reality of self expression; a do-it-yourself magazine in the truest sense, not a get-it-done-for-you magazine. We have always offered encouragement in the face of all odds, removing the mystique from the experts, winkling out their techniques and secrets in order to tell you where to look for pitfalls in whatever you undertook so that you could do it well. That has been our aim – and our pleasure. You in turn rewarded us with what matters most – your enthusiasm and trust. Hearing the stories of your achievements, your discovery of unsuspected talents, has made producing Womancraft marvellously worthwhile."

And that is how we were supposed to say goodbye and invite the readers to buy the next issue of *Sewing & Knitting with Womancraft* (within a year the title was turned round to be *Womancraft with Sewing & Knitting*). The staff decided we would do it differently, by changing page 3 to add our farewell – and it required subterfuge.

As is usual with magazines, Page 3 is the first editorial page, listing the issue's contents along with small 'taster' pictures of the subjects. The first page 3 was completed and taken by the chief sub for Laurie's signature before being sent to the printer. But we had a second page 3: with a drawing done by Malcolm Bird of the staff waving goodbye. Somehow Jeff got Laurie's signature on that – and it was the one that appeared in our last issue.

Petty. Bolshie. Not the right thing to do at all. There were some emotive words exchanged when printed copies arrived at Chestergate House, but what could Jack and Laurie do – we already had our marching orders. We felt sad rather than smug because we wanted the readers to know just who they'd been dealing with for three years.

Before we left we were visited by Terry Mansfield, who was in line to be managing director, to wish the staff well, and that was much appreciated. [Terry, sadly, was an early victim of coronavirus, dying aged 81 in March 2020. He had a long and highly regarded career with NatMags and Hearst UK and when he retired did a lot of voluntary work, particularly in arts and education which earned him an OBE.]

I can't remember Marcus saying goodbye. In his obituary in *The Independent* in 1989, written by Ruari McLean, designer of the popular comic *Eagle* who then supervised the design of *Girl*, *Swift* and *Robin* (all successful publications), Marcus was described as hard-drinking and chain smoking – not a side of him I saw.

It was sad to archive everything relating to *Womancraft* and pack it into boxes. My job then was to take it by taxi to a huge tower block called Kings Reach, on the Waterloo station side of Waterloo Bridge, which is where IPC had moved to in 1974. There was an official handover to the new publisher Jane Reed who was actually most sympathetic, but that didn't improve my feelings.

Worse still, as I was about to leave the smoked glass and brown aluminium building, I met Ita Buttrose on her way in – and she obviously knew what had happened. "What have they done to your lovely magazine?" she asked. Even with tears clouding my eyes I could see she looked as fabulous as ever.

Ita, by now very much a big wig in Australian journalism, was visiting the UK on a publishing trip with Kerry Packer, head of Consolidated Press (he was also setting up his sport-changing world cricket series).

By the end of May, my links with *Womancraft* and the National Magazine Company at Chestergate House were over. I had three months' redundancy money and needed to find a way to earn my living in journalism. Could any magazine be as rewarding or creative as the one I'd left?

7

GOING IT ALONE

L aurie Purden left the National Magazine Company about the same time as I did. She intended having a breathing space, some thinking time, she said, after many years of employment by big publishers: George Newnes, IPC, Hultons and then NatMags. Soon she would be enticed back to IPC by a friend, Pat Lamburn, the only woman on the Board, to work her magic on the monthly *Woman's Journal.*

Laurie's reputation had been enhanced by another friend and colleague Brian Braithwaite who invented a verb to describe her talent for changing a magazine: 'purdened'. He never thought it happened with *Womancraft*, yet her experience with *Housewife* in the 1960s should have stood her in good stead.

Cynthia White's *Women's Magazines 1693-1968* says that *Housewife* would reflect "every aspect of successful living for the young wife and mother". It would focus on 'lively women between 25 and 35'...for whom 'the house is still a vital part of life...a creative workshop...a place to experiment...a base for full and happy living'.

"The new Housewife was created for the woman who was gay [not a description publicists would use in today's world of LGBTQ+], fashion-conscious, and 'interested in new opinion, new ideas, new patterns of behaviour', able to 'think for herself' and 'set her own trends', an outlook which the magazine was committed to share...guiding young housewives through their first attempts at homemaking, in particular how to get value for money..."

Michael Bird's 1970s research showed that readers of *Womancraft* were more like those of *Housewife* than either *Good Housekeeping* or *Woman's Journal*. Both are in the 'glossy' category and appeal to middle and upper class readers who allegedly have more disposable income.

A MATTER OF CLASS

It is very British to have a 'class' designation for magazines. Readers, in shorthand, are known as As, Bs, Cs and Ds and advertisers like to know what percentage of each read the magazines so they know how their ads will fare. The glossy magazines, with better paper and more colour pages, aim to attract the As and Bs who are less restrained in their spending. In reality the buying market comprises more Cs and Ds, who read the weeklies (hence higher circulations), and they are as likely to be disloyal as loyal.

Did 'class' mean anything to the *Womancraft* reader? It doesn't to me as an Australian, but who knows? The magazine was inspirational, encouraging those who bought it – possibly more maverick and individual than run of the mill – to find and use their skills, getting pleasure from what they were able to do themselves. To my mind they were early 'greens', thinking of the planet, not approving of waste. These attitudes have come into their own today with greater recognition of environmental dangers we all face.

Looking back through my collection, I am surprised by the number of advertisements, even advertorials or 'paid content' promotions arranged by Gabi Tubbs and Sylvia Madden working directly with the public relations side. Sylvia had come from this world, and had the highly rated 'address book of contacts'.

If *Womancraft* were to come out now – well into the 21st century when many of the conditions that existed in the 1970s have, as if by some dreadful bad luck, reappeared – real estate queen Kirstie Allsop has clearly seen the future. On television she has successfully encouraged domestic creativity, guided by experts into making cushions and curtains and home decorating. Apart from being in full colour, it is, indeed, much like *Womancraft* come to life. The web is a great help to her and craft courses are coming into their own along with magazines at newsagents to inspire a new generation.

My daughters knit and sew, just as I did, and my granddaughters do too – perhaps this has come through the genes of my mother who gave up crocheting and knitting at 90 when her sight was affected by macular degeneration (and she lived to 101!).

There's been an upsurge in DIY too – I read in *Prima*, summer 2020, that 60% of UK women now take charge of

household DIY tasks, and skills are encouraged via
courses in many places including Manchester, London,
Brighton and Bristol.

* * *

Back to 1977: with no job on the horizon, I opted to
be self employed. It meant altering my membership
of the National Union of Journalists to join the freelance
branch. It had not been compulsory to be a union member
at NatMags but I never let my membership lapse. This
wasn't a problem as I didn't have a hiring and firing role;
Laurie took this on. I also told the tax people I would now
be paying my stamp myself.

'Stamp' was the word used for National Insurance
Contributions and as a freelance it literally was a stamp
that I bought weekly from the DHSS (Department of
Health and Social Security, now the Department of Work
and Pensions) and placed on a record card.

Unlike the popular Green Shield Stamps of the 20th
century – which you collected from stores to buy something from a catalogue – the government stamps would
only come into their own at retirement age (60 then, for
women, and 65 for men) and influence how much state
pension (at that time called the old age pension) you
received. In those days, for a full pension, females had to
have been employed for 39 years, men for 44.

From the time I started work in the UK, I paid the full
NIC stamp (it was deducted from my pay). I didn't – as
many married working women chose to do – opt for a
lower amount, possibly because the stamp was too high a

proportion of their earnings. Why this was legal is incomprehensible, and it was a poor decision. Many of those women, on reaching 60, would be distressed to discover that their state pension was dependent on their husbands' NIC records. If divorced they could use their ex's NICs as their own but if still married the amount received could be lower than expected.

My first freelance assignment came from Dee Remmington at *Woman*. For six weeks I helped her with a filing cabinet full of articles needing to be re-angled, rewritten or written off – talk about shades of the past. Dee, who'd weathered the storms and vicissitudes of Fleet Street and was rarely at a loss for ideas or inspiration, felt under pressure from the demands of Jo Sandilands, the new editor. I was glad to catch up with Renee, my former secretary, who stayed at IPC after *First Lady*'s demise and was now the editor's personal assistant.

It was obvious that the staff were still shocked by Peter Lawrence's death, at the age of 38, from carcinomatosis. This, uncannily, was the same as that which had taken the life of Robert Bruce, his *Woman's Own* colleague, a few years earlier. Peter had married Sue, the managing editor's secretary at *Woman's Own*, and they had two small children. It was a tragedy. The sudden death plus the new regime affected all the staff. No job is perfect and there is always something to grumble about. Somehow these mutterings seemed different.

The gossip was riveting: darkened rooms and closed doors, erratic direction, calamitous conferences that often went on until well after midnight. The main beneficiaries were the taxi drivers who were called to take people to their homes, miles away from this part of London, in the wee small hours. The department heads could not leave the building until what they'd submitted to the conference had been accepted. Every week was like sitting an horrendous exam. Such irony. This was a woman's magazine, ostensibly interested in the quality of women's lives.

At this time, Brenda Polan was deputy to *Woman* features editor Diana Hutchinson and they felt under siege. They were rewriting and re-angling stories right up to press time when the final pages had to be retrieved (indeed often wrenched) from their hands by the chief sub to be sent to the printer.

For Brenda, the final straw was a major confrontation over the length of what she called "a cobbled-up story about the newly elected President Jimmy Carter and the women in his life", and she threw in her hand. It was a good decision as it took her to *The Guardian* – as a sub in the features department! That was something.

Female subs on Fleet Street (or nearby Farringdon Road in this case) were rare though the much revered Mary Stott had set a precedent at *The Manchester Guardian* years before. Months after I started at *Woman's Own* in 1966, I heard that an 'Aussie sheila' had been employed on shifts at *The Daily Mirror*, and others were casuals on other dailies. Lynn Corbyn went from the *Woman's Own* fiction department to be the first female sub on *The Sun* in Manchester; Patricia Pett survived many years subbing on *The Sunday Express* (she was the last taken on the staff by legendary newspaperman Sir John Junor, she told me).

Dee invited me to lunch to meet her good friend Patsy Brougham, associate editor, who'd been chief sub at

Woman under Barbara Buss (the editor after Mary Grieve). Miss Buss (or Barbie, as she was known by the staff) refused to allow women employees to wear trousers (she died in 2017, aged 84). Though I didn't meet her then, Patsy's protegée was Rose Wild, a very tall and bright young woman who was in the fiction department.

From what Patsy told me, *Woman*, the first colour magazine, born in 1937, was ground-breaking and included a range of subjects not normally tackled by women's magazines. Back then, aspirations of working class girls were shaped by by the need for respectability, fear of poverty and a wish to escape the hardship and domestic burden of their mothers' lives. In the 1970s, although circulation was diminishing, it retained an edge.

The ActionWoman spread regularly homed in on things that affected readers – like poor equipment or directions or instructions or labelling. Many famous journalists worked in this section under Patience Bulkley: Lyn Faulds Wood, married John Stapleton with whom she later had a highly regarded consumer show on TV (she died in 2020, aged 72); Jan Walsh, went on become a consumer champion on several Fleet Street papers; and Davina Lloyd was an agony aunt, then launch editor of *Practical Parenting* (a Jill Churchill production from *Family Circle*). About to leave the department then was chirpy Essex girl Jenny Glew, pregnant with her first child.

INSPIRATION AND ROMANCE
Star interviews were stock in trade for *Woman* and one writer used them well. Christine Sparks wrote articles about the really big Hollywood heart-throbs like

Charlton Heston, Roger Moore and Warren Beatty. She had a wealth of material at hand when a few years later she became Lucy Gordon, a full-time writer of successful romantic fiction with her own website. Her own story was the impetus: on holiday in Venice she'd fallen for a gondolier called Roberto who she married and they lived happily ever after.

It wasn't to be the same for Janet Horwood, who Dee had enticed from *Woman's Own* because of her skilful rewriting ability. I liked Janet and felt desperately sorry for her. Her marriage was in turmoil because her husband William, a journalist working on *The Daily Mail*, was having an affair with a Californian woman. His inamorata turned out to be Leslie Kenton whose life had crossed with mine several times.

She fascinated me. After *Harpers & Queen*, as the guru of health and vitality, publicity came naturally to her. In the late 70s she was forthright about her healthful minimalist lifestyle, the choices she made to encourage self-awareness. Shown in her signature floaty white garments, she said she had eschewed a bed for floorboards and talked of her children – each one had a different father – as being lent to her while growing up.

I never met William but I had always been impressed by Janet and her ability to work while bringing up her daughter Rachel, born with cerebral palsy. After the marriage break-up William had a bestseller with *Skallagrigg*, made into a film in 1987 starring musician and actor Ian Dury who was physically disabled by polio. It is a testament to his daughter and others who fight for existence against the odds, I read on the web.

William, too, had an eye for publicity, even if it hurt those he left behind. In a 1993 interview in *The Independent*, William said the idea for *Duncton Wood*, his first bestseller, in 1980, was planted by Leslie (to whom the book is dedicated). "I feel like a mole," she told him, during what he described as "a lie-in". "I want you to write me a story about moles." He told the interviewer, Christine Hardyment: "She's Rebecca, I'm Bracken. It's our story."

My stint at *Woman* put me back in touch with George Cannon, as unflappable as ever. At the conference these days, he said, he didn't know where to put his eyes as they were drawn magnetically to features editor Wendy Henry's cleavage displayed at table-height. His remark made me laugh as I'm sure I'd have felt the same about such a sight. I never met her, but I discovered that she had an upfront career too, going from *Woman* to Fleet Street, to the huge-selling daily *The Sun*, where she came up with the famous *"Gotcha"* – the headline which editor Kelvin McKenzie used after the Argentinian cruiser *Belgrano* was sunk during the Falklands War in 1982.

Wendy was allegedly the first journalist to reveal the relationship between Princess Margaret and Roddy Llewellyn, and went on to edit, at the end of the 1980s, the high-circulation popular Sundays *The News of the World* and *Sunday People*. She had a stint as 'Professor of Anecdotes' at the London Journalism Training Centre. What a job title, a raconteur's dream!

Woman and *Woman's Own* still regarded each other as enemies, fighting for readers to prevent their circulations falling, though each six months' ABC (Audit Bureau of Circulation) figures were worse than the previous. *Woman's World*, which was going to start in the same year as *First Lady* (1974), was now launched and selling well via Terry Hornett's Carlton Publishing.

The Hornett package brought a new element to magazine production: it did the development, chose the staff to create the editorial, then leased the magazine to IPC which became the publisher and sold advertising for it. Hornett also had an exceptional eye for recruiting staff.

Judith Hall, ex *First Lady*, was working there along with others who would in the future be influential in women's magazines (and in Fleet Street as well): Sally O'Sullivan, Bridget Rowe and Richard Barber. Before this, both Sally and Richard were columnists for *Hi*, a teen magazine that took over *Petticoat*, and was edited by Bill Williamson (after *First Lady*). Bill moved later to *Good Life*, similar in size to *Home & Freezer Digest*, a monthly version of *Woman's Weekly*.

One of the most popular TV programmes of the time (1975–1978), *The Good Life* was about a couple (Tom and Barbara Good, played by Richard Briers – who died in 2013 – and Felicity Kendall) in search of self sufficiency, and their neighbours who measured happiness by what they owned. Readers of *Good Life* magazine couldn't have connected it to the funny and heartwarming screen stories. It only lasted a couple of years and Bill moved on successfully to magazines produced for the 20somethings in the metropolis: *Ms London* and *Midweek*.

* * *

At *Woman* Dee confided that she was considering becoming freelance. It shocked me. As a single woman she'd always favoured being employed, for security. Now in her mid 50s she felt there were no options for her at IPC. Thinking of my future, she arranged for me to meet Pat Lamburn, Laurie's friend on the IPC board, and Lady Georgina Coleridge (editor of *Homes & Gardens*). Pat, ardent supporter of Terry Hornett and Bill Williamson (they were known as 'her young men'), had a special interest in monthly publications. We discussed placements at possible magazines, one aimed at young mums, another at those on a permanent diet. I couldn't see myself contributing successfully to either.

This is a perfect example of reaching a fork in the road and having to make a choice. I failed. In career terms it was undoubtedly bad on my part not to show keenness. The magazines were launchpads for some well-known journalists (Tessa Hilton, for example, went from editing *Mother* to top jobs on *The Sun, Daily Mail, Sunday Mirror and Daily Express*). And the subject matter of each are top themes all these years later. Before I had too much time to regret my response, however, something else came up which led me to another type of magazine.

I was asked to edit a book for Collins, the publishers, called *The Complete Book of Children's Clothes*. Many of the garments – for babies through to teenagers and sometimes adult – had appeared in an Italian publication called *Il Filo*, published by Fratelli Fabbri Editori, Milan.

The instructions had been translated but needed to be checked and rewritten, with new art work for patterns and cutting-out guides created. I would be working again with Lorry Spooner who had left *Woman's Own* to join her husband Trevor in book-packaging, handling the preparation and production for publishers. Trevor had been art editor on many magazines, including *Woman's Own* and *Modern Woman* (whose end came with the arrival of *Cosmopolitan* in 1972).

I knew I couldn't do it all by myself, and fortunately there was a budget. I called on the talents of the *Womancraft* freelancers who knew everything there was to know about knitting, crocheting, sewing and crafts such as embroidery, smocking, tie-dyeing and batik. More photography was done, using my children Dani, Sally and Christopher, and friends' children, as models. The new pictures joined seamlessly with the Italian.

The book, a large format, full colour hardback with 224 pages, took over a year to come together. Every garment was made or created in full (for photography) or in miniature so materials to buy could be accurately calculated. Instructions were in metric and imperial.

Knitting instructions in the UK took a lot of space: every row of a pattern was always given because the wool company wanted the knitter to use their recommended brand. On the Continent, the method simply gave the correct tension achieved by using the correct size needles and ply, along with abbreviations.

For Trevor to assemble the book, the instructions were

galleyed – it was just like working as a sub back at *Woman's Own*, except now I was working from the kitchen table at home. Then I was contacted by a publishing company called Orbis.

* * *

The timing of the phonecall was extraordinary because, through the aforementioned *Il Filo*, I had just become aware of what is best described as education by instalments: part works. These weekly publications produced by European companies had no ads (except their own, for binders or back issues) and had a clear purpose to provide accurate information on a subject.

In 1969 I came across *Cordon Bleu Cookery Course* (subline *be a better cook in your own home*) in which the techniques of the venerated French chefs were clearly explained. I still have No 4: shortcrust pastry. It cost 4s 6d which seemed expensive, especially as a set of three top quality saucepans in shining aluminium (long before non-stick) were offered at 80s/£4. This was a weekly part work, just like *Golden Hands* and *Stitch* that focused on handicrafts. Behind these examples lay a huge industry.

The person who called me from Orbis was Brian Innes. He'd set up the company with Martin Heller, a colleague from Purnell, part work publishers (one of their successes was *The History of the Second World War*, in 1966.)

Orbis worked in conjunction with publishers DeAgostini in Italy, a country with a high regard for self education. This concept was certainly understood by Martin Heller who was born behind the Iron Curtain, as was the corpulent, black-eyebrowed Robert Maxwell, owner of the British Printing Corporation of which Purnell was a part. After coming to the UK both changed their names.

It was in London, so the story goes, among tourists in Trafalgar Square, that Martin spied someone holding a copy of *Catch 22*, the runaway bestseller at the time. He liked the author's name and so Heller he became, said his obituary in 2016.

Brian also had an interesting background, having been a member of the trad jazz band The Temperance Seven which, I learnt from his obituary (he died in July 2014, aged 86, leaving orders that he was to be cremated to the sound of Benny Goodman's *Smoke Gets in Your Eyes*), was formed at the Royal College of Art in 1957 with nine members. One over the eight ostensibly means intemperance. He called himself Professor Emeritus, was the percussionist, and also the band's leader for a decade.

The band had its first hit single in 1961: *You're Driving Me Crazy*. It was produced by the soon-to-be-very-famous George Martin who was instrumental to The Beatles' success (he died in 2016). And Orbis had its own jazz band as well: the Orbis All-Stars. Being able to play an instrument was almost a guarantee of a job!

* * *

In 1977 Orbis filled several floors of a converted warehouse on the edge of Covent Garden, just round the corner from the world-famous men's clothing hire store Moss Bros and not too far from Southampton Street where I'd worked on *Woman's Own*. The luvvies club for men only, The Garrick, was just up the road, but so was Charing Cross Road and Leicester Square where *First Lady*, a supposedly humorous weekly for women, died in 1974. Nearby was Gollancz, famous left-wing publishers.

Marie-Jacqueline Lancaster, known as MJ, had edited the *Cordon Bleu* course at Purnell and had come with Brian and Martin to Orbis where she was working on a gardening publication, *Green Fingers*, that was selling well. I had met her at a press do when I was at *Womancraft* and it was she who gave my name to Brian. In publishing, getting a job by word of mouth is not unusual.

MJ and Brian explained that the new project was to be international cookery, to be created in conjunction with French, Italian, German and Scandinavian material for which Orbis had UK publication rights. Having joined Europe in 1973 we could look in detail at the cuisines of Continental countries and around the world too.

The interview veered all over the place. I knew almost nothing about part works, and Brian questioned me about cookery. "When would you put tomato puree into a dish, early on with the oil, for instance, or later?" he asked. I wondered for ages about my reply (I put it in at the start to develop the flavour, but not always). But it wasn't for this answer that I would be editor.

The experience I'd had in previous magazine jobs was what was needed: to create from scratch, with the help of experts, a weekly publication that would provide the reader, and collector, with everything to be known about cooking. It was to be called *The Complete Cook* and before any work could start I had to decide what would fill a 20-page issue each week for three years!

* * *

T he skill of living in the future, drummed into me all those years ago at *Woman's Own*, when magazines were produced on a 12-week roller coaster schedule, now came to the fore. But planning a few months ahead is a doddle compared to what has to be included over years.

In the 1970s, several cookery part works had been successful: *Cordon Bleu, Supercook, Good Cooking*. Each had a different approach, and I concluded that *The Complete Cook* could be an alphabet of ingredients. Interspersing these would be spreads of traditional cuisines around the world, the countries where more and more people were travelling to.

You wouldn't believe how many recipes we had on offer! But recipes on their own, without a distinct theme, can be indigestible, overwhelming. They had to be categorised by the major ingredient, or an essential ingredient, as a base for communication. We would find relevant pictures and recipes – from our French, Italian, Swedish and German sources – and allocate them from A to Z through the full-colour volumes. Our input would be recipes from the British Isles, and photography for the ingredients and the world's cuisines.

Do you think this sounds simple? It wasn't. There was a big catch. Before a word was written or before recipes were examined or translated, I had to know what exactly the ingredients would be, how many pages each would need and how many there would be in a volume.

The reason behind this was simple: part works are designed to be constantly referred to, so binders are made available to buy to house the collection. I was told that *The Complete Cook*'s content over three years would fill 10 binders, each with a stick-on label designating the alphabetical range of subject matter inside: for example, AL–BE, BI–CH, CH–DI, and so on.

What went on these labels had to be decided before the start so the binders were ready and their stickers printed and in the warehouse from the moment *The Complete Cook* was regarded as a goer – usually six weeks after launch. (I couldn't help but think of the reply to that old joke, when seeking directions to somewhere: I wouldn't start from here...)

The search for the foodie alphabet began. I had a large collection of cookery books, including some I had brought with me from Australia, plus I had an English dictionary, the French classic *Larousse Gastronomique*, and *The Joy of Cooking* (from the US). I went to markets in those parts of London where different ethnic groups lived and to Harrods to check out its remarkable food hall. Today it still a tourist attraction as well as being a high class grocery source for the Knightsbridge locals.

As the ingredients list grew, I expanded the content to make it truly a 'complete' compendium. It wasn't necessary to think of each issue as a weekly magazine but I wanted to add contrast. In came food groupings called 'generics': Alcohol, Biscuits, Bread, Fruit, Cake, Herbs, Liqueurs, Meats, Spices. In went basics about eating: Diet, Macrobiotics (a buzz word then!), Menu planning, Nutrition, Vegetarian. And, as so many dishes relied on them for success, basic cooking techniques slipped into the alphabet: Liaisons,

Sauces, Stocks. Photos or drawings showed the 'how to'.

The index for each volume listed recipes under starters, soups, main meals, vegetables, desserts, lunches, salads, tea-time, appetizers/party snacks, sauces/dressings/spreads, drinks, preserves, techniques, and cuisines of the world. Each issue had a small space for corrections – in any publication, even with the best intentions and constant monitoring, there will always be things that slip through and we put them right when we could. Somewhere in the future lay the comprehensive index that would cover everything published in *The Complete Cook* and its place in which volume.

I had let myself in for an experience that had all the elements of Alice pursuing the White Rabbit through unknown territory! Today an algorithm (a word much denigrated during the Covid crisis) could probably work out the contents of 10 volumes; then, it was just me.

The AL-BE label on Volume 1 had been a guess, but it worked out! It began with Alcohol (*Cooking with wine and spirits*) and finished with Bergamot (*Herb of the new world*) 12 issues and 244 pages later, whetting the tastebuds of cooks and travellers as well with the lifestyle and dishes of Algeria, Alsace-Lorraine, Australia, Austria, the Balkans and Belgium.

* * *

Let me explain a little about what are known as part works. Commercially produced weeklies and monthlies have a designated market, aim constantly to increase circulation, and can alter the number of pages in an issue if they attract more or less advertising. On the other hand, part works (generally speaking, though there are exceptions) have a continually diminishing number of readers and each issue is the same size during its life – from one, two or four years.

The business proposition is different, too. The major investment is made at the beginning, when the publication is heavily promoted, mostly on TV, which aims to bring huge sales. Heavy 'boredom times' – after Christmas, for instance, or the end of the summer holidays – are usually the best to tempt people.

In the first few crucial weeks, the strategy is to get buyers hooked on the subject so they place a regular order with the newsagent. With luck inertia then sets in and it would be too much trouble to cancel. It seemed hit and miss, but the procedures had made part works successful for years so what did I know!

There were some odd facts to digest. Women would be the prime market but mostly it would be the husbands who placed the order and paid. It wasn't uncommon for the buyers not to read the issue they picked up every week; but they bought the binders and religiously filed the magazines inside. Research didn't reveal how often they were read or consulted. This rang alarm bells.

From my experience of women's magazines the readers had huge expectations of each new arrival and couldn't wait to devour its contents. (In fact, if they hesitated they were lost to future sales. If an issue remained unread – for lack of time or whatever – why buy it?)

On the web I found a company specialising in vintage

part works where there was a full set of *The Complete Cook*, so at least one person must have stayed the course! I have always hoped it would be a valued and relied on part of people's lives. But that may be difficult for it started over 40 years ago, in 1977, and sold for four years in its first run, as I'll explain.

I still cook from my collection in their brown, table-cloth-style, wipeable binders, with pages smeared with dustings of icing sugar or flour, or notes I've scribbled. I use it just as I intended the buyer would use it: to find a different way of presenting a food, to make a meal in a hurry or to take advantage of a glut. All very useful at the time of the coronavirus crisis.

* * *

Life in the 1970s wasn't lived 24/7 and 'sell by' or 'use by' dates didn't exist. Shops often shut after lunch on Saturday and few opened on Sunday. You didn't do huge shops as people do now at the supermarkets, piling their trolleys high any time of the week, day and night. You had to plan for long weekends – like the four days of Easter. You stocked up for longer breaks like Christmas, particularly if Christmas Eve fell on a Thursday or Friday and shops didn't open again until Tuesday or Wednesday.

Supermarkets were getting bigger but were nothing like they are today. They hadn't started offering prepared meals to buy and cook at home, though some were available in the large freezers. But there were cans (usually called tins), and dried food as well (peas and potato, pasta and rice) which were good storecupboard standbys. If you had a delicatessen on your high street you had a more exotic choice. With the increase in newcomers from other countries, there was demand for foods of their homelands and these were now appearing on shelves.

The two domestic themes of the 1970s, home freezing and microwaving, were beginning to have an impact. Even so, most homes only had small refrigerators – tiny compared to today's monsters. Some people still had ice boxes, or ice chests, the hessian-wrapped blocks of frozen water brought to the door by a delivery man (in the street where I lived in southwest London, he drove a horse and cart – in 1977!). Only when more women went out to work did they see the advantage of having a fridge (often written as 'frig' then), freezer and microwave.

* * *

I did the planning at my kitchen table while working on the children's clothes book, craft on one side, cookery on the other. When my concept seemed to jell, I presented it to Orbis. Suddenly I had a new job: the contract said I would remain a freelance, working four days a week for 11 months out of 12. (Only staff members worked for five days.) It was a bit scary but I would be earning and it would be a challenge.

Two other partners at Orbis were integral to a part work's success. The accounts man acquainted me with the editorial budget, and how much new photography could be done to go alongside the European pictures which were not free but cost less than if we had to do them ourselves. The promotions man asked me to come up with something special, a bonus for those who bought the first few issues.

Brian, who'd been an art editor on other part works, worked with a designer to create the 'look' – the choice of type and layout would remain constant throughout its life on sale. When we launched, a reviewer on *The Daily Mail* (Sheila Fullarton, who'd been a feature writer on *Woman*) approved of the clarity and the fact that recipes were in both metric and imperial.

Most importantly the ingredients in a recipe were listed in the order in which they were used so your eye didn't have to roam all over the place looking for what to use when. We gave timings for preparation and cooking, what equipment was needed, and freezing guidance (whether it could or couldn't be frozen, and length of storage time). This was quite innovative I assure you, though this is how recipes are generally presented today.

The staff were mostly concerned with producing the issues: researching, editing and proofing text, and checking pictures. My former colleague at *Woman's Own*, Jose Northey, was my knowledgeable deputy; she worked with MJ on *Cordon Bleu* as well as *Home & Freezer Digest*.

Eventually we had a full-time tester in house, but at the start freelancers were essential: the home economists tested the recipes, the researchers wrote the required number of words that introduced each ingredient, and a nutrition expert checked it. We used photographers local to Covent Garden and the picture editor arranged and supervised the photography.

The first few weeks of *The Complete Cook* – the practical guide to better cooking – were exhausting. I quickly discovered that I needed help and advice on the nitty gritty of food. Fortunately a part work company called Phoebus – which had produced in four volumes *The Story of Pop* for the BBC in 1973 – had come to an abrupt end and from the ashes stepped Gilly Cubitt. Her background was home economics and her special interest was organising photo shoots.

I couldn't have asked for better. She hadn't long been married to Allan Cubitt, then a schoolteacher but who would later become a TV scriptwriter (among his credits was the very popular *Prime Suspect*, starring Helen Mirren, created by Lynda La Plante, and later *The Fall* with Gillian Anderson in the lead role), and her enthusiasm was inspiring. She would certainly know the right time to add tomato puree.

8

A FOOD-LOVER'S WORLD

Orbis's warehouse on the edge of Covent Garden was a hive of industry with a range of publications being created on several floors. It was a labyrinth. While Brian Innes, as editorial director, stood tallish on his cuban heels overseeing the part works, Martin Heller concerned himself with producing magnificent coffee table tomes on esoteric subjects – probably collectors' items today. Later, there was a good market in spin offs from the part works; books which reused material but presented it in a different way. *The Complete Cook,* with its many facets, would provide an amazing collection of hard and soft cover books in the future.

Our little team became culinary linguists, with French, German, Italian and Swedish dictionaries close at hand. Hoots of laughter accompanied our discoveries of ingredients unknown in Britain then, such as the German cream cheese quark, or the Scandinavian reindeer horn (hartshorn) used in cakes as a raising agent. Radicchio wasn't a holiday town in Italy but a cross between a large brussels sprout and a tiny red cabbage. As for dudis and palm hearts, samphire and sea eggs...they all seemed rarified at that time (and may still be to some today!).

We created an efficient, essential, aide memoire: an expanding envelope-style filing system so that recipes ended up under the right ingredient entry, cross-referencing could be done and the previously mentioned comprehensive index could be compiled at the very end of the run (years away!).

Certain decisions were taken early: egg plant, quite unknown apart from its use in the Greek dish moussaka, would be Aubergine; there were entries for Courgette and Zucchini, though they were the same vegetable (but needed for the final entry under Z); Bilberries (*myrtilles* to the French) covered what we now know as the ubiquitous blueberry as well as "huckleberries, whinberries, hurts, whorts and bowberries"; brightly-coloured bell-shaped peppers went under Capsicum.

Jose was fluent in French, as was assistant editor Kate Laughton, a former teacher. Having young children of my own, my heart almost stopped when she told the story of how she and another teacher took a group of primary school children to the Tower of London and how one had wandered off just as a bomb scare was announced.

While her colleague ushered the youngsters outside as calmly as she could, Kate ran back through the crowds pushing their way out until she found the remarkably insouciant child staring at one of the exhibits. She scooped her up in her arms and ran. Bomb scares related to the troubles in Northern Ireland were a feature of

London at this time. The bombing at Harrods, the store of the super rich, horrified and alarmed Londoners and visitors alike. Everyone knew they had to be alert.

The two people people who had to have eyes in the back of their heads at *The Complete Cook* were the other assistant editor Rosemary Hiscock (who'd been chief sub on the ill-fated *Woman's Mirror*) and chief sub Judith Howlett who came from part works and was well versed in production.

KEEPING UP WITH THE ALPHABET
Let me give you a little insight into one of the complications of an A-Z project designed to run for a number of years! Though we had our eyes on the future, that future (in work terms) was proscribed from the start. The ingredients were the most important element and if a recipe did not make it under what was listed as its main ingredient then we could quickly put it under its second ingredient – so long as it was further on in the alphabet!

Food and its influence on our lives was different in the 1970s. Most people shopped at grocery stores, with apron-wearing staff behind the counter to weigh out big or small amounts, often still using old-fashioned scales with weights in a range of sizes (collectibles today!) and plastic bags were unknown. Greengrocers, bakers, corner shops, small off licences: you expected to find all these in suburbs and high streets everywhere. Such personal service was eventually considered far too expensive, yet it couldn't be anything like the cost today of pre-packaging of goods and stocking shelves in supermarkets. In those days you bought according to your needs, not as though preparing for a siege.

Too much waste occurs because of either buying too far ahead or buying too much – the BOGOF (buy one, get one free) marketing ploy was particularly insidious as you end up with more than you can immediately use. Fortunately this selling technique has mostly been outlawed.

Pre-packed ingredients can be far too large and making meals for one or two takes planning if you want to cook from scratch. For those otherwise inclined, the supermarkets proffer prepared and chilled, ready-to-cook meals that require no more effort than removing the covering and placing the pack in a traditional oven or microwave. And ordering in takeaways and eating out is normal, even with people whose incomes are precarious – at least it was until the coronavirus crisis.

Covid 19's appalling effects on people who are overweight brought new focus on food and obesity and forced the Government to come up with viable health strategies for the future. They will need to grasp a very nasty nettle.

* * *

Looking back, did I realise we were part of a revolution? I know that a great deal was changing then in the world of food and eating: we'd become part of Europe and the world seemed to be shrinking. *The Complete Cook* was innovative, providing logically detailed information about every single food we could lay our hands and lens on at that time in the UK.

There was no concept that each had an ecological footprint – the cost of getting it from one part of the world to another which has been so well explained in the last few years by *Financial Times* journalist Sarah Murray in *Moveable Feasts* (subline: *the incredible journeys of the things we eat*) and *Guardian* journalist Felicity Lawrence in *Eat Your Heart Out* (subline: *why the food business is bad for the planet and your health*).

At the end of the 1970s it was exciting to discover these foods, the countries they came from, and reveal their flavour, use and nutritional value. Martin Heller, returning via France from a book fair, either the big general one at Frankfurt in Germany or that for children's books at Bologna in Italy, told of his visit to a most newsworthy *nouvelle cuisine* restaurant, all the rage then.

The focus was on freshness, lightness, clarity of flavour, a reaction to the rich, calorie-laden extravagances of classic French cuisine. There was no menu but he was bewildered and dissatisfied by the nine small, insubstantial, courses he'd had. He couldn't recall what had actually been on the plates, whether it resembled anything he knew. He and his companions imbibed some excellent wines, ordering more as the time lapse between plates grew longer. Not a report to rely on!

Nouvelle cuisine was in no way linked to dieting. The food-loving French had their own approach to weight loss called *cuisine minceur* (nothing to do with British mince). The idea behind the movement was to reduce what should be served to prevent the eater putting on weight, or putting less on the plate to reduce what was gathering round the waist and hips.

With the help of the French part work we could talk about the wonderful culinary inheritance of France and also show how longstanding recipes could be adapted for modern times. The best of both worlds.

We had a great team of testers at *The Complete Cook*. They were used to preparing dishes for photo shoots, where a little leeway might be taken and the end result altered for a better picture. But not in our case. One rule was paramount: the recipes had to work in ordinary kitchens and the results had to look like the photos.

One tester, New Zealander Clare Ferguson, whose husband Ian worked in administration at Orbis, had a sister, Alison Holst, who was well known in their home country for her cookery books, newspaper columns and radio programmes. Both knew fellow Kiwi Graham Kerr, the Galloping Gourmet, whose British TV cookery programme was fuelled by his wine tasting. (I got a taste for it too when I lived out there, when vineyards invited you in to sip their products.)

Another tester Val Barrett was, like Gilly Cubitt, a home economics graduate and both had worked at the Good Housekeeping Institute; Val had also contributed to *Womancraft*. She told a great story about one of her first jobs, as a 'cookery stylist' on a Fanny Cradock TV programme; according to Wikipedia, she had 24 series between 1955 and 1975. It reminded me that I'd bought the first issue of the Fanny and Johnnie Cradock Cookery Programme, a Purnell part work, published in 1970 – a time when colour photography and printing left a lot to be desired and cooking styles were changing. But Fanny was a legend, renowned for her domineering, authoritative approach and her cooking garb of balldress and pearls. Val remembered well Fanny's demonstration of omelette making and the part she played.

FANNY MAKES AN OMELETTE

Val and Fanny's second assistant, usually a teenage boy, had to have bowls, pans and an abundance of eggs at the ready. Each stood by a four-burner hob. Around them the floor was covered with newspaper spread over a tarpaulin. At the first hob, Fanny put the lightly beaten eggs into the bubbling butter, swirling and manoeuvring until it was ready to turn. If she didn't like the way it looked, she flipped it onto the floor and moved to the other hob – and did it all over again. The cameras recorded it all. Val reckoned 50 three-egg omelettes were discarded before Britain's distinctly different cook produced her ideal, which viewers saw.

Sheena Davis, Lorna Walker, Maria Bird, Elaine Bastable, Joyce Hughes, Carole Handslip, Jennifer Kay, Hilary Foster and Cathy Gallop tested the recipes in the *Complete Cook*'s first year. All had worked for other part works and often told tales of things that went wrong.

One ingredient that frequently proved difficult was gelatine. A reader who had followed a recipe for mousse sent in the result by mail: an apricot concoction that you could almost bounce! The recipe should have been four *teaspoons* of the setting agent but instead four *tablespoons* had been published.

The warnings were appreciated. We would watch carefully how much gelatine was called for in any future recipe, and it also made me aware of the need for clear abbreviations. I could see that the commonly used 'tsp' and 'tbsp' were far too similar to the eye and opted for teasp and tbsp.

And then there was the ever present problem of being healthy and not putting on weight. Each issue presented enticing dishes to whet the tastebuds. Our nutrition adviser Jill Leslie, who was down to earth and practical, said it was no good knowing about food if you don't know what it is made up of – ie, the nutrients. This information was included on each ingredient. What was needed was a guide to not eating too much of anything.

A wall chart was the answer. Devised by Jill and Gilly it was given away with one of the early promoted issues. Called *Follow the Stars to Healthy Eating*, it was an effective way of choosing the right amount of food each day. But not by counting calories. This was a concept too far for most people with the added problem, because of metrication, of kiloJoules; 1 calorie, known as a kcal, equalled 4.2kJ (kiloJoules). Far too difficult.

[Much later, magazines included with recipes the calorie content per serving of a finished dish. But did cooks take any notice? Did they understand how much physical energy was needed to burn up the calories in the serving? Was it ever satisfactorily explained?]

Jill and Gilly chose a star route for the chart. They put everyday foods in their seven nutrient categories: protein, calcium, Vitamin A, Vitamin B, Vitamin C, iron, Vitamin D – all of which are essential to good health. The number of stars allotted to foods in each category showed their value in a day's eating. If any had a red dot, you cross-referred to a separate section called Top-up Foods.

Listed here were everyday foods containing carbohydrates and fats – the starches that the body burns up if you are active. Any meat, for instance, under protein, also has fat. If you are inactive, these so-called fuel foods are converted to fat and stored (causing weight increase). In nutritional terms, the best foods for topping up are high in roughage or fibre (fresh or dried vegetables, fruit and wholegrains) and have no fat.

The idea was to choose 10 stars from each category, and divide them between breakfast, lunch and evening meal: 70 stars altogether which gave you a balanced diet.

The NHS advice on ideal daily intake is 2,000kcal/8,400kJ for women and 2,500kcal/10,500kJ for men (though this does depend on age, metabolism and physical activity). With the star system, it was fascinating to see how little you should eat to give your body what it needs to be healthy. The chart's assumption was that you would create each meal from scratch (in a world of takeaways it wouldn't work) and would be physically active.

HOW FIBRE BROUGHT CHANGE
The importance of fibre was hardly known in the 1970s, and would not revolutionise the world of the overweight until 1982. This is when Audrey Eyton, editor of *Slimming* magazine, produced the amazingly successful *F-Plan Diet*. Joyce Hughes, one of our testers, worked with her to create many of the recipes featuring ingredients that would find their way out of the body and not not end up being stored as fat. That

book was followed by two other bestsellers still available today: *The F Plan Calorie and Fibre Chart,* **and** *F-Plus High Fibre Menus for the Whole Family.*

I was interested to read on a website run by Dr Donald Norfolk that the inspiration for the *F-Plan* was probably Dr Denis Burkitt. (Audrey Eyton, who died in 2019, aged 83, never made any public mention of him, says Dr Norfolk, though her obituarists did.)

Dr Burkitt was a member of Britain's Medical Research Council and from epidemiological research in Africa he concluded that many of the chronic diseases of western civilisation (constipation, diverticulosis, bowel cancer, coronary disease, obesity and type-2 diabetes) were the result of eating a diet lacking in roughage. In African tribes who ate foods rich in fruit and vegetables containing a high proportion of indigestible fibres, these maladies were rare.

Burkitt's suggestion to all in the developed world was that they should supplement their daily diet with just two tablespoons of bran or five ounces of wholemeal bread (two slices). This was explained by one of Burkitt's colleagues Dr Andrew Taylor in *Taking the Rough with the Smooth* published in 1976, and the suggestion was eventually upheld by the Royal College of Physicians.

* * *

T*he Complete Cook's* second 'extra', free with issue 3, brought about a veritable storm. It was a 12-page booklet: *A-Z of Cookery Terms and Equipment.* In a way, it was the essence of the whole continuity series. In one fell swoop the booklet managed to offend both Jews and Muslims when it stated that "Kosher was a Jewish method of killing meat or preparing food according to the Koran".

On women's magazines, readers never hesitate to make their views known, but this wasn't usual with part works and feedback was rare. On the day issue 3 of *The Complete Cook* went on sale, the number of phone calls was unprecedented at Orbis. They did not bring a smile to the face of the marketing manager in particular.

We on the editorial side were devastated. We went back to the page proofs and the word Torah was there, not Koran. We had worked long hours getting *The Complete Cook* launched and preparing the extras, and many eyes had seen the page at every stage of production. Yet somehow it went wrong. Our first correction, and apology, was on its way. To this day, I blush when I think about it, and don't understand why we didn't have an entry for Halal. It was upsetting, but was a valuable lesson.

Gilly, like me, was a nearly-full-time freelancer. The sad fact was that it cost money to have staff who were entitled to a range of benefits. Part work companies ran a risky business and had to lay people off when sales were bad. Better to have workers on a renewable contract (which is exactly what happened years later on magazines and newspapers), in some cases verbal.

It supposedly gave us the freedom to do other work though we had our hands full getting *The Complete Cook* out each week. I found and briefed the contributors and Gilly, as picture editor and recipe adviser, organised the photography. Men predominated in this field then.

It saddened me to read the obituary of Peter Williams, a big bear of a man who memorably created the meat spreads. Carcasses of beef, lamb and pork were dissected by a butcher from Smithfield Market, near Farringdon, into every known cut and delivered to Peter's studio in Covent Garden. Here he painstakingly photographed them so they were in proportion to each other. The meat wasn't wasted. Its cost was covered by production expenses, but the staff bought the cuts for a nominal sum and the money was reserved for a future office celebration. Peter won quite a few awards and his pictures illustrated many cookery books. He died far too young in 2008, aged 72.

A range of writers provided copy for the country cuisines and Gilly found experts to help us set an authentic-looking table for photography. The embassies in particular were happy to verify the words and food choice and often recommended a speciality restaurant or a members' club where a photo shoot could be done. Otherwise the shoot took place in a studio.

France was the only country with multiple spreads, a decision taken simply because it was impossible to describe the wide variety of dishes and styles of cooking in just one article. Instead we threaded the renowned regions through the alphabet: Alsace-Lorraine, Brittany, Picardy, Southern France, and The Wine Route (from Paris to Marseille).

We thought that the islands of the Mediterranean – Sicily, Sardinia, Malta, Corsica, Corfu and the Balearics – had similar cuisines so their dishes were combined effectively, giving an insight into what today is called the

Mediterranean diet with its emphasis on fish, garlic, olives and olive oil. Each of which had its own entry, of course, and showed how the countries used these ingredients.

* * *

There was no entry for eating habits, a subject that crops up occasionally. I remember what my father said when I was in my teens: "When you choose someone to marry, remember you are going to be sitting at the same table, looking at the way he eats, for the rest of your life." (As a Catholic he never considered divorce.) Being a bootmaker and repairer, he also warned me to check that the shoes on the feet of my possible intended were well looked after, his message implying that if he cared for his shoes, he'd treat me well. I've always felt the eating one more reliable.

How do you learn to eat attractively so that you don't offend another at the table, or nearby? Should you talk with your mouth full? Mouth open as you chew? Knife and fork held upright between mouthfuls? Or held like pens in both hands? Today in the UK it is a free-for-all with no real etiquette to rely on; in other countries the way you eat depends on the food served.

At the table of my upbringing in Nowra, a small country town in New South Wales, we each had a knife, fork and dessertspoon, used for just about everything we ate. Except for an occasional Sunday treat. My father collected fresh prawns and oysters from the fishermen's shed on the Shoalhaven River, and brought them home wrapped in newspaper which he unfolded on the table next to a pile of bread Mum had buttered. We dived in.

With our fingers we tackled the prawns, pinching off the tail, then the head, the legs and shell until the luscious, fleshy body could be popped into the mouth. Wonderful. Cooking was to become a favourite activity but I learnt to peel prawns and shuck an oyster (using the blunt, short-bladed knife designed for the purpose) before I boiled an egg or baked a cake.

When I left home at 17 I didn't know a table could be set with an array of cutlery, and I certainly didn't know why they were different or what they were used for until I came to Europe. I can't remember when I heard the useful guide "work from the outside in", very helpful with the glistening line-up at very posh affairs. In a restaurant, I only ordered food I knew how to eat.

The one exception was escargots, which I tried during a fantastic press trip to Paris before I started work in the UK. (It had been arranged by the incoming French Ambassador to New Zealand. He was the last person I interviewed before I went abroad.)

The Kiwi embassy hosts took us first to the Opera, then to the restaurant at the Tour Eiffel. I couldn't resist trying the snails which I'd never seen on a menu Down Under. After the sizzling dish was put in front of me, the waiter placed a bib around my neck and handed me a small two-pronged fork and an object that looked like it should hold tea leaves (an old way of infusing tea, before tea bags). Across the table someone else had the same: I saw him use the object to lift up a shell with his left hand,

and pick out the garlicky, meaty body with the fork in his right hand. I was away.

I still have a quartet of deep red ceramic escargot dishes I bought in Paris in the 1970s. They had a lot of use before the fashion for these land succulents died out. (Could this have been the reason my three children chose to become vegetarians I wonder?)

It helps to know how some foods are eaten. For instance, it was not common then to find whole artichokes as a starter on a British menu, but *Complete Cook* readers were prepared should the occasion arise. They would know that each petal is to be pulled off and nibbled at the base before the tender heart is revealed, and that a finger bowl would be provided to rinse your fingers along with a fabric napkin to dry them.

With the cuisines, too, customs were explained. The Chinese, for instance, have no need of knives at the table because food is always cut into bite-size pieces for cooking. And by holding the bowl just under the chin, an eater can deftly move food into the mouth with chopsticks (which, naturally, we showed how to hold).

No space was wasted in each issue. The inside back cover and back cover (when not used for an index or the promotion of binders to buy) gave opportunities to enhance the world of cookery. We discussed all types of kitchen equipment, showed the art of tablecraft by combining cloths, candles, cutlery, china and flowers in different ways, used historical paintings to recount the history of eating and how culinary traditions – such as the use of cutlery – developed. And each week there was a menu, with dishes from any of the previous issues, plus a helpful countdown of what to prepare and when. It had everything you needed to know about cooking and eating!

Once the part work became established – strange as it may seem, I never ever knew how many people bought it each week – the staff was reduced and freelancers came and went. Our main researcher was Anne Crane, ex BBC, and she was helped by a young American, Scott Ewing, who introduced us to a daily dose of cider vinegar as a cure for arthritis (a popular practice today). They came up with detailed information about the ingredients.

The year 1979 brought Margaret Thatcher to power as Britain's first female prime minister. But it started badly, continuing the dreadful winter of discontent (the coldest for 16 years), there were strikes over pay and struggles everywhere. Bodies were not being buried, rubbish was not being collected in the streets. My mother-in-law Molly was staying with me when she had a stroke in the early morning and it took me a couple of hours of desperate phone calls before an ambulance took her to hospital.

Only some hospitals were accepting emergencies, there was a work-to-rule in place and ambulance drivers were answering emergency calls at their own pace. Ian was in the US and although he changed his flight to get back, Molly died just as his plane was landing next morning. She was nearly 79, born in 1900 as was my father.

Towards the end of the year Keith Kotch, Laurie Purden's husband who was only in his 50s, died suddenly, a terrible shock to the family. A memorial service held at the famous St Bride's Church in Fleet Street was packed with men and women he'd worked with at Hulton Press and Fleet Street papers. Laurie looked amazing and self-composed, her feelings well hidden.

She was enjoying her job as a consultant at IPC, working instinctively to bring new life to *Woman's Journal*. Cynthia White (*Women's Magazines 1693–1968*) described it as a title, started in 1927, "for a slightly higher class of readership" (as opposed to others "intended for middle and lower-middle class consumption"). They were the sort of words used then.

In summer I learnt my father was ill again, with cancer, and Ian and I decided to take the family to Australia to see him. This would solve another problem, too. Our part of London was having difficulties providing places for all the children moving from primary to middle school – the offer for Dani was either of two on the edges of the borough and no direct bus route. It would have meant having three children at three different schools so far apart we would never get them there on time. As we both had full-time jobs (Ian in Brighton, me in London) we couldn't accept it.

There was uproar over the school assignations, just as there is in many boroughs of London (and other parts of the UK) even today. How can this under-estimation happen? Everyone seems taken by surprise by the number of children there are to be educated. Obviously there is an ebb and flow in the birthrate which causes local authorities to close schools one year then have to add extra classrooms in another. Knowing that didn't help.

I talked to some mothers and teachers about the situation, and from reading between the lines it seemed Dani had a better chance of getting into the school we had chosen, nearer our home, if she applied to start in the second term, and Sally, as her sibling, would follow naturally a year later.

One of my younger sisters in Australia, a teacher, agreed to let the girls stay with her family for a term to attend a country-town school in New South Wales, and they would fly back for Christmas. The plan worked. Gai borrowed uniforms for them and they had a taste of life Down Under with cousins they hadn't met. Looking back, I think they were remarkably brave to do it aged 10 and nine but their resilience was superb.

We left the UK in August – the Australian winter – and were only away for three weeks, but it was the one time when a crisis was to occur at *The Complete Cook*.

It was the first issue of Volume 6 that tested all resources. The genesis of the problem was the alphabetical breakers that readers stuck on the spine of each volume's binder: eg, on the first five were: AL–BE, BI–CH, CH–DI, DU–HA, HA–LA.

As I explained earlier, these were chosen before the part work even began, so up till this time we must have had a charmed life, finding an ingredient to get us from one sticker to the next. With Volume 6, designated LE–ME, Gilly calculated that there was only one way to reach the goal of 12 issues: information about, and recipes using lettuce, had to fill a whole issue and five pages of another!

Never have so many words been written about something that is so uniquely insubstantial. Being 90% water, lettuce doesn't have a lot going for it. But the team in my absence should have won an award for care and diligence, coming up with enticing recipes from around the world, even finding apt illustrations to accompany them. No leaf was left unturned, as they were to say later with pride. We celebrated with champagne, my treat for them all.

* * *

In the world of part works, the weeks leading up to Christmas were either filled with joy or fraught with worry. This was when runs were coming to an end or new publications were ready for take off. It was also when the company announced whether it would pay a bonus (if it had been a good year). That was the way of giving rises to the staff then. For the long-term freelancers, the bonus was relief that you wouldn't be out there looking for work in the new year.

As I've said, I had no idea how many readers/buyers we had so I was surprised, in the third year, to be asked what could be done to fill another volume of 12 issues! By this time, *The Complete Cook* was a fine example of home economics both in the written sense and as a production. I was pressured constantly to reduce costs, and while we had some regular contributors, Gilly and I wrote a lot of the text and used bought-in illustrations.

We had established an efficient routine with recipe testing, copy production and processing and were meeting the promise of 'everything you ever needed to know about cooking'. We were never lost for ideas and freelancers were more than willing to write about elements relating to the subject.

The back-cover articles added insight into food and eating. *'The History of Eating'* ran for 22 weeks, ending with the *Age of Nutrition* which revealed staggering information about health in Britain. This is an extract:

THE RESULTS OF FOOD POVERTY

"The major breakthrough in nutrition came with the discovery that disease could be caused by a lack of something in the diet. With the introduction of conscription in 1916, British military authorities were horrified to discover the extent of undernourishment throughout the country. Over one million men, almost half the number examined, were quite unfit for any military service at all."

Famous Characters in Cooking enhanced the parts in Volume 10, starting with the great reformer Alexis Soyer whose life encompassed the horrendous potato famine in Ireland and the Crimean War where he encountered the famous innovative nurse Florence Nightingale. [Her statue stood in the foyer of the Sydney hospital where once I thought I might become a nurse.]

We learnt about Louis Pasteur whose discoveries about bacteria contaminating food led to pasteurisation, and Clarence Birdseye, American scientist and inventor who in the early 20th century caused the revolution in food preservation allowing us to eat out of season all year.

With all of this in their hands, I was sure the readers of *The Complete Cook* would be able to cook anything under the sun and do a master's degree at the same time! What else could possibly follow? And could it be done on a limited budget?

Gilly, continually adaptable, wasn't fazed. For the 11th volume, we agreed on the proposition of mixing science and craft: *Practical guide to kitchen craft*. It started from planning a kitchen, choosing and using available equipment and explaining in great detail exactly how each cooking process works, what happens to the food during it, and what can hinder success.

It's quite amusing to read what we wrote in 1980/81 about 'Tomorrow'. The highlight was the microwave (which, we predicted, you could prime by phone to start cooking while on your way home from work – but we had no foresight relating to the many hand-held smart devices which can be programmed for so much). We talked of ovens that would have fans for efficiency, be controlled by touching a panel, and be self-cleaning.

"It's all part of the technological age where the emphasis is on making machines work for you, rather than the other way round," we stated. The microwave ovens then were heavy and cumbersome to work, looking like a smaller version of the huge computers that took up whole rooms in universities and large companies.

Today's cooking equipment has lived up to many of the promises made but we didn't foresee all the wondrous things that can be part of the modern kitchen, from boiling water on tap, taps that can disappear from the surface, to the silicone dishes that transformed baking.

It's hard to believe now, but cling film and plastic bags were welcomed with open arms during the run of *The*

Complete Cook. Both are now anathema because of their effects on the environment but were any downsides raised then? Who'd have thought that the lives of ocean animals would be so tragically endangered as a result of these and other 'useful' inventions like plastic bottles?

* * *

The 11th volume aimed to take away all the mysteries of preparing and presenting food. It was home economics at its best, encouraging understanding of food and cooking and how not to waste time or money in the process. Gilly oversaw the original photography, which from our present standpoint has shades of Hester Blumenthal in it. (He's the celebrity chef whose avant-garde cuisine is described as 'molecular gastronomy'– in which the ingredients' taste alters through physical and chemical changes.)

Aristology – the art and science of cooking – is a never-ending preoccupation. You can almost feel the heat in the shots taken by Dave Elliott, life-like actions representing the basic processes of boiling, steaming, braising and baking. Some pictures were accomplished using glass double saucepans which were a passing fad.

Gilly and stylist Lorrie Mack borrowed props, which were duly credited, from stores and companies, so readers would know where to buy the equipment shown. Original art work, done by Kate Simunek, illustrated techniques. It would have made a fine video, us glued to the sight of Gilly boning, stuffing, carving meat and poultry, while Kate sketched. It was a cookery course anyone could succeed at in his or her own home – or on *Mastermind*.

The four years and 11 volumes of *The Complete Cook* would never have been achieved without the knowledgeable contributors: Josephine Bacon, Helen Triggs, Sue Lacey, Sue Gold, Hilary Walden, Joy Langridge, Jeni Wright, Jackie Burrow, Caroline Moulsdale, Sandra Pruski and Marion Milne. Their copy gave credibility and insight into an amazing variety of elements of a subject that is part of everyone's everyday life.

* * *

R eading it today, the material is as pertinent and all-embracing as it was over 40 years ago. But styles do change, especially in photography and presentation. Even the work we did on getting the dietetic advice right would need updating as more has become known about vitamins and minerals and their role in general health, more particularly in planning parenthood, and preventing diabetes and obesity – both problematical in many countries and affecting young and old.

Over those four years, the one ingredient I missed was feijoa, a fruit that had not left its southern homelands when *The Complete Cook* was being compiled. Now new ingredients are coming on to the market all the time, proliferating almost as fast as the number of chefs coming up with ways of using them.

Still to come were 'e' numbers representing additives: colours, preservatives, antioxidants, thickeners, emulsifiers, stabilisers, acidity regulators, flavour enhancers, sweeteners, foaming agents and gases. Any of these if used has to be on the list of ingredients contained in a prepared food on the outside of a can or packet according to proportion (from the greatest to the least).

Much more critical was the invention and use of two additives: olestra and high-fructose corn syrup (also called glucose/fructose syrup) which are thought to play a big part in weight increase that becomes obesity.

AN APPALLING ADDITION

In 2010 *Time Magazine* listed olestra among the "50 Worst Inventions". It has zero calories, cholesterol or fat (so doesn't even have to be listed as an additive), removes unwanted fat from foods but also negates the body's ability to absorb essential fat-soluble vitamins and nutrients, particularly carotenoids which protect our organs from damage. Side effects include "cramps, gas and loose bowels". Doctors and scientists in the US have expressed concern about the longtime effects: it was "clear folly to introduce this product into the diet of children," said one. For the manufacturers the bonus is that they cost little to add but because they increase the 'mouth-feel' of foods (savoury, such as pizzas, coleslaw, meat, bread; and sweet, like yogurt and cereal bars), eaters want more and more, ensuring an on-going demand. This 'maximum palatability', as it is known, is one of the most frightening modern developments.

In that final year of preparing and selling Volume 11, I turned 40 (my present was a Kenwood food processor, very new on the market) and we moved house, to another part of Wimbledon. Ian decided to leave paid employment to write books and articles on maritime and military history, so now we were both freelancers.

Gilly and I were the last of the original team left by the time *The Complete Cook* finished in 1981. One of her many skills was cake decorating and she excelled with one shaped like a typewriter, with faces of staff members as keys on the qwerty keyboard, and all waving goodbye.

It was a year of austerity, Britain was in another recession, with protests a frequent occurrence, and I was out of work again. After four years eating, breathing and sleeping cookery I was back in the job market.

9

THE POWER OF PART WORKS

W hen the run of a part work comes to an end, original material used (text and photographs) are archived for possible reuse. I freelanced at Orbis for a short time to do this and to plan spin-offs – a range of books reusing what had appeared in *The Complete Cook* – for Alison Cathie. She was running the book department with Martin Heller, and would eventually move to Conran Octopus, owned by publisher and philanthropist Paul Hamlyn, before forming her own successful publishing company Kyle Cathie.

My name went on the 20 or so attractive publications, including three hefty hardbacks, and two of the compilers – Gill Edden and Norma MacMillan – were given co-author status. I never met them, yet they and I sit together on my shelves. Norma, I have learnt, had worked on *Woman's Mirror*, and Gill at *Good Housekeeping*.

I was fascinated by the concept of part works and tried to think of subjects that would respond to the premise of educating by drip-feeding information. Health was a natural, money was another – subjects which everyone, it seemed to me, has a vested interest in – but I obviously hadn't got the angles on either right as there was no positive reaction from Brian.

To run a part work company requires an instinct that's unquantifiable and thanks to Brian, Martin and their team Orbis had had some fantastic successes in the 1970s and 80s. Subjects have to be universal, or able to be adapted. Orbis's market places – listed on the inside cover of each part work – include Australia, New Zealand, South Africa, Europe, Eire and Malta.

Cars are a winner. *On Four Wheels* (comprising 165 parts in 11 volumes of everything you ever wanted to know about cars) even today has a cult following according to the web. There was also *On Two Wheels*, nearly as popular with eight volumes.

The Unexplained was filled with real-life stories of odd and inexplicable happenings from around the world. As can be seen by the success of American author Dan Brown's books, there is a huge appetite for information about the paranormal and downright suspicious. In 13 volumes, it has had a very long life, reissued several times.

It may even be out there now for all I know along with one of Brian's earliest successes, when he was art director at Purnell. *Man, Myth and Magic*, 112 weekly issues in seven volumes, lifted the lid on the supernatural, magic, mythology and religion. Over 200 academics, writing in what came to be known as 'accessible style' (popular, not dry), were the contributors.

The conspiracy theorists loved *The Unexplained* as it

was packed with troubling stories for which there didn't seem to be a full explanation. Anastasia was a great topic (it would be years before DNA tests could prove a woman who claimed to be the murdered Tsar's daughter was a fantasist), the deaths of President Kennedy and Marilyn Monroe, the Profumo Affair which combined spies and sexual shenanigans, Chappaquiddick and Ted Kennedy (an appalling story of a young woman left to die in a sinking car), Carlos the Jackal (the most famous international terrorist before Osama bin Laden, who eluded capture for years). There was no problem finding stories in which a mystery was paramount.

Brian was actually quite kind in the way he rejected my ideas. "Do you honestly want to move onto another part work?" he asked. While I was thinking about my reply, I was approached by Whinfrey Strachan which aimed to branch out into DIY. Four years after *Womancraft* was sold to IPC, in 1977, DIY became all the rage, and everyone was doing it.

There is a magical osmosis in publishing. Once an idea is stated or written down it gets into the atmosphere and almost immediately someone else will be working on it as well. It happened to me time and time again throughout my career as a journalist. But nowhere was it more apparent than in part works.

While I was at Orbis, a series called *Know-How* had done well, lasting for 120 parts, and opposition at the time, from Marshall Cavendish, were *Fix-it* and *Do It Right*, both of which followed *Golden Homes*. Health, as I said, was a universal topic: Whinfrey Strachan's weekly guide to health and medicine called *Advice* came out in

1981 almost simultaneously with *Doctor's Answers* from Marshall Cavendish. But that was ahead.

The name of the new project was *Jobmate*. Though women occasionally appeared on the pages, *Jobmate* was basically made for men, a part work that would build into a complete manual of do-it-yourself techniques. It was not to be over-macho, dark and gloomy, but bright and cheerful and very well illustrated. I was offered the role of editor, my experience with *Womancraft* and *The Complete Cook* being in my favour, but so was the fact that I was Australian and knew a little of that market.

Richard Carlisle, the consultant editor, was a Nordic-style Brit: tall, blond and bearded with a droll sense of humour. Illustrated publications were his forte, having worked at leading companies Marshall Cavendish and Dorling Kindersley. He had at his back the skilled and unflappable art director Kelly Flynn.

It seemed to me that *Jobmate* planned to do the impossible: to sell in the UK, Australia and New Zealand. It had been a long time since I lived out there, but I knew that any project involving electricity or plumbing was not done by the untrained or unqualified. It wasn't that people were disinclined (Aussies and Kiwis are renowned for their ability to have a go at anything), it was that the law said so. There are laws, too, here but I had found that DIYers would tackle anything, preferably with guidance.

Whinfrey Strachan, in partnership with Rigby International, Australian publishers, had had a success with *Joy of Knowledge*, a comprehensive home reference library. Now the challenge was to provide a part work about DIY that would sell in both hemispheres.

The cleverness came in replacing pages on subjects that would just not work Down Under, mostly involving the aforementioned electricity and plumbing. The useful rider was that anyone planning new installations would know exactly what to do from reading *Jobmate*.

We went ahead with ordinary and ambitious projects – plumbing in baths and basins, doing emergency pipe repairs and electrical rewiring – photographing each tiny step in full colour. Richard was a stickler for detail and photo shoots were planned to cover every conceivable angle and step. None of us forgot *Reader's Digest* was out there, watching keenly for anything that might resemble their manual!

Lorrie Mack, ex *The Complete Cook*, sought appropriate props for photography. Bathrooms and kitchens were a problem, mostly because the style of furnishings differ north and south of the equator. One early stalemate was finding a suitable vanity unit that could be tiled around – British ones just did not look right to the Australasians. Eventually one passed muster. All this did for the Australians, who have a reputation for their showers and wet rooms, was to reinforce the belief that Brits don't much like bathing.

Richard steered the direction of *Jobmate*, with a technical editor and technical consultants planning the 20-page issues which would eventually build up to six volumes. There were six colour-coded strands for techniques, of which three would appear in each issue, covering building, decorating, plumbing, carpentry, electrical, home maintenance and repairs. There was a Fact Finder section (backing up the strands with information about materials, tools and equipment), and a Jobspot (practical projects putting to use techniques already featured, with working plans and drawings).

All was going swimmingly when lo and behold, as *Jobmate* was ready for take off, out came *The Knack*, from Marshall Cavendish, and that was the end of my time there. While work would go on in creating *Jobmate*, the launch date was put on hold. But I didn't want to continue; it was much too male orientated for me and Richard considered me pedantic for wanting to make sure all instructions and directions were as clear as possible. He and the subs believed that men just know things about DIY that women don't, with no explanation necessary.

I had, however, learnt much from the project. I had overseen a lot of photography, using the hands of Dave, a local plumber who'd worked on our Wimbledon house, for some bathroom features, and the bricklaying lecturer at a technical college who'd done work at *Womancraft* was a malleable and co-operative model for the hard stuff.

And it wasn't all wasted effort. Having worked on the 'Papering Walls' feature, I spent weeks decorating different rooms of our three-storey Victorian house, built in 1884, with a staircase wall that from top to bottom took more than a whole roll of wallpaper. Hanging that certainly concentrated the mind.

In fact, I was still up the ladder and pasting when *Jobmate* eventually appeared in early 1982, issue one proudly displaying tool-wielding, overalled men on the cover and with issue two free inside. *Jobmate* thrived and survived, running successfully against *The Knack* for years. And despite my concerns, it was fully accepted in the

southern hemisphere. Both are regarded as vintage magazines, I gather, ripe for collectors.

I wasn't surprised to learn that Richard Carlisle started
a successful publishing company, Templar, specialising in
children's books, which he ran alongside his consultancy
work with continuity publication specialists. I don't think
Whinfrey Strachan survived for long in the UK after one
of the founders died tragically young. My dilemma, after
my short experience at this company, was that it left me
really wondering what I was going to do in the future.

* * *

I'd reached this stage before in my working life but this
time I was at a crossroads. I had no idea about me,
what I was, who I was. I'd been a journalist for over half
my life, but had never had a career plan as such. Going
from reporting on newspapers to the unknown world of
women's magazines in one of the lowliest positions and
moving on to editing two 'collectable' magazines could be
put down to luck, a mix of success and failure.

It is par for the course in journalism that jobs either
last or they don't, but it is still a shock when redundancy –
it means no longer needed – happens to you. Lack of
confidence made me feel I should change direction, do
something else. I thought I could be a taxi driver as I was
beginning to know London like the back of my hand. But
Ian was now a fulltime author and with three school-age
children and a house and mortgage to look after, and both
of us in the same freelance situation, it made sense to stick
with what I knew. I needed a job in journalism. The big

preoccupation at the time was the Falklands War but industrial action for better pay was a frequent threat as the increased cost of living made life difficult for most. Equal pay and equal opportunities were becoming goals to reckon with while unemployment grew.

I had worked out a synopsis and chapter plan for a book on recycling which came from doing a piece for Brenda Polan, editor of *The Guardian*'s women's page, about getting the most from your dustbin. While it was being considered by a publisher (it was never taken up), I edited a book called *Cooking for Two* for Octopus. Then I heard about changes at *Woman*.

While at Orbis, I kept in touch with women's magazines. While part works were not considered in any way related to an industry regarded as an offshoot of Fleet Street, everyone in publishing, whatever their job, always reads the Positions Vacant ads, to see what's going on where. The service side of magazines, the practical subjects, were still given a lot of space and many who worked on cookery and craft part works had the experience the magazines needed.

The place for the get-together of the two was *The Daily Mail*'s annual Ideal Home exhibition at Earls Court, a vast enterprise drawing in an extraordinary range of manufacturers and sellers of everything you might possibly conceive as relating to the way you lived. Gilly and I both arranged an invite to the Press Day and met there.

I'd provided a reference for her when she joined the staff at *Woman*, as deputy to the cookery editor Frances Naldrett. She was learning at first hand the pressure everyone was under to come up with ideas and at times things appeared to verge on chaotic. The big news was that *Woman's* editor Jo Sandilands had left to join Capital Radio; the enterprising Michael Barry, who'd contributed to *Womancraft*, had been one of the people behind its start and became its programme controller. Surprisingly, Jane Reed had moved from her job as a publisher with IPC Magazines to try and resuscitate the flailing magazine.

At Earls Court, I also caught up with Dee Remmington, who'd left *Woman* to freelance, but even with her long experience in Fleet Street and women's magazines she was not finding life as easy as she'd hoped. And I heard, too, that Jill Churchill was leaving *Home & Freezer Digest* to edit *Family Circle*, the magazine that enticed shoppers at Sainsbury's supermarket or Woolworths.

In the US *Family Circle* has a very long, and successful, history of doing the same and the owners of the British one, Thomson, followed suit with the sales method when the title launched in 1964. Why bother competing with other magazines at newsagents (and there weren't nearly so many then as there are now) when you had ready-made unique sales spots?

The target audience was the young housewife whose interest was in feeding her family and FC catered for that perfectly, devoting a third of its pages to many aspects of food. Special Sainsbury supplements, known today as advertorials or 'paid content', were also included in every issue, a sort of quid pro quo for providing the selling space in the stores. It was a monthly service magazine, reasonably priced with a high percentage of colour pages jam-packed with the practical elements that the women's weeklies specialised in, but with no fiction.

It was a good formula. In 1967, when FC's circulation passed a million and it became the UK's biggest-selling women's monthly magazine, Thomson produced *Living*, devoted to leisure, home style and furnishings. Displayed side by side, near where the shopper stood in the checkout queue, *Family Circle* and *Living*, with eye-catching and bright, busy, covers, were designed to meet the needs of young cash-strapped parents with homes to furnish.

And, as seems inevitable in this highly competitive world of publishing, the arrival of *Living* had another effect: it caused the demise of *Housewife*, owned by Odhams and once edited by Laurie Purden, which disappeared into the pages of the IPC monthly *Ideal Home*.

The supermarket twosome did well until the 1980s, when both magazines were looking tired. Thomson achieved a bullseye by employing Jill at FC and Dena Vane at *Living*. Dena had been Jill's deputy at *Home & Freezer Digest* and both were brimming with ideas for change. They even campaigned to lose their magazines' protected position in the supermarkets preferring them to be on show on the bookstalls, taking their chance alongside others aimed at women. This brought them under the rules and regulations of the Audit Bureau of Circulation.

THE 'SCIENCE' OF MAGAZINES

There is a 'science' behind why magazines are different: their content is tailored to meet the needs and aspirations of certain ages and social grades. It isn't as simple as upper, middle and lower classes; these, too, are divided. So uppers, are A and B; middles, C1 and C2; lower, D and E. As a rough guide, few magazines cater for the As; Bs, C1s and C2s are the biggest market; Ds and Es are less likely to buy (but respond to TV). Ages are profiled: 15-24, 23-34, 35-44, 45-54, 55-64 and 65+. Advertisers are mainly interested in the 15-54 groups, for they are the spenders. It doesn't bode well if the readership has too many 55-65+ or too many Ds and Es. Behind the magazine publishing I came to know, the plan was to get them young and keep them. Teenagers bought the weeklies with content specific to their interests (music, clothes, make-up). Later, the adult weeklies' design will seem familiar and inviting. What's changed is that today's tailor-made magazines are created for earlier ages, an adjunct to increasingly significant children's TV and films, and online sites.

In the early 1980s, times were very dreary. Printing methods had not changed much and the cost of production was still very high. The magazines didn't look very different from 10 years earlier though the elements within them had a harder edge than previously. And, typically, the country was going through another financial crisis, unemployment was high and money tight.

I wrote to Jane Reed, congratulating her on her new role as editor-in-chief of *Woman* magazine, and told her that I was freelance again but looking for a permanent job. She rang almost on receipt and asked me to King's Reach to talk about a position that was about to become vacant, assistant editor in charge of practicals.

Blow me down if I didn't also get a phone call from Jill Churchill asking me to lunch. She was looking for a deputy editor at *Family Circle*. It was, unfortunately, the waiting for the bus syndrome – and I was terribly torn. I really liked Jill. She was always positive and bouncy, with big plans for the magazine. But I also liked Jane, though she was far more daunting with her authoritative approach, and I'd worked with her before.

In the end, I decided I was much more at home with a weekly schedule and I said yes to Jane and was utterly distressed at having to say no to Jill. She was, understandably, furious. We had got on very well over lunch and I'd been fired up by her enthusiasm. In passing I mentioned that Dee was looking for work, a fortunate lead because the real-life stories that Dee went on to dig up and write for FC were a mainstay of the magazine for many years. And I helped get Gilly there, too, but much later.

After being in charge of small teams in small circulation publications, I was now returning to one of the bigger sellers in a new role. With Jane Reed in charge, how different would *Woman* be from *Woman's Own* which I'd left nearly a decade before when she was editor there?

LEGENDARY WOMAN

I t took me a while to appreciate the irony of getting the job at *Woman*. It was the one that Jill Churchill had had, that I had applied for when *First Lady* ended in 1974 and didn't get. Now it was vacant because Billie Figg was 60, the age when women had to retire at IPC. I would be stepping into the shoes of another legend.

I went to meet the department heads a week before I started and was reunited with Gilly Cubitt who was now deputy cookery editor. Billie had not yet vacated her office and as I made my way along the 'practicals' corridor' towards it, Gilly told me to be wary. "You'll probably find her lying on the floor, stretched out, meditating. It de-stresses her." And that's exactly where she was. Her eyes were shut and I decided to leave her to it. By the time we met, years later, glaucoma affected her badly but she told me about her working life in magazines. Sadly she died in 2015, aged 92.

BILLIE'S INSIGHT AND INFLUENCE
Billie Figg worked at *Woman* under Mary Grieve but left to run her own public relations company. When she returned to the magazine – and the new editor Barbara Buss – she was full of ideas to help readers and advertisers. Her place in the history of these publications deserves to be remembered.

At 60, she did not retire and take the Old Age Pension (as it was called then) but started a new career doing exactly what she'd always wanted to do, to write on a wide variety of subjects (for *Family Circle* in particular). She did even more, as a script adviser for Thames TV, on the soap opera *Gems* – about the world of fashion designing. As you'll read below, she was well qualified to recount the dramas and disasters behind a magazine's fashion department. *Gems* was shown on daytime TV and as I was working I never saw it.

Within days of starting my new job, I was on a train to Harrogate, Yorkshire, for the *Woman* British Fashion Awards, a glamorous event to be shown on ITV. The awards were a brainchild of Billie's in the mid 1960s, when she was fashion editor writing under the house name Veronica Scott. At this time magazines that sold nationally could not always tell readers where they could buy the clothes and accessories shown on the pages. I'd learnt this as a sub at *Woman's Own*. Today a stockists' list or website or phone number is usual.

Billie began her career at Amalgamated Press, originally started by Alfred Harmsworth in the 1890s to publish comics but which eventually became Fleetway

Publications. She left to be a PR for three years and was full of ideas when she rejoined *Woman*. One was a reader fashion service which, she convinced the new editor Barbara Buss, would publicise the magazine. There would be an annual event at which buyers from department stores and shops could see what was available for the coming season.

The first of the 'dress shows', as they were known, was held at the stately home Woburn Abbey in 1965, and later at the Royal Garden Hotel in London's Kensington. It took Billie and her staff four months of preparation, having elicited from the fashion houses and manufacturers the trends for spring – the colours, fabrics and shapes. Between 50 and 80 samples of garments considered to be 'on trend' were ordered, after which models were chosen and fittings arranged.

All the clothes were accessorised, and the fashion assistants recorded what went with what, who made it, etc. These details would be published months later in *Woman* over several weeks, a service to the readers that justified all the expense of the show.

A theme was worked out, a commentary written for the compere (amiable broadcaster Michael Aspel, who succeeded Eamonn Andrews as presenter of TV's *This is Your Life* in 1988, was a favourite for this role) and separate scripts were prepared for the musicians, electricians and dressers. Other skilled specialists were involved to do hair and make-up, and take photographs.

For the journalists it was valuable experience that couldn't be learnt at a desk. Among them, at the end of the 1960s, were Ann Christine Wallis, props girl then, who went on to edit *Woman's Realm* and, later, *OK!* magazine; and Jackie Modlinger who became fashion editor of *Bride and Home* and one of Fleet Street's top fashion writers.

Billie stage-managed from the wings, and Jane Burgin, who was head of publicity at IPC in my time there, supervised the lighting from the electricians' box. In the audience of the October show were buyers, people from the fashion houses, *Woman* staff and IPC executives.

Fashion was normally the prerogative of the glossy monthlies and I imagine the rather superior beings working on them thought it outrageous that a weekly would have any influence at all. On the other hand, they may not have noticed or cared – there was a huge gap between the publications, including the people likely to be employed on them.

But the *Woman* Fashion Awards, as the annual event became, put the magazine in a different league to the other weeklies. In 1980 Billie persuaded designer Jeff Banks, husband of barefooted singer Sandie Shaw who won the 1967 Eurovision Song Contest with *Puppet on a String*, to join the judges, and the very elegant Princess Michael of Kent (before she was known as Princess Pushy) presented the prizes on the show filmed by Yorkshire TV.

In 1981, designers and manufacturers were able to submit garments themselves in various categories (for example, coats, casual co-ordinates, daywear, after-six wear, knits and ballgowns). Billie, now assistant editor, helped by her replacement as fashion editor Geraldine Gobby, whittled 300 entries down to 175. The judges chose 80 to appear on the TV show.

Among the judges was a couple who would become

known as the 'designers royal', Elizabeth and David Emanuel, whose wedding dress for 20-year-old Lady Diana Spencer, marrying the heir to the British throne in 1981, would always be described as "fairytale". It was the ultimate in meringue-shapes, a combination of creamy-coloured silk taffeta, antique lace, pearls and hand embroidery, with a 7.5metre-long train.

Like the marriage of Diana and Charles, that of the Emanuels did not last either but they certainly established their names as designers and continued to have a link with *Woman* through reader offers. One designed by Elizabeth sold very well: a fuchsia pink satin, bias-cut dress and longline jacket with the big shoulders so popular at the time (remember TV's *Dallas?*). I still have the sample which was used for photography. It is dressy and elegant, definitely vintage.

A BAD AND SAD TIME

What a year of contrast 1982 was. Just before the show at Harrogate, a BBC2 drama series created by Alan Bleasdale captivated the country with its devastating representation of unemployment that was affecting families everywhere. *Boys from the Black Stuff* was the grim but very moving tale of Liverpudlian tarmac layers who had been made redundant. Anyone who saw it could never forget the poignant cries of Yosser Hughes (played by Bernard Hill): "Gissa job", and "I can do that." Brought to the edge of insanity from losing his job and family, he would try anything so that he could earn money.

* * *

W oman, though sales were nothing like the glory days, was still a big magazine and had a large staff. Jane Reed, as editor-in-chief, having been a publisher, a job that is about money and budgets, was tasked with setting up an administration for editorial that would work efficiently and successfully when she left. One theory behind top appointments is to do yourself out of a job, but this was my first experience of it. It was a time of enormous tension. The staff had been affected by the many changes: Peter Lawrence's editorship, then death, then Jo Sandilands' appointment and departure.

Jane had appointed Jo Foley as editor (Jo had worked with her at *Woman's Own*). From the time I started, I was aware that the line of authority was less than clear. And the departments I was responsible for – as assistant editor, practicals – were in flux.

Cookery (headed by Frances Naldrett), knitting (Lesley Stansfield) and home (Jane Graining) were stable. The others were not. Geraldine Gobby went to head fashion at *Good Housekeeping* and Arline Usden left the beauty department to edit *Beauty Plus* magazine. She then went on to *Successful Slimming* and, much later, *The Lady* where she stayed 18 years and brought it into modern times (it is the oldest weekly magazine and survives still. Arlene died in 2013, aged 75). Vickie Bramwell became beauty editor but left after a short time and Alison Plummer was appointed. She'd previously worked for DC Thomson in Scotland on their young magazines.

Jaki Bell, once Jo Foley's secretary, had not long been

in the fashion department and her elevation to editor of it seemed sudden. But she and Jo were as one regarding the *Woman* Fashion Awards: get as much publicity from them as possible. And they were innovative: the Young Designer of the Year award brought to the fore many whose influence continues still.

Jane's second task as editor-in-chief was to cut staff numbers. She gave me 'a watching brief' on the correspondence department, a roomful of women at the end of the practicals' corridor where my office was. They opened mail, answered readers' queries and passed on possible leads for ideas to the editorial departments. How important was this group to the functioning of the magazine?

As all the departments had their own secretaries who should have been able to handle letters, I was asked to find evidence to show that the ones going out in *Woman*'s name needed improvement. Jane undertook the negotiations with the unions to make the letter writers redundant. It was a protracted affair and not pleasant. But it met Jane's plan: 20 at one blow was better than trimming here and there, though that too would have to happen. I did not like my part in these women losing their jobs. But I learnt that the higher you go the greater the chance of having to do things that go against the grain.

The departments were all well staffed, with an arrangement new to me. In cookery, for instance, there were three recipe testers, a secretary and a junior to do the washing up and cleaning. There was a writer called Deborah Murdoch who worked with Frances, the cookery editor. The department presented a 'package' to the Thursday conference: headline, sell, captions, interviews where necessary, to top and tail the chosen recipes. I couldn't understand why a separate writer was necessary, and nor could Gilly. Writing copy for publication should have been part of the job description. Were words in a recipe or knitting instructions a journalist's job? Not everyone thought so. As readers want both to be accurate, I thought journalists were needed.

Jane had promoted Jo to beauty editor at *Woman's Own* after Jenny Greene left to edit *Country Life* and must have seen she had editor potential or she wouldn't have brought her to *Woman*. She put Dee Nolan, an Australian, in charge of features, a decision helped by a personal letter from Ita Buttrose. Ita, the Tweedledee who'd sat with me at the *Woman's Own* subs' desk in the late 1960s, had soared to celebrity status in Australia and was Dee's inspiration. Ita had told her that she couldn't do better than work for Jane Reed when she got to London. And thus it came to pass. This was *Woman* as I found it, with an atmosphere that was challenging and at times electric.

I knew Jane's style of working from old: the constant rewriting, the search for something different, always looking for what seemingly couldn't be expressed in words or pictures. Those first six months were a baptism of fire for me, getting to know a lot of new people and their ways of working, to find my role in it all. I was back in the world of long-distance planning, of the fraught conference and the concomitant late nights, the divided corridors – features on one, practicals on another – and a new element: the jockeying for position at the top.

One of the children's books I liked to read my daughters when they were small involved good and bad fairies and what they could bestow. It was fun to act out – Who makes you frown? Who makes you giggle? – and always made them go to sleep happy.

At *Woman* there were no laughs or giggles for me, just disapproval. I didn't seem to be doing what was expected with regard to the practical subjects: to me, the department heads were the specialists and my job was to encourage them to produce ever-better ideas. It wasn't working. We just couldn't grasp what we were missing. It fazed me.

I t was good to see that Gilly was as effervescent as I remembered, and I was delighted to find an ally in George Cannon, an assistant editor like me, but in charge of production. Terry Brown, also ex *Woman's Own*, ran the art department. Boyish looking and outwardly calm, he hid the turmoil he must have felt as the layouts from his department faced a minefield at each dummy meeting.

The 'dummy' was the issue put together after the conference; layouts with photo-copied pictures and text in place had been changed according to diktat and in their new form were presented to the editor for approval before the next stage of production could begin. 'Going back to the drawing board' was an expression we came to know well. 'A ripping time' described the way layouts were discarded.

Jane's plan had been to stay until staff changes were put in place but about six months after I started she must have decided that it was too confusing to have two people at the helm. She left it to Jo while continuing to oversee from a distance in her new role as publisher of *Woman's Journal* and *Woman & Home*, a move that was not to Laurie Purden's liking. She was in charge of both.

Laurie was one of my saviours at this time. *Journal* was housed on a nearby corridor, and it was to her office that I sped when I found things too overwhelming at *Woman*. When Laurie took over in 1978 she had hoped to bring in Sally Brampton as *Journal*'s editor (she had won *Vogue*'s talent competition for new writing, much prized) but Sally went to *The Observer* and became the first editor of *Elle* in 1985. Anne Gregg who had been deputy editor at *Good Housekeeping* was appointed *Journal*'s editor.

After two two years in the role a new world opened for her. With her gentle Northern Irish accent, Anne became one of the best-known and cheerful faces on the box, on BBC's Holiday Programme, for 11 years. [Anne died of cancer in 2006 and a service of thanksgiving was held at St Bride's, Fleet Street, to celebrate her life.]

As contracted editor-in-chief of *Woman's Journal*, Laurie worked solidly for a decade to give the magazine a new lease of life, reaching out to middle class women just like her (as she explained it to me), reflecting their lives and ambitions. Having inherited *Woman & Home* at the same time, she was able, too, to alter its fortunes, working with editor Sue Dobson to add more fiction, which had been her love since she worked all those years ago at George Newnes, and travel features.

Woman & Home was also chosen to be the guinea pig in the changeover to computers which would revolutionise magazine production in the company.

* * *

I was convinced that I was having such a hard time at *Woman* because I had given up smoking. My memory, my emotions, my clarity of thinking were all over the place. Each weekday was allocated to an issue that was well in the future or in front of my eyes. Six-monthly planning sessions with the five practical departments, then three monthly, then monthly, then fortnightly, then press time – all were part of the creative process.

Keeping track of the different stages of each project of each department took some doing, and I knew what it meant to be caught on the hop. Jo had a similar power of put-down as Mrs Thatcher, her remarks as cutting on men as on women. She brandished 'wimp' as devastatingly as a boning knife.

But it wasn't the absence of nicotine causing the problems (though it may have had some effect). In technical terms I was suffering from advanced pre-menstrual syndrome or the peri-menopause: my hormones were in freefall. I found this out from reading a bulging file in one of the filing cabinets I had inherited and it was a revelation. In 1983 I was a year older than my mother was when she had her seventh and last child at 43, and my symptoms (which included erratic periods) were linked to an oestrogen imbalance. I had thought menopause only related to women over 50, but I learnt that the end of menstruation is not the whole story. I found the name of a leading Harley Street specialist and made an appointment to interview him, ostensibly for a future health special.

John Studd, a gynaecologist and obstetrician, was a

physically big man whose strong views often conflicted with traditional medics. He was the first to promote in Britain the use of the twice-yearly hormone replacement implant (combination of oestrogen and testosterone which the body could use as needed) instead of daily oestrogen and progestogen tablets which are processed via the liver. [Today there is an option for this combination as skin patches, avoiding the digestive system.]

We sat in his office at 6.15, after he'd seen his last patient for the day, and talked for perhaps 15 minutes about the pros and cons of the HRT implant/tablet debate while I made notes. He then opened a bottle of red wine and poured two glasses. At which point I burst into tears and he started asking me questions.

My symptoms were obvious to him and before I left, an hour later, he'd put in an implant, given me a prescription for progesterone tablets to take for a week every month (so that I would shed the womb lining as a monthly period), and arranged a bone scan for me (to check for signs of osteoporosis, related to lack of oestrogen) and blood tests for hormone levels.

It was some interview and it certainly helped me understand women's need for clearer knowledge about their bodies. Many years later I would edit a book along these lines but during my time at *Woman*, no in-depth article focused on this element that affects all women, possibly because menopause was seen as a subject only for old women. But it isn't.

Now that I have reached four score years, I am pleased that determined women today can find out a lot about menstruation and menopause and understand how both can affect them, at school, at work, in retirement. And importantly that they have a choice of using hormone-based methods to stop periods altogether.

The monthly bleed can incapacitate females with endometriosis and depression (known as Pmdd) and those with gender dysphoria. I don't understand why it has taken so long to recognise the suffering this event causes.

As it is relevant to half the population of the world, its importance in the lives of women who produce children or have problems with fertility is huge. I can't find out why medically it isn't a subject in its own right and is lumped in with gynaecology and obstetrics, which deal with health difficulties and end results. Menstruation demands to be the focus of attention as a prime influence on the female body after puberty (perhaps even before).

Professor Studd gained worldwide acclaim for his positive approach to the use of hormones and in 2008 received the Blair Bell Gold Medal of the Royal Society of Medicine, an award given every five years to the obstetrician/gynaecologist who has made the greatest lifetime contribution to the speciality. Depression is common in women who are going through 'the change' and his reproach to psychiatrists is forthright: they have little idea how to treat it because they refuse to learn how to treat hormone responsive depression with hormones. [Read more on his website: studd.co.uk]

For me, the advantage of the HRT implant (which is inserted in a fatty area such as the groin or buttock, numbed by local anaesthetic) was the speed at which it kicked in. I was amazed at the change in me, quite restoring my spirit, as my husband noted with relief. It was costly because it was done privately but no matter how skint I was I found the money every six to eight months for this HRT until I retired. I couldn't have worked at my job without it.

* * *

At *Woman* I felt I was back in control. Well, as much as I could be. It would have been a rare conference when everything went through smoothly. I found myself holding my breath as the people around the table took agin the look of a food, or a cloth, a knit or an accessory – what could they see that I couldn't? My only way to survive was not to fight them, but I did take it personally. What I couldn't do was show my emotions to the departments I was responsible for. Being cheerful was essential.

But I was affected by the atmosphere around us, as was George. We talked about it but felt helpless. We could see, but not alter, the effect constant criticism was having on the work output. I know from *The Devil Wore Prada*, that very clever novel (and film) that described the stunning arrogance of a powerful (if flawed) woman in publishing, that I had to avoid head-on collisions.

Unfortunately George and I put ourselves on the outer when we made our excuses not to join the editor's party at the British Society of Editors' Awards at the end of 1983, the year *Woman* won the best weekly category. A lot of money had been poured into promotion, into features about pop stars, and of course the Fashion Awards. The circulation had increased a little, and effort was rewarded.

Then came 1984. That was some year. The Miners'

Strike was the main event, considered the defining moment in British industrial relations (says Wikipedia) as the once-powerful National Union of Mineworkers took on Margaret Thatcher. She was at her most adamant, determined to control the coal-mining industry with pit closures and job losses.

The miners weren't after more money, they just wanted to keep their jobs, and in the process there were deaths, horrible confrontations and political mayhem that altered completely the concept of trade unionism as a shared endeavour for the good of all. The words 'scabs' and 'pickets' were in everyday usage. Smear campaigns came into their own.

Ten years earlier, an NUM strike had effectively killed *First Lady*, the weekly I was working on (there were other reasons as well), and brought down the Heath government. This time the effects on the ordinary person at home weren't as great. Then we relied on candlepower and camping stoves, spirit lamps and open fires if we had them, when electricity (which depended entirely on coal) was stopped. Now we had oil and gas to counteract the lack of coal. Even so times were tough.

The miners' strike went on for almost a year, into 1985, with calamitous results for the pit men and their communities, personal disaster for a seemingly obstinate rebel and 'militant' – a nasty word used frequently as a synonym for single mindedness – called Arthur Scargill who led the NUM. It brought to the fore a group of indomitable women, the wives, partners and mothers of the miners who called themselves Women Against Pit Closures (their story wasn't sought by the women's magazines but was touched on in the brilliant film *Brassed Off* made years later). Politics and Margaret Thatcher won.

The right of the worker to strike, to withhold his or her labour in pursuit of a valid claim, would never again have real substance. And while Britain no longer has a coal industry to speak of its entire disappearance is top of the agenda of the worldwide movement to save the planet.

DANCE TO THE MUSIC OF TIME

History has its own ironical last word. It is possible that the disastrous miners' strike will be remembered thanks to the success of a stage play called *Billy Elliot* written by Lee Hall. It became a world award-winning musical, then a film, about a miner's child living in abject poverty because of the strike who overcomes all to be a dancer. With a young boy as the lead character, it bent the rules of homophobia and manliness, challenging misconceptions head on. The story in any of its presentations has the feel-good factor – worth its weight in gold in the entertainment world.

In publishing, 1984 wasn't Orwellian, but Maxwellian. Havoc ensued when Reed International, owners of IPC since 1970, sold Mirror Group Newspapers to Robert Maxwell, soon to be known, courtesy of the wits at the satirical magazine *Private Eye*, as The Bouncing Czech.

This man whose name I had encountered in part works, when he owned the British Printing Corporation, already had had some dicey financial dealings. In 1973 it was declared that "he could not be trusted to exercise proper stewardship of a public quoted company".

At IPC, with the annual National Union of Journalists' pay negotiations about to get underway, a mass meeting of members took place at the Friends' Meeting House, Euston, London. For several years we'd had a pay freeze or almost non existent rises and with inflation a permanent presence the journalists decided that the negotiators should ask for a percentage increase to restore what might, even should, have been their due.

[The strongest memory I have of that day is watching *Woman's* knitting department in a row near where George and I sat in the gallery, their needles working on four new garments, a modern version of Madame Defarge and her knitting circle – *les tricoteuses* – sitting by the guillotine during the French revolution. At long last they were recognized as journalists and had joined the union.]

When management chose not to discuss a percentage increase, the NUJ balloted the members, which it had to do by law, who chose a work-to-rule. Our salaries were stopped. We were, in effect, sacked – and the view of management was that we had sacked ourselves.

Defiantly the journalists opted to go to work every day, to stay at their desks from 10 am to 6 pm, with an hour for lunch. Kings Reach had pickets at the door, though in actuality they were almost a guard of honour for the editors to walk through, with ne'er a glance sideways. Editors did not have to belong to the NUJ.

At *Woman* the atmosphere was putrid. Our practicals' corridor might have been an isolation ward harbouring consumptives. Everyone believed the action would come to an end quickly and the departments continued to plan future projects though no photography was being done or props called in. The normal fast pace of daily life just stopped dead. The quietness was eerie. No phones rang and conversations seemed to be hushed as in a church.

It was weeks before an agreement was reached; it was nothing like the one sought but accepted as being the best in the circumstances. The slight increase was not back dated and pay for those work-to-rule weeks was lost. It was a hard blow for all of us with mortgages to meet, and children to keep. Though the NUJ had officers who could advise on claiming benefits there was little point because our action was regarded by Reed as illegal. It was a mess.

While we were in this hiatus, the editors tried to produce issues of their magazines with whatever non-union or freelance help they could get. They prepared the pages but they had to get them to the printer. As I've explained before, several unions were involved in magazine publishing and some hoped that if the NUJ secured an increase they could follow suit and get one as well. They chose not to be helpful in the preparation of the magazines while the stalemate existed.

Woman's bottleneck was the production department. What eventuated was almost legerdemain: one minute Suzanne, George's assistant, a member of another union, had the signed-off pages in her hands ready for the printer at Watford; next minute they couldn't be found. I wonder if that young woman went into acting, for her ability to outbluff her editor was stunning.

The air was blue, as they used to say about swearing, but she was nonchalant and stood her ground. Miraculously the pages reappeared as soon as the strike was over and even though they made it to the printer, the allocated slot on the machines was probably missed so the number of issues printed would have been reduced, affecting the audited circulation.

It hurt us all, of course. But there's no easy way of doing these things. Fences were never mended. The gulf between the features' corridor and the practicals' corridor widened even further, almost with a flowing lava stream between them. Journalists from all departments only ever met in the loo, which during the time of turmoil had many a woman sobbing there. It was a strange situation. I was also concerned about my two emerging-from-childhood daughters, my hormones were not completely stabilised and I had started smoking again. That's what stress does to you.

Gilly was by now working with Jill Churchill at *Family Circle* (and would eventually become deputy editor), and Frances Naldrett had left to join Hamlyn, publishers owned by Reed, to work on their very successful cookery books; later, publishing innovator Paul Hamlyn bought back his old imprint and incorporated it into his new company Conran Octopus. *Woman*'s cookery department had been slimmed down and its new editor, Joy Davies, was settling in when the strike occurred. Joy had been on the short-lived *Now!*, the political and news magazine owned by wealthy Sir James Goldsmith who had no background in publishing. *Now!* never achieved the circulation it needed to survive.

* * *

As well as overseeing the practical departments, I had my own strand, gardening, and only articles tied to a celebrity were considered. An early success was an interview with Miriam Rothschild, who had found fame for making the Israeli desert bloom with wild-flowers She described in detail the wild garden she created for Prince Charles at Highgrove.

I relished the subject as it took me on some superb press jaunts and meetings with the now long gone veterans of gardening journalism whose conversations about plants and planting were liberally interlaced with Latin. On one trip I met Stefan Buczacki and Daphne Ledward, from BBC Gardeners' Question Time, who became contributors.

Another trip, to Portugal (for the launch of a new hover mower – and why not? PRs had to think months ahead, and Portugal, in winter, had specially cultivated grass), revived my interest in astrology. Among the writers were Topline Broadhurst, Roddy Llewellyn and Rosie Atkins, all born on the same October date, but not year. Roddy ('friend' of Princess Margaret) became Sir Roderic, 5th baronet of Bwllfa, and did well as a journalist. So did Rosie who launched award-winning *Gardens Illustrated* in 1991, editing it until 2001; then she became curator of the Chelsea Physic Garden until 2010.

The trio's eldest, Topline, a nickname from World War 2 (real name Creighton), was the original voice of West-ward TV – "soothing and agreeable", said a report on the station which tuned out for good in 2008. "Many West Country folk over a certain age smile with fondness when his name is mentioned," wrote the reporter. Topline was born in 1919 and died in 2015 (I wrote his obituary for *The Guardian*). Roses were his speciality.

* * *

E veryone on my corridor tried hard to be positive but we were subdued by what had taken place. I could not help but appreciate that being in charge of a magazine like *Woman* must have been exceedingly challenging with or without a staff wanting better pay. From my own experience I knew how essential it was to have reliable backup.

Jo's deputy was Gaythorne Silvester, an effete young man who had come from the young magazines sector. He had the owlish look of (a not yet created) Harry Potter and was quite introspective, quite droll. The role of deputy editor is probably the hardest one of all in magazine publishing: unless you are a clone, you cannot be what the editor is, yet you are expected to act as if you were in his or her absence.

IPC once considered sending its editors on management courses, but I heard Jo dismiss these as completely unnecessary as you either had the ability, or you didn't, to get the best out of people. She must have known which category she fell into as ahead of her lay a highly regarded career in magazines and newspapers (editor of *Options*, the *Observer Magazine*, executive editor of *The Times*, managing editor of the *Daily Mirror*, woman's editor of *The Sun*) plus international standing as an authority on 'Wellness and Wellbeing'.

At *Woman* at this time, her 'stamp' – the special some-thing an editor gives to a publication – was the pursuit of pop celebrities. As years later this is almost the *raison d'être* for all the weeklies, it could be said Jo was well ahead of her time.

Unfortunately, when we worked together I was never in her good books, rarely meeting her undefined criteria. After the strike, working life did not return to normal and the atmosphere was tense. I sensed I was in danger of being forced out. I could not afford to resign unless I had another job in place and had started looking around when, quite suddenly, Jo left for Fleet Street. She had an offer from Robert Maxwell that she couldn't refuse.

RETURN TO RELIABLE TRADITION

The appointment of Richard Barber as editor was both fast and unexpected. He had not been at *Woman's Realm* for long and the new life he'd brought to it was only just starting to be seen in the circulation. He stayed until a new editor was found for *Realm*, but in those weeks he got to know *Woman* too, talking to the assistant editors and department heads individually.

From the first meeting, I was a fan. He was personable and quick witted, and he laughed easily which was a tremendous asset in the post-strike gloom. Happily married to Patti, a teacher, and with young children, he made it known that he intended to be there for them every evening at bath-time, so there would be no staying late at the office. Except on Thursdays, of course. The conference would still go on but the late hours of the past were not replicated. A man was able to do what women editors before him didn't, accepting that the staff have a family life as well.

Richard had the same brief as all IPC editors: cut costs and increase circulation. I thought him a good manager because he appreciated that the department heads were the specialists. He didn't want to do their job or think he knew better, but he wanted them to tell him what was best for the *Woman* reader. He did not bludgeon; he was firm but courteous. By the time he arrived to take up the job, however, the practicals' corridor was like a moving conveyer – and there was no time to hold the handrail while travelling.

Woman was taking to the road and it affected the fashion, beauty and cookery departments, and me. Sponsored by Flora, the first company to create a low-fat spread (as opposed to margarine), the road show went to three cities in the UK – a stage manager, lighting experts and transport people packed it all up and moved it on.

The show combined real-life reader makeovers on stage and a parade of the latest fashions which, in the mid-1980s, were either dreary or outrageous, a mix of chic and clump (the sound of Doc Martens' boots hitting the floor). I wrote the script which was read – over the thumping beat of the vibrant catwalk music – by Jaki Bell, Alison Plummer and me; we each did a show. Eating healthily and losing weight was a big element and involved a nutritionist. Joy Davies was there to talk to readers about cookery and low-fat meals.

It strained every sinew of those in the departments who had to coordinate the readers taking part, the clothes and the experts in each place, and keep a record so that when a report eventually appeared in *Woman* all relevant details were known. Fashionistas Val Savage and

Mary Weaver dressed the newly made-over readers as well as the models. Alison and Sue Cooper from beauty worked with bald-headed and bearded Harold from Harrods, a showman-hairdresser who was great fun on stage, and make-up people from Boots. Even now, if I hear the music from the film *Ghostbusters* – the choice for the catwalk – I feel myself preparing to take the microphone: "Welcome to the Woman and Flora Road Show…"

With the diet culture growing apace, Flora was a breakthrough in the low-fat/dieting arena but problems lay ahead. First there was the 'trans fats' issue: unhealthy substances created through the chemical hydrogenation of oils which allowed the spread to solidify. Investment went into removing them and reformulating the product.

With increased concern over cholesterol, Flora produced the ProActiv range aimed at reducing this. The arguments about 'good' and 'bad' fats raged for many years. When poly-unsaturated butter emerged as 'natural', as opposed to 'processed', sales of spreads and margarines fell. Unilever sold the section making Flora and Stork.

* * *

Real life returned all too soon and we were back at our desks and into the routine of living in the future. The atmosphere was better and team spirit revived but changes occurred on the 'other' corridor. Dee Nolan left to join *The Mail on Sunday* and to start the very successful *You* magazine. Mary Fletcher, also Australian, became features editor, backed up by writers Ann-Marie

Sapsted, Alison McDonald, Sue Thomas, Janet Horwood and others.

Alison left suddenly to join a new left-wing weekly tabloid, *The News on Sunday*, produced in Manchester. Behind it were some radical journalists including John Pilger, an Australian who I had known a lifetime ago before he found his crusading platform on *The Daily Mirror* in the UK. Though he was editor-in-chief, he left before the paper began publication. Lori Miles (who had been in charge of *Woman*'s London supplement) was made editor but the paper achieved only a quarter of the 800,000 needed sales, and lasted from April to November 1987. But that was still some time ahead.

Richard opted for tradition rather than innovation for *Woman*: useful but inspiring practical features, solid interviews with glamorous mainstream stars, focus on the challenges which the 'badly done by' faced in every community in Britain, adding in humour and warmth and as many enticements as possible to induce readers to buy each week. The frequent appearance of Royalty was a must, particularly Princess Diana or Fergie, her sister in law. The former Sarah Ferguson had an uncanny proclivity for attracting the 'wrong' type of publicity.

All the women's weeklies, from the earliest days of their creation, have sought a Royal connection. *Woman* and *Woman's Own* (with Bridget Rowe as editor) now vied in earnest to get one a week if they could. But a strange thing happened. Often the lead story would be the same in both, or near enough to make you wonder which magazine you were reading. The reason may simply have been that the editors of both magazines knew each other's minds very well. Richard had been Bridget's deputy on *Woman's World*, and both were protégées of Terry Hornett. The constant pressure to prevent such calamitous and costly coincidence brought much stress. I remember Mary Fletcher suggesting ruefully at a conference that feature ideas should be submitted to the publishers of each magazine so that a choice could be made of what went into which. This went against every inherent instinct of journalism, that a story remain secret until published. And publishers, the money people, usually have no direct input in editorial matters.

The problem with the similarities became apparent when the magazines were being promoted. The IPC PRs who were given the task of getting extra mileage out of the material in the issues via radio, TV and newspaper interviews found themselves flogging the same personalities and revelations about them.

This might not seem odd today, when there's hardly a hair's breadth of difference between the magazines whose permanent preoccupation with the minutiae of celebrities (known and wannabe) make them all look exactly the same. Back then the editors tried to make them different.

* * *

Though this clash of scoops was a worrying development, *Woman* had the edge with the practicals. The knitting, for instance, was outstanding. Some garments were literally works of art – one sweater was based on the magnificent Book of Kells, gloriously illustrated gospels of 800AD, a cherished possession of Trinity

College, Dublin, where it is kept in a locked glass case. The pattern created by the talented knitters, and instructions, worked a treat.

Fashion produced stylish ready-to-wear offers but Val Savage's biggest coup was organising reproductions of the spectacular jewellery of the Duchess of Windsor. After her death in 1987 the collection of the woman who might have been queen went for £31m (six times higher than expected) at auction in Switzerland but the discerning *Woman* reader, for just a few pounds, could adorn herself with remarkable pieces. Paste yes, but it was panache for pence. Importantly, the auction money went to the Pasteur Institute in Paris, where research concentrated on the rising horror of the 1980s – AIDS and cancer.

From beauty came absolutely fabulous transformations. Alison and her team brought readers to London from all over the country to produce a coverline such as '50 marvellous reader makeovers'. I treasured the leather-clad biker in her late 40s who wanted a hairstyle that was intact and attractive when she removed her helmet.

Slimming remained an essential element; at one stage we seemed to run a diet a week. I'll never forget the look of bewilderment on the face of Sue Cooper, deputy beauty editor, who supported a reader through a weight-loss programme. Pleased that the reader had shed over three stone, when Sue saw the excess skin deprived of its fatty filling hanging off the poor woman's body it was too much reality. But it inspired a feature on what could be done about it.

Home came up with incredible house makeovers, or reported what people had done themselves; if anyone turned a semi into a castle, or a terrace into a mansion, it found its way into *Woman*. This department had many talented journalists: Jane Graining, Helen Chislett, Nicole Swengley, Margaret Caselton – whose names I have often seen in more upmarket publications.

I remember Richard interviewing a young woman called Julie Pike who was applying to be secretary in the department. When he asked her about her ambitions she told him she wanted his job. Within a few years, as Julie Savill, she would become editor of the BBC magazine *Good Homes*.

Cookery, too, made its mark though the inspirational food spreads produced by Joy deserved to be printed on much better paper. She was stunningly attuned to the trendsetters – 'influencers' as they are now known – and brought their thoughts, faces and fare to *Woman* readers. Anton Mosimann, Ken Hom, Rabbi Blue, Glyn Christian, Colin Spencer, Keith Floyd, all well known then, provided interesting storylines along with recipes.

She found story/photo opportunities in the US, about people and their restaurants making differences where food was concerned. While the country has a very high obesity rating, one of her reports was about children who didn't have enough to eat. The school in New York was serving breakfast to its pupils, mostly African American, improving their concentration and achievements. It wasn't published, perhaps thought too esoteric for *Woman*.

Many years later Michelle Obama, wife of the President, in her memoir *Becoming* described how successful this project had been during her husband's tenure. In the UK the short-lived 'Every Child Matters' initiative, introduced by Prime Minister Gordon Brown, saw providing breakfast at school as a major step forward in helping children of low or no income families. In present-day Britain, ensuring children are fed well remains a subject of great concern.

I worked with Alison Plummer on *Beautiful Woman*, an annual with pretentions to being *Vogue*. With striking pictures and artistic white space, it covered health and beauty in far more depth than was possible in the weekly magazine. Printed on better paper, it made the hard work of preparation worth it. The designer was Reg, an old timer from the art department, who never looked you in the eye or brooked any criticism. We tiptoed round him, though Alison could wheedle him into making a change here and there. His taciturnity allowed much to be accomplished in silence but the end result was always pleasing.

In early 1986, Alison decided to go to Australia to join her New Zealander partner Ken Martin, a photographer with whom she had worked on some glorious photoshoots in exotic places for *Woman* and *Beautiful Woman*. She went on to become managing editor of *Vogue Australia*. Later, after marrying Ken at an idyllic spot in the South Pacific, they ran a photographic/film/media business specialising in travel and health. Vickie Bramwell returned to *Woman* in her stead.

Going abroad to do photographic shoots was common practice at *Woman*, and a lot of (deodorized) sweat went into it. The department heads arranged it all: chose the location (for its scenery and better light), got the flights for free in exchange for credits in the magazine, chatted up PRs to provide and pay for hair and makeup stylists to accompany them, sweet talked a photographer into going with the group which would include one or two models and suitcases full of clothes borrowed from designers or stores. That week or ten days away would provide material for many future features.

One in particular I think was well ahead of its time: the backdrop of the rose red city of Petra, in Jordan, for a range of knits in complementary hues was breathtaking. Lesley Stansfield must have had amazing powers of persuasion to organise such a trip to a country whose borders were hardly open. Often the superb photography was lost when printed on *Woman* stock, but was impressive in *Knitting Woman*, an annual with better paper. One featuring knits for Princess Di was particularly successful.

For magazines and newspapers, 1986 was a breakthrough year. Peter Davis who was assistant managing director of Sainsbury's (whose HQ was in the tower block alongside Kings Reach) became chief executive of Reed. Richard Barber invited a few of us to go with him to his 'welcome' reception on the 29th floor of the tower. There we heard him promise to try and bring more equality to the wages paid in the company: 80% of the employees were women yet their earnings were far less than the 20% of men. Needless to say, his words didn't translate into achievement.

By the time he returned to the top job at Sainsbury's in 2000, after having brokered a partnership between Reed and the Dutch publishing company Elsevier, and a few years as the 'man from the Pru' – CEO of the financial institution the Prudential – the Reed Elsevier wage structure still favoured employed males. But Davis did get a sort-of comeuppance.

The Independent in 2004 reported on the newly knighted business guru facing shareholder revolt over a promised £2.4 million bonus after dismal trading. The Sainsbury's board defused the situation by ending his tenure. But we need shed no tears – he had his luxury yacht and country pile to escape to, said the report.

* * *

*T*he Independent was one of three new – all unusual – newspapers, that appeared in 1986. It was the most traditional, aiming to challenge long-standing broadsheets, *The Guardian* and *The Telegraph*, and was refreshing in its approach. A mix of traditional with a hint of tabloid, 'accessible' as it was known, suitable for all.

The second was *The Sunday Sport*, up against the *News of the World* and *The Sunday People*, and was not unlike the Sundays of Down Under, with lots of bare breasts and bums and quite ludicrous stories. It called itself the most outrageous newspaper in the world but its 25-year run ended in April 2011 when it went into administration. Then its original publisher, David Sullivan, bought it for £50,000 – and you can now read it online, taking everything you see with a pinch of salt. It could be considered a hive of 'fake news'.

1986 was revolutionary in printing terms – and a fight to the finish between old methods and the new. It began in January when Rupert Murdoch moved production of *The Times* and *Sunday Times* to a site across the Thames at Wapping where journalists used modern computer facilities to input copy. The print unions tried to block distribution of the Sunday paper and were fired. The 54-week Wapping Dispute, as it was called, was a victory for Margaret Thatcher's determination to reduce power of the unions.

The new direction owed much to Eddie Shah, a newspaper proprietor from Warrington, Cheshire. A year before the miners' strike (1984-5) he made the news by using non-union labour to directly input onto computers. At this time national newspaper journalists, because of demarcation or union rules, could touch nothing more technical than paper or typewriters. The resulting conflict with the trade unions led to near-eradication of the old printing industry and its power in newspaper production.

Shah was behind the third paper to launch: *Today*, a new tabloid which hit the streets in March. Jane Reed left her job as managing director of IPC's Holborn Publishing to be the paper's managing editor in charge of features.

Today was different (Wikipedia says the paper's motto, hung in the newsroom, was 'propa truth, not propaganda'). Produced by the offset printing method, it had colour throughout. Because of the untried technology (later to be called desk-top publishing) the paper had a difficult start.

Within four months it had a new proprietor: multi-millionaire Tiny Rowland whose Lonrho Group owned *The Observer*, a Sunday newspaper (now part of *The Guardian* group). Prime Minister Edward Heath had described Rowland's company in the 1970s as "the unacceptable face of capitalism" because of its attempt to avoid paying tax. Rowland made the headlines himself as he and Mohamed Al Fayed battled to buy Harrods, the prestigious London store. He lost and destroyed his successful conglomerate in the process. (He died in 1998, aged 80.)

Rowland's ownership of *Today* lasted about a year, after which it became part of Murdoch's News International (where Jane Reed was Director of Corporate Affairs). It was eventually killed off in 1995, but it was the catalyst that forced all the national newspapers to change to electronic production. And that in itself changed the future of British newspapers – and magazines.

* * *

At *Woman*, I worked quite closely with the managing editor, Betty Hale. She had been with IPC for many years, working mostly on teen mags, and was a good friend of one-time IPC chief Ron Chilton, a former printer who had reached the top (a rare occurrence). Her job loosely fell into the category called 'promotion and reader offers' and she was a whizz at making deals. In 1987, *Woman*'s 50th anniversary, she arranged a cover-mount for half a million issues: a tiny phial of perfume in which floated fine flakes of gold. Her 'reader special' events, though, were memorable because often nothing went right. The one promoted as a rare happening in the grounds of Leeds Castle is a perfect example.

The London Ballet's performance was something to look forward to. British weather was at its unreliable best and we trekked there on one of the coldest and wettest days of the summer, let alone the year. Despite heaters placed around the back of the outdoor stage, the muscles of the poor ballet dancers went rigid, a not dissimilar happening in the bodies of readers shivering under blankets and brollies on the grass in front. My long-suffering husband was with me and we wrapped ourselves in plastic dry cleaning covers found in the boot of our car. To no avail. It was utter misery.

Then there was the day's outing to France, at a very special price for readers, with non-stop entertainment arranged by Betty on board the ferry going to and fro. On offer were face and hair makeovers while a young, very noisy, band made music in one of the lounges. We had to be at Ramsgate very early to meet the readers who gathered in the amusement pavilion before boarding. Calamity soon ensued. Our awaited ferry broke down at sea so another had to be found and brought to us. This meant there was no time for the promised couple of hours on French soil.

The decision was made to go to France and back, keeping the readers as good humoured as we could at sea. There was just nowhere to hide – and the bars did a roaring trade. I think I got home at midnight. There were no mobile phones then so I don't suppose I could let my husband know where I was. I doubt, however, that anything surprised him about my movements at that time.

Betty retired early, just before her 60th birthday, and began a new life. Just as Billie Figg had done, she went on to another career – as an agent. She promoted the up-and-coming astrologer Jonathan Cainer into the public's consciousness. Cainer, whose first column was in *Today* in

1986, became one of the world's best known sun-sign predictors via mainstream newspapers. [He died in 2016, aged 58, of a heart attack possibly after taking cocaine – there was an open verdict at the inquest.]

* * *

R ichard chose not to fill the managing editor position (part of the general cost cutting) and my job changed too: at his behest, I found myself working on special promotions and contributing features. One involved Fergie, married to Prince Andrew, who was continually criticised for the clothes she chose. With the help of the *Woman* fashion department and a new computer system at Selfridge's store in Oxford Street, London, I was able to 're-dress' her.

It worked like this: a naked outline with Fergie's face on top was placed on the computer and various styles were added. These were photographed for *Woman* so readers could see how she could look if she changed her preferences. And the practice caught on – 25 years later Tesco and others trialled similar 'avatar' systems so shoppers can see what they look like without having to try on the clothes instore. These systems may well come into their own in the future with restrictions on handling garments imposed by the Covid pandemic.

I commissioned Stefan Buczacki from BBC's *Gardeners' Question Time* to create a garden for Carol Thatcher when she moved into her newly bought terraced house in London's Fulham just after her mother's extraordinary re-election 100-seat victory. We ran step-by-step pictures, shot from an upstairs window by the leaning out Colin Thomas, a lanky and easy going photographer.

Later I interviewed Mary Quant and her husband Alexander Plunket Greene, and we ran exclusive pictures of their garden, in every way as charming as they were. He was a good friend of Terence Conran and died in 1990.

Woman under Richard Barber was far more fun, much better natured, than my first years there. Somewhere along the line in his early 20s he made the decision to be a journalist but really he might have gone into acting, with his declamatory style tinged with a touch of camp.

Having brought with him a good business head, instilled by Terry Hornett into all who worked for him at the higher levels, he knew about magazine housekeeping: making every penny of the money allocated to editorial work increase by getting as much free help as possible from PRs, paid by businesses to get their names and products before the readers' eyes.

Competitions with fantastic prizes, such as winning a 'dream home', were very rewarding. The new house we featured, in Haslemere, Surrey, was done up by TV's DIY dynamo Harry Greene (father of *Blue Peter* star Sarah Greene) under the watchful eye of Margaret Caselton. Another long-running competition had a Beazer home in the north as the major prize. In both instances readers had to buy the magazine for several issues in order to be considered for the prize, and with weeks of promotion involved it did the trick of upping circulation.

* * *

Press trips or 'jollies' were a feature of journalism in the 1980s. PRs invited journalists to go to amazing places with the hope of later publicity in their weekly or monthly publications. Richard offered me one to the Caribbean which was on a par with my wonderful Paris experience in 1966 (when I went to the Opera, dined at the Tour Eiffel restaurant and learnt how to eat snails).

In the depths of February 1987 our small party boarded Concorde for a fast and well-irrigated flight to Barbados. Concorde was an extraordinary plane – stunning to see in the air, nose aimed upwards like a sniffy pointer in the hunt. We had a clear view of it from our Wimbledon home at about 6 o'clock every evening (not that I was there very much at that time).

But I had another link with it, too: in 1976 I had been in Bristol with my husband whose firm Angus & Robertson was publishing Concorde's story, about how the British and French worked together on this innovative creation. The press hovered round the prototype on display, all trying for a different angle on a craft that had truly broken the mould – British Airways would introduce the first commercial flight from London Heathrow to Bahrain that year.

Press attending do's like this in those days were invariably men and Paul Callan, the diarist from *The Daily Mirror*, suggested I join him in the cockpit. Next day there was a picture of us in the paper and me described as "cuddly Wendy" – which was perfectly accurate as I had not long given birth to my son and extra pounds were not yet gone. [Callan died in 2020.]

The trip to Barbados in 1987 was fantastic. Supersonic Concorde was supported by celebrities and business people who thought the cost worth it because of the hours saved in crossing the Atlantic. It carried just 100 passengers, travelled at twice the speed of sound and champagne was served as a matter of course. The press trip was organised to promote the start of twice-weekly flights, from London Heathrow, taking only four hours to Britain's loyal and lovely former colony and the superb hotels and holiday options available. And it was a dream.

There were just five in the group, and one was Jean Rook, the so-called Queen of Fleet Street, whose youngish but gravelly voice indicated her smoking habit. (I had given up yet again so I was feeling superior.) We discovered we were both Scorpios (she was eight years older) and we never stopped talking.

She too loved tennis so we had a hit in the early morning with hotel racquets, walked on the golden beaches, were awed by the vast colonial houses that could have been the setting for the slave-owning families in *Gone With The Wind*, and imbibed gently as the sun set magnificently in front of the exquisite Sandy Lane Hotel. I couldn't believe that this was the woman known to be the scourge of subs and liable to create havoc if anyone touched a word of her copy.

On the third day Jean was called by her news editor at the *Daily Express*. Prince Edward was to represent the Queen in the Bahamas, his first official duty since leaving the Marines just weeks before, an exit that excited outrage as he hadn't been in long but had quickly discovered that this way of life was not for him. Her employer thought that as Jean was 'in the vicinity' (broadly speaking) she might obtain the first interview, if she could get there in time. There was just one problem, she had no 'formal' clothes with her. But as I had never learnt to travel light I had what she needed, from silky dress with matching jacket, to shoes and tights – all of which fitted.

Next day she went one way and the rest of us boarded the ordinary flight back to the UK, cramped into economy for an excruciating 10 hours. Jean got the interview and sent me a nice thank-you when returning what she'd borrowed. Within a year her life was turned upside down.

THE JEAN ROOK STORY

Jean's husband Geoffrey Nash, who was her first news editor at Sheffield when she began in journalism, died of a brain tumour in 1988 on their 25th wedding anniversary. She used her *Express* page to talk about her experience of widowhood and breast cancer, which appeared about the same time, revelations that endeared her to her readers. She sent me a note when I changed jobs in 1989, wishing me well, and we made plans meet but it didn't happen. In 1990 Sue Lawley introduced Jean on BBC radio's *Desert Island Discs* as "a Yorkshire journalist who [it has been said] prefers brassiness to classiness" but I think she was an actress who enjoyed her reputation as an outspoken, hard-hitting columnist. She died in 1991, before her 60th birthday. Not that she would have retired. Writing was her life, deadlines her fuel — she'd missed just two: when her son was born in 1971 and when she learnt of her cancer diagnosis, which knocked her for six.

* * *

Having fewer people on the staff doing the same number of jobs was now a fact of life on all the weeklies which, with falling circulations, had to trim their spending as the publishers received less income. Board member Pat Lamburn got the editors together to look at the problems the company faced and it was on this committee that Richard and Laurie Purden forged a long-lasting friendship. 'Think ins', when an editor and the staff spent a day or a weekend in earnest pursuit of a miraculous way forward, were nerve-racking for all.

Laurie was discovering how hard it was to give an A personality to a magazine run by IPC which saw big bucks only in pursuing C1 category readers. Along with C2s, these were the prime targets of the weeklies. They were the most likely to be profligate, spend money on impulse, build up debt (a very common four-letter word in women's magazines). The real fact was that they had no loyalty at all.

By the mid 1980s IPC was huge, inviolable, all knowing. Or was it. There were rumours about a challenge coming from across the channel. The Germans, it was said, had plans to launch in the UK, but what and when? In 1986 and 1987 there was gossip about different editors being seen on flights to Germany, of people meeting unknown strangers at places like the bar of the Savoy Hotel on the Strand. Iris Burton, Jill Churchill, Gaythorne Silvester were all mentioned in these murmurings. No one seemed to realise that a shake-up was on the way.

Gaythorne was an enigma to me. He had worked at

DC Thomson in Scotland on teen magazines which is how he knew Alison Plummer who'd been on *Jackie* (whose content was much more advanced than *Girl* of my adolescence) along with the phenomenally prolific children's writer Jacqueline Wilson. But the web (ever problematical with facts, remember) says someone of the same name as Gaythorne edited 'sexually provocative teen magazines *My Guy* and *Oh Boy!*' which were immensely popular 'with girls – and gays'. These were magazines Betty Hale had also been involved with before *Woman*.

When Gaythorne left *Woman* for pastures new – first for a short stint at *Today* newspaper, then to contract publishers Redwood and much later to the German group Bauer – Richard needed a new deputy editor. I thought I was in with more than a chance, but no. He chose Rose Wild, the urbane and erudite fiction editor who years before had been picked by *Woman* talent spotter Patsy Brougham as someone who was going places – and did. (After magazines, Rose went into newspapers and became Feedback and Archive Editor at *The Times*). For me, it was not a good time.

'Kings Retch', ie Kings Reach, IPC's home in Stamford Street, was in two parts: a 29-storey tower and, in front of it, a lower four-floored building. Each was continually being rearranged, and magazines relocated. *Woman's* practicals' corridor, in the low building, saw changes as offices became available and new faces appeared.

My secretary Gill Doran and I were moved to a sort of ensuite, an office with a front area large enough to hold a table and chairs for small meetings, or better still for occasional drinks after work. Next to us was a larger office where Mike Matthew, destined eventually to be chief executive of IPC, was installed. His background was production and he moved smoothly up the greasy pole, never tempering his tongue and its proclivity for the liberal use of the word fuck. No sentence was complete without it, in his mouth it was adjective, noun and verb.

He must have had far more going for him than met the eye (or ear) for he held the position of CEO of what was termed the Ministry of Magazines for seven years, shepherding IPC through the Cinven-backed management buyout from Reed Elsevier in 1998 (when the very tall David Arculus, ex Emap, was chairman).

Then in October 1999 he suddenly and inexplicably resigned, leaving the company in the hands of 38-year-old Sly Bailey. At last, a woman at the top of IPC. Would she do for the large number of women employees what the men had failed to do? No, but she did well for herself.

THE RISE OF SLY

Sly Bailey (her birth name was Sylvia) had started out at Emap and left Reed Elsevier in 2003 to be head of the Trinity Mirror group, publishers of three of the UK's biggest newspapers: *Daily Mirror, Sunday Mirror* and *The People*. In February 2012 shareholders demanded she take a pay cut because of the huge slump in the share price. "Investors are furious," said a report in *The Guardian*, "that Bailey has collected about £12.5m during her nine years at the helm." This was made up of pay, bonus and pension awards – she was effectively being rewarded for failure, said one pension fund manager. When she moved on she had a £900,000

payoff to keep her buoyant. After the Trinity Mirror
group bought the *Express* titles (including *OK!*
magazine, which Richard Barber had edited in the
1990s) from Richard Desmond in 2018 it changed its
name to Reach plc – the biggest newspaper, magazine
and digital publisher in the UK.

* * *

The news report of the changes at IPC (in *Marketing Week*, which I found on the web) said that Mike was only 51 when he left, and that he was "an old school manager who was never happy unless he was in control of everything". Old school? Hardly in the English sense surely! As for his age, I never thought of him as young. I liked his wife though, when we met occasionally. She worked at *The Guardian*.

When the editorship of *Woman's Weekly* became vacant in 1987 I saw this as perfect for me, the next move in a career in magazines that had come about more by accident than planning. After I applied I was interviewed by Mike. It brought back memories of my meeting with Peter Lawrence, editor of *Woman*, when *First Lady* died in 1974.

Both were alike physically, quite lean, and I found both inscrutable, which probably says more about me than them, and each spoke with a nasal twang that hinted of allergic rhinitis. I thought I had all the right answers to Mike's questions and put forward ideas about making *Woman's Weekly*, still thought of as the old pink-and-blue magazine though it had been full colour for many years, a brilliant success. I didn't get the job.

It went to Judith Hall, fiction editor of *Woman's Journal* and – from my past – my co-worker at *First Lady*. In her favour she had the Hornett inheritance, having worked on *Woman's World* with Richard Barber, and was steeped in the intricacies of fiction, agents and bidding wars. She was also blonde, exceedingly tall and elegant. I'm not being catty here; many female editors seem to be blonde. As a redhead, it was something I noticed.

Almost five years to the day after I'd joined *Woman* I received a call from someone out of the past, a phone call that brought unusual and unexpected challenges in a new era of magazines.

BELLA MAKES AN ENTRANCE

'The Germans are coming' was a cry heard for some time in the corridors of Kings Reach before anything actually happened. In 1979 Brian Braithwaite and Joan Barrell (writing in *The Business of Women's Magazines*) had speculated that there were at least two consumer groups in Germany that "may well begin to look at our market". But in mid-1980s UK, did anyone know the depth of the rivalry between the two companies and the dramatic impact it would have on women's magazines on their home ground?

Gruner+Jahr, part of the huge Bertelsmann group, cheekily stole a march on Bauer, Europe's biggest private publishing firm at the time, by launching two magazines in the UK in 1986. The monthly *Prima* and the weekly *Best* appeared suddenly and were immediately successful with British women. From Braithwaite's book I learnt that there'd been a *Prima* here in the mid-1970s: "published by the BSR gramophone turntable company it was doomed to failure".

Not so the new *Prima* from Germany, edited by Iris Burton (ex-IPC). This had a well-tried formula with domesticity at its heart, according to Jean Elgie, a production journalist who worked on the launch. "Sections of the magazine were easily identifiable and there was a dress pattern in the middle," she said. *Best*, based on the G+J French magazine *Voici*, was also very well received following strong TV ad campaigns. (Iris edited the weekly too and became editorial director of both magazines.)

The German TV campaigns were bright and cheerful, simple, nothing outrageous. *Prima* and *Best* were a modern take on the old-fashioned values of information, education and entertainment, offering tempting ways for readers to make money by sending in their own story or useful household tips.

Mike Matthew let it be known vociferously that the German influx was certain to fail, adding a lot of f-words to his unrestrained description. Jean Elgie said he didn't appear to be aware that that the Germans regarded IPC as a dinosaur, far too slow to bring products to the market. But I'd lost interest in IPC and simply seethed. I knew I wanted to move on.

I was at my desk, finishing my day's work, when a call came from a woman I had known in the *Womancraft* years. She was a PR, promoting decorative ideas using ribbons, and now she told me she had a new editorial job and there was one there that might interest me. Could she get someone to call me? Well why not, I said.

Within minutes of putting down the phone, he called. His name was Dennis Neeld and we arranged to meet at 6.30 the next evening at his office in Camden, an area of north London that I only knew as a place with a very popular Sunday market specialising in trendy clothes.

His 'office' was a vast, almost empty room and when I walked in the first person I saw was Alison McDonald, formerly of *Woman's* features department. She looked exactly as I remembered: in a black dress, fine-denier black tights and high heels, little black gloves and brighter than bright red lipstick which set off her blonde Marilyn-Monroe-style locks.

Her smile was a great welcome. She took me to a partitioned-off area where Dennis sat. She put on her pillbox-shaped hat, complete with teeny veil, and went off to the pub with several others leaving me with this grey-whiskered man with close-cropped grey hair. He was the one who would broker for Bauer in Britain. I don't remember him as a smiler.

"Eve tells me," he said, 'that you are very good at practical subjects." He looked at me rather sceptically over the top of his unrimmed glasses, his voice more querulous than warm. I answered his questions as best I could; I was quite clued up about the who's who of fashion, beauty, knitting, sewing, cookery and home in women's magazines and our conversation covered some of this. By the time I left, an hour later, I wasn't sure what job we had been discussing.

But the next day I knew: to be the senior editor, practicals, for the new Bauer weekly – called *Bella* – whose launch was imminent, so imminent that it was frightening. I had no idea what I was letting myself in for, but the offer made my heart beat faster.

The pay was certainly an improvement on that at IPC – in fact, it was the higher salaries being paid at *Best* and *Prima* that influenced salaries for the better throughout the women's magazine industry for some while. The German companies chose to pay more because they were working to produce publications at speed. They used salary as the inducement to obtain the right employees.

When I put in my resignation at *Woman*, I like to think it was a bombshell, but journalism isn't like that. The printing ink closes fast over the one who was there before, leaving no trace. Richard said I could go immediately rather than serve out the required notice period (well, after I had sorted out a few things that I was responsible for). He gave me a terrific send-off, as did the others I'd worked with for years. And I was pleased to receive from the knitting department the sweater inspired by the Book of Kells (which I went to see years later in Dublin). All the well-wishing made me quite tearful, but off I sailed into the unknown world of Bauer.

* * *

I started work at Camden on September 26, the same date I'd joined *Woman's Own* in 1966, 21 years before. I quickly learnt of the one major hurdle for the new enterprise: that huge room needed to be filled with staff, and I had to find many of them.

Those who were there already had been secured by Dennis. He'd worked for years in Fleet Street before going to the US and joining *The National Enquirer*, a newspaper with a reputation for revelling in the scurrilous (and sells well today in the UK). From this he joined *Woman's World*, a magazine owned by Bauer. The one thing both have in common is that they are 'supermarket weeklies'. This is where they are sold – and do very well indeed.

The rumour (possibly fake news, though the expression wasn't in use then) got round that everyone who worked for Bauer in the US had to spend time working in a supermarket to understand the readership. But *Woman's World* was a phenomenon, simply because it wasn't sold by subscription as other magazines were.

Dennis was editor-in-chief, as he was at what was to be *Bella*. While he was in the UK, editor Stephanie Saible ran *Woman's World* (she had formerly been his secretary) and despite the geographical distance he kept a close grasp on it. At his right hand in Camden was his secretary Eileen who would be a fixture for many years at *Bella*. He'd been in town for some time scouting for staff.

Jean Elgie, who moved from *Prima* to be production editor at *Bella*, told me that Bauer's informant and adviser was Geoffrey Perry, the original publisher of *Family Circle* and *Living*, and later of *Home & Freezer Digest*. With time short Dennis called in a recruitment agency as well. He'd found Alison after she returned to London; her sojourn in the north on the John Pilger weekly *The News on Sunday* had been brief. By the time it folded in November she was well into her stride as *Bella*'s senior editor, features, adept at handling a wide range of material that had to be tailored to a strict formula.

Working with her was features editor, Sue Reid, who I'd known at IPC's *Woman & Home*. In 1986 she left to edit *Working Woman*, a monthly launched two years earlier by Audrey Slaughter and husband Charles Wintour (father of the famous fashion influencer, Anna, of American *Vogue*), backed financially by the original US magazine of the same name. The publication struggled to grab the mind and pocketbooks of the UK women executives it was aimed at. There were just too few of those then, just as there is today, so it was always going to be tough.

Audrey left when millionaire Peter Cadbury became its owner in early 1986, as did her successor Pandora Wodehouse (Fleet Street journalist and self-declared non-feminist). Sue's letter to readers in the October/November issue was reassuring: "A few people have suggested that this magazine would disappear altogether. We say, certainly not; I say, we're here to stay."

She didn't know that the owner had decided otherwise and her words appeared in what turned out to be the last *Working Woman* published. Such dreadful treatment is not uncommon in magazines. [Audrey Slaughter died in 2020, aged 91.]

Bella's one full-time feature writer was Deborah Ross, an instinctive wordsmith who quickly showed her penchant for the cheekily humorous. She is today active as a columnist in various newspapers. Gareth Powell was showbiz writer, aided by Jonathan Bowman, who would go on to edit a successful TV magazine.

Andrew McKenna was to write short funny pieces.

Former Fleet Street reporter Steve Ellis did the regular health page. Then there was Skippy, a young Australian philosophy student. So named by Alison after a children's TV programme about a kangaroo, Skippy was the magazine's runner, at the beck and call of all. With his long blond dreadlocks, Doc Martens boots and cheerful demeanour, he was good to have around.

Hans Gotta, a Bauer man from Germany, established the art and production side. He was a whizz at shoehorning a lot of information into a small space yet making it readable. This design skill would be effective much later in TV magazines with their voracious demands for programme details.

The soft spoken Phil Tristram was art editor, assisted by the sharper Steve Holder. There were two picture researchers: Patricia Elkins and Mark Garland, who would eventually marry Sue Reid.

This was the team that was overseen by the eagle-eyed Dennis. He was the one with the ultimate vision of *Bella*, what each page should look like, how each feature should 'sound'. Dennis's chosen aid in this was Helen Massey, chief sub, whose husband Patrick was head of the international news agency, Reuters, and had worked with Dennis in the past.

The inspiration or blueprint was *Tina*, Bauer's classic women's magazine that had a strong history in Germany. From the cover to the last page of *Bella* and *Tina* there was just one intention: to make the buyer eager for more. After several purchases, the reader was assured that there was nothing distasteful on any page and she would find much to enjoy in the range of subjects which had her interests at heart.

Dennis checked out the freelance branch of the NUJ where he found Eve Harlow, who'd done me the favour of giving her new boss my name. She was a tall, buxom lady who cheerfully flirted with Dennis and worked as a one-woman band arranging features based on needles: knitting, sewing and embroidery.

Petsa Kaffens, an Australian, was essential to *Bella*'s success. Her brief was the beauty angle – the covers (fresh-faced models with the healthy girl next door look), the true-life reader makeovers, the latest lotions and potions. Aided by the very quiet Angela Covington, she produced what Dennis wanted. (If he ever said "she looked better before" they knew they'd done wrong.)

This was my first meeting with Petsa though she had worked on *Home & Freezer Digest* and *Woman's Own*. (She was very helpful jogging my memory about women's magazines; in 2004 she began inspiring media students as visiting lecturer in fashion journalism at the University of Westminster, but retired in 2018).

In one of the room's far corners, a freelancer, Jillie Murphy, created the fashion features, up to three spreads an issue. She was assisted by a couple of young women who looked like students and seemed constantly to be pushing rails of clothing between the desks. One of them, Mimi Spencer, would go on to become one of the UK's best known journalists having compiled a range of hugely successful 'fast diet' books based on the 5:2 principle (five days of eating, two of fasting) artfully promoted by TV health guru Dr Michael Mosley. Her website photo shows an elegant woman, slim as a rake and beautifully dressed.

At this early stage of *Bella*, Dennis worked with free-lancers to create home and cookery spreads using bought-in agency pictures. Barbara Jeffery, who had a Fleet Street background, organised two pages of travel in each issue. Dennis had found a gardening writer, Elizabeth Arter, who was unknown to me, who happily filled a page each week to a set of instructions. Astrology, which came from *Woman's World*, was manipulated and de-Americanised for British readers by the subs (and the predictions were happily accepted).

The problem page was given lively treatment, illustrated by posed black and white situation dramas, like stills from films with captions, the shoots for which were overseen by the picture editor. Whole magazines are made like this in Europe and have large readerships – if that's the right word for publications where pictures predominate over words.

Fiction was the sole operation of Linda O'Byrne, also ex-IPC, whose desk was near the fashion area. Like me, I think she also may have thought she would be editor of *Woman's Weekly* where she had worked for many years.

FICTION GETS A BOOST
In developing her role at *Bella* Linda O'Byrne established a new influence in fiction writing in the UK. The short stories in each issue either had a twist in the tail or entertained – and as neither type took long to read they were very popular indeed with *Bella* buyers. Just as they were with writers who were well

paid for their efforts. *Prima* did the same, encouraging
would-be authors. The market for short fiction
continues to thrive here, as a quarterly magazine,
MsLexia, bought by subscription, shows.

Dennis challenged me to find a crossword compiler (it
had to fill a whole page, often with a theme), an agony
aunt, a home editor, a fashion editor, a letters editor and
freelancers to provide words and pictures for two cookery
features an issue plus cookery cards. Relying on my
contacts book, I made a lot of phone calls and arranged
meetings. The Germans' attitude to lunching was
different from that at IPC. I needed Dennis's permission
to have more than an hour and drinking alcohol then was
frowned upon. It was best to meet prospective contributors or staff at the end of the day.

While I was at *Woman*, I got to know Anne Lovell well.
I felt great sympathy with her situation as a mother of two
daughters with cystic fibrosis, an inherited life-threat-
ening disease (both parents have to carry the faulty gene
that causes it). As secretary on ActionWoman, the
consumer pages, she was used to both researching
subjects and answering letters. She jumped at the chance
of joining *Bella*. It worked out wonderfully for eventually
she was to become the magazine's agony aunt and author
of several books on relationships and health.

The news was getting around about *Bella*'s imminent
appearance and freelancers starting ringing in, eager to
bring in their portfolios. Among them was Eddie
Waltham, a 'puzzle specialist', who would provide the big
crosswords and other tempting word games. I couldn't

believe my luck! He was a miracle on legs and could come up with requested themes almost overnight without turning a hair.

Roger Tuff, a photographer I'd known in the days of *The Complete Cook*, came in with his partner Catherine Redington who'd been in the cookery team at *Woman* under Joy Davies. I introduced them to Dennis who agreed a fee for all work, pictures and words, to be done to order. Our cookery was oven-ready (as Boris Johnson is wont to say) for the foreseeable future!

HIPS AND THIGHS SUCCESS
At IPC I'd often encountered a 'media liaison' person, part of the PR contingent, called Lewis Mantus, a big bear of a man who decided to become a freelance agent with the name Media Angles Ltd. He was a reticent, unpushy person and I couldn't imagine him selling anything to anyone, but he came up trumps for *Bella*. He rang me about a book he was promoting, featuring self-help, do-it-yourself dieting for specific body areas.

Thus it was that Bauer's baby was in at the start of Rosemary Conley's soaring success with *The Hip and Thigh Diet* which topped the best seller list in 1988. *Bella* also offered its sequel containing recipes. Both of these launched Rosemary Conley Enterprises which did phenomenal business worldwide and earned her a CBE in 2004 for services to the fitness and diet industries. She now runs an online weight-loss club.

Within two weeks of me joining the staff, the first issue of *Bella* was on the streets, an event marked by

Konrad (Konnie) Wiederholz, the president of Bauer Publishing, with cars decorated with *Bella* billboards driving backwards and forwards in front of the Gruner+Jahr offices in London. He thought it was great fun to show off his bouncing baby to the enemy.

It wasn't until issue six that I was involved in putting the magazine together and the whole room seemed to be in perpetual motion. What made *Bella* out of the ordinary at this point – and for the first year of publication – was that each issue contained only four ads, to be placed where Dennis decided, not the advertisers.

He was aided and abetted by The Publishing Consultancy whose job it was to entice advertisers onto a waiting list. The promise was that *Bella*'s sales would reach a million, and that the handpicked advertisers would benefit. Being part of the Bauer bandwagon would also bring them favourable rates in their magazines on the Continent, an appealing prospect. Konnie was backed up on the business/advertising side by Henning Lauer, his very tall right-hand man.

They had spent years in the US with Bauer and obviously knew Dennis well. They liked to play jokes on each other, using what I believe is known as testosterone-fuelled humour. One that caused them most hilarity was cutting off someone's tie about two inches below the knot. The other was spiking beers with vodka, a tasteless and lethal spirit. The idea appalled me.

The worst case occurred at a pub gathering after work to celebrate someone's birthday. Fortunately I didn't go, but the reports of how much he drank were all round the office next day. He was so ill he couldn't work for several days. Nobody seemed to realise just how dangerous this practice could be. Like refusing to wear a mask during the coronavirus crisis.

A YEAR OF HORROR

1987 was a year of horrible happenings. In March there was the Zeebrugge ferry disaster when the ro-ro (roll on, roll off) *Herald of Free Enterprise* capsized killing 193 people (many on board had been *Sun* newspaper readers, paying just £1 for the trip). Two weeks after *Bella* launched in October, Black Monday occurred, the biggest fall in financial history that affected world stock markets. In November the horrific Kings Cross Underground fire killed 31 people and caused widespread disruption. Most of the staff came to work by public transport and travelling by tube was plagued by holdups and irritations for months. There was no need to make up an excuse for being late as Kings Cross was where you changed to the Camden line.

* * *

When Dennis had to return to the US for some time, he left in his place German-born Sieglinde Uetzfeld who had worked on *Woman's World* for many years and knew the Bauer style inside out. She sat opposite me on the central desk, where Alison and I worked side by side, and trained me in the nuances of successful Bauer magazines. My smoking habit had, alas, returned and this time I was encouraged by the smiling Sieglinde. Nothing fazed her. Her patience was fantastic. We needed this and good humour to create the *Bella* that Bauer expected.

It was tricky at first to angle the words in the right way so the readers felt the magazine was speaking just to them. Think of the problem: English wasn't Sieglinde's first language and I was still getting used to its nuances even though I'd lived here for some time! Alison did it instinctively. She was alert to the choice of words, whether in a caption or in promoting the issue on sale the following week. Our new vocabulary included empathetic words and phrases such as light-hearted, heart-warming, uplifting, feel-good, affordable, inspirational. All were motivations in the mix.

As this was a newly created magazine, it was interesting to see how the working practices evolved. At *Woman* the pattern of the days revolved around issues going to press or being processed or planned, and the many inevitable meetings that these engendered.

At *Bella*, meetings were kept to a minimum, but a strict production schedule had to meet the demands of the Bauer printing house in Germany. Jean Elgie went to and fro by plane with the page proofs and the turnaround time for checking, colour in particular, got shorter.

Despite his British background, Dennis was used to working in the US and could not accept that employees here expected to get more than two weeks annual leave and all bank holidays off. I received a call from him over the Christmas break – at the office. A few of us had come in simply because of pressure of work and he thought everyone should be there. Another time, when we contacted *Woman's World* to speak to him, it was a religious holiday in the US. He complained about that too because he was the only one working!

Much of the time I was so busy I felt I was running to keep up. After a while a routine did develop so I knew what had to be accomplished each day. I don't know whether it was because I was new to Bauer's ways, but I became aware of a strange atmosphere in the room; there was a wariness I couldn't understand.

Alison and I started to notice that Dennis made comments about things we'd spoken about, when he hadn't been present, most particularly if we'd been in any way derogatory about something. Of course we joked a lot – it's a welcome relief when you are working constantly against the clock. Perhaps irony and sarcasm can't be picked up by 'the walls have ears' syndrome.

Then we discovered that overheard conversations were reported back to him and the rumour got round that phone calls were taped. Whose job was it, we wondered, to go through it all, tuning into an ever-flowing stream of voices? Did they listen day by day or save them up for an all-in-one session? Were they looking for signs of insurrection or working with the enemy? So, end of joking remarks. Any personal discussions took place out of the office, not because we were disloyal but because we objected to anyone spying on us. And we could still grimace at each other, shrug our shoulders and and nod knowingly, communication that was beyond ear-scrutiny.

* * *

What was amazing was that the near-empty room I first saw was now full of desks and people. Emma Powell had come from *Family Circle*, a move suggested by Dee Remmington when she knew that Emma, who was deputy editor, was about to be retired (and Gilly Cubitt took her place). At first Emma worked with Anne Lovell and then took over the letters which were coming from readers in abundance.

Bonnie Spencer, who was to die tragically young in 1993, a year before the death of her husband the publisher Clive Labovitch, joined as a staff writer. Freelancer Ingrid Millar worked regularly with Alison; she went on to become the agony aunt of *Chat*, one of *Bella*'s rivals.

Bella was not unionised though there were many NUJ members on the staff with a father of the chapel to represent them and with whom Bauer agreed to speak. It took months for pay grades to be formalised, holiday entitlement and hours of work agreed, after which each staff member was given a personal contract to sign.

Incredibly, after four months of publication, *Bella* was on track to reach the magic million. All departments were now established and working to a dominating timetable, as is always the case with a weekly magazine. Then the time came for Dennis to relinquish his UK post. Alison and I both thought one of us would be appointed editor-in-chief but without any warning the chair's new incumbent, Jackie Highe, was suddenly there among us.

Before returning to the US and *Woman's World*, Dennis told each of us privately that we weren't ever in the running for the top spot, Konnie had made the decision and he agreed with it. What else could we do but say what the hell...

Jackie, who would go on to have a very long and productive association with Bauer in the UK and the US, has her own website now so I was able to find out about her glittering career. What a woman! Such confidence, such certainty! She tells how she had been associate editor at *Living*, under Dena Vane, and was instrumental in revamping it, taking the circulation to over 400,000 – "phenomenal for the 1980s".

She was then headhunted to edit *Parents* magazine, doubling its circulation within 18 months, and then was enticed to *Bella* which, she says, within a year was selling in excess of a million a week. (True, but she doesn't mention the part Dennis played in this.) It seems she clicked with Konnie. In 1989 she went Stateside, to Bauer headquarters in New Jersey, to edit a new monthly, *First for Women*, which had 3.5m sales within 18 months.

"The biggest single copy sales in the US women's market," she declares. I was riveted by what she said about this period, summed up best (my words) as a superior example of efficient networking. Jackie's former editor Dena had become editor-in-chief of *Woman's World* [Dennis having been compulsorily retired, I heard from Sieglinde] and when Jackie returned to *Bella*, Dena eventually moved to *First for Women* which unfortunately did not have the envisaged staying power and came to an end. This news brought to mind the demise of the also badly named *First Lady* on which I had lost a few metaphorical teeth. But Jackie and Dena appeared to be unscathed.

This part of Bauer's history established extraordinary

precedents in UK magazine publishing. Jackie, again I'm grateful for information on her illuminating website, devised and developed *Take A Break* which she says took four months from concept to launch and a few weeks to get onto the shelves. And, of course, at the same time she was mistressing *Bella*'s sales to 1.35m a week.

Not quite like the old days of the early 1960s when *Woman* and *Woman's Own* hovered round the 3m mark but times were different then. In the cut-throat 1980s and 1990s magazines fought to stay attractive enough for readers to want to buy. And Ms Highe obviously had the magic touch.

* * *

Into this fizzingly creative group came Lori Miles. After *Woman* she went on to have an astonishing career. She launched the young women's mag *Mizz* in 1985, *Chat* in 1986 (produced on newsprint, the first colour magazine to benefit from new technology – see Chapter 14). In 1987 she was in Fleet Street editing the *Evening News*, a daily created by Associated Newspapers to cruel the pitch of notorious Robert Maxwell's venture the *London Daily News*.

For eight months London had three evening newspapers but only one survived: the *Evening Standard,* now a free full colour tabloid with a Russian owner Evgeny Lebedev. Former Chancellor of the Exchequer George Osborne (inheritor of the wallpaper company Osborne & Little) was editor until the Covid crisis struck, causing a reassessment of the economics of free publishing. He was replaced by Emily Sheffield, formerly deputy editor of *Vogue* and sister-in-law of former Prime Minister David Cameron, Osborne's co-conspirator in the UK's austerity programme after the global financial crisis of 2008/9.

In 2011, a year after he became a British citizen with dual nationality, Lebedev bought the Independent Group whose newspapers were struggling. To cut costs, he merged with the *Standard* two of the editorial areas – sport and business, an unusual combo. *The Independent* became an online-only newspaper which Lebedev sold to JPI Media in 2016. When the company, overwhelmed by debt, was put into administration, the Daily Mail and General Trust bought the *i* newspaper and website. [In 2020 Evgeny Lebedev was made a cross-bench peer by Boris Johnson.]

Lori Miles, after a short and sweet experience in Fleet Street, worked for two years in an ad agency before joining Bauer. In March 1990, she was launch editor of the aforementioned *Take a Break*, a magazine that combines true-life stories with puzzles and prizes, a competitions-plus-confessions formula. It has been most successful and still leads the women's market today though its sales aren't the 1.3 million a week of earlier years. Lori, like her successor John Dale, received the Editor of the Year award or nominations many times from the British Society of Magazine Editors. This is a real sign of appreciation.

She attributed the prime reason for the magazine's popularity (I read in an interview she did with the *Press Gazette*) to the fact that every letter was answered, customer care that paid off. Readers brought their stories to them, and got paid for it. Britain was used to cheque book journalism on national newspapers, but now it spread to women's magazines and anonymity was no longer possible. In 2009 the Press Complaints Commission said 5% of complaints were about magazines, the greater proportion from people who were featured in 'real-life stories'.

Jackie Highe, writing evocatively on her website, says at this time she was working on new concepts. I don't know whether these were the same ones that Lori was also involved in, but three new Bauer magazines – *TV Quick*, *TV Choice* and *Total TV Guide* – appeared that shook the status quo in TV publications, knocking stalwarts *TV Times* and *Radio Times* off their perch. Hans Gotta designed all of them.

Then came *That's Life*, a winning formula that was reader-led, the title and a concept for which I'd had in 1986. My real-life quirky stories were a tribute more to the deceased popular paper *Titbits* and the unusual people found in every byway of Britain, many of whom were revealed through Esther Rantzen's TV show. At this time we were all looking for new ideas. Gaythorne Silvester was constantly championing magazines for men that were not pornographic, though he was not against a lot of bare flesh, and this was a phenomenon to come.

In 2002 Ms Highe left Bauer, after 14 years, to become a freelance publishing consultant and a vocalist with a swing band. I don't know why that doesn't surprise me as she is obviously multi-talented. She's written two successful books covering older people (her parents) and younger (five granddaughters). Lori departed in 2004, after 15 years, when David Goodchild became managing director, taking over from Alan Urry who'd been enticed away to Burda, another huge German competitor, to bring out a copycat title called *Full House* in the UK.

Urry, renowned for the 'corporate silence' he instituted as Bauer UK head, had not long before won the Marcus Morris Award for longstanding contribution to publishing. Janice Turner, a columnist at *The Times* and a former Bauer editor (*Real* magazine, a fortnightly, launched 2001) revealed in the *Press Gazette* that Urry and Bauer supremo Konnie Wiederholz were best friends and that "Alan's job was to smooth ruffled feathers and impose Konnie's will." I remember Urry only for his ferocious scrutiny of expenses.

Lori hardly missed a step in her progression and did a variety of jobs, including returning to *Woman* in 2005 as Acting Editor. Like all former employees in senior positions, when she left Bauer she was careful when speaking about the company. In a press interview she called her former boss Mr Bauer, describing him as a very shy man. "But," she said, "there is no doubt when you meet him that he is...powerful." Not many will have that experience: the family so predominant in world publishing is very private.

THE POWER BEHIND BAUER

In an article for *MediaGuardian* in 2008 (after *First* and *New Woman* were closed by Bauer Consumer Media) journalist Helen Pidd said that publicly available information on the German company could fit on one sheet of A4. This is exactly what Emap employees were given after the Bauer buyout the previous December.

The line of ownership went from father Alfred (died 1984) to son Heinz whose four daughters worked in various capacities for the company. Yvonne, Chief Executive Officer, is the fifth generation to run the family-owned business. Perhaps one day someone will write the story about what prompted this German printing firm that started in 1875 to expand to the US where it made publishing history before taking on the rest of the world, including Australia and New Zealand.

Bauer is a privately owned company with a clear mission: "to be media innovators who create and deliver influential brands that connect audiences with excellent content wherever, whenever and however they want it." In the UK, their intention to have the cheapest products brought them the description 'the Morrisons of the magazine world'. [Morrisons' approach has now been bettered by German supermarkets Aldi and Lidl.]

Konnie Wiederholz is on record, in the US, talking about Bauer's success there. He said one of the purposes of publishing is to build a family, the responsibility of publisher and editor being to create a community within the magazine, for readers and advertisers. He puts the success of the company down to the "Harvard Business Plan called 4P: product, place, price and promotion".

Woman's World, **the product**, was launched regionally in 1981 and went national in 1984. **The place** (of sale) was supermarkets and convenience stores. **The price** was kept low. **Promotion**: *Woman's World* was launched without any advertising and awareness was raised, with positive results, through a 16-page sample edition inserted into Sunday newspapers.

"Readers liked the 'compactness' of the new magazine," he said. Only the "complete romance" was more than a page long; the format was consistent, with everything always in the same place (his analogy was: like a familiar apartment, you know where all the rooms are); and only about 5% of pages are advertisements. When *First for Women* appeared in 1989, 8m copies went to grocery stores at 25c a copy – "only the price of a telephone call," said Wiederholz. A month later the price rose to $1, 7m copies were distributed and the ads were few. "We think the customer...cares about the editorial."

* * *

At *Bella* Jackie bustled in on her high heels and a big smile. With the support of the boss, Konnie, and backed by rigid working methods laid down by the former editor-in-chief Dennis, she set about manoeuvring all departments into the mould she wanted.

She was undoubtedly in charge, even when she was hopping around with her leg in a plaster cast, having fallen down a stationary escalator at Camden (there were continuing problems there for commuters, as a result of the Kings Cross fire months earlier and she was fortunate not to be more badly injured). The atmosphere, however, was very intense.

The staff at departmental level was long lasting but it was different at the top. When Jackie went to the US in 1989, Sharon Brown became editor and Jean Elgie was promoted to be her deputy. But it was a roundabout as Jackie eventually returned to *Bella*, Sharon left, followed by Jean – both going to IPC's *Living*, from where Jackie had made her leap to fame and fortune! Sue Garland (nee Reid) was headhunted by IPC in 1992 to edit *Woman's Realm*. It sounds like it was a tempestuous few years.

I wasn't part of it. In 1988 I was having grave doubts that I would last in the pressured environment when I received a phone call. I still wonder whether I should have just said 'sorry, not interested' and put the phone down.

13

THIS MORNING AND AFTER

It was headline news when Richard Madely and Judy Finnigan announced they were to leave ITV's *This Morning* programme after 13 years. For me it brought back dreadful memories. I had gone from the frying pan into the fire (some clichés really are very apt), leaving *Bella* in 1988 after just 11 months to take a job that was flawed. I was flattered to be headhunted (always fatal, I've learnt) and the money was very attractive, but everything occurred far too fast.

The launch of the TV show was very well received and made before-lunch viewing attractive to people – women in particular – at home. Transmitted from a studio that had as its back view the Albert Dock in Liverpool, its presenters were journalists, a married couple known by all as Richard and Judy. With four children between them, they came over as cheerful and relaxed and brought a little glamour, allied to practicality, into viewers' homes.

The times were not good, with economic problems for

house owners and savers alike, so money – particularly debt, the most common four-letter word for families – was an ever-present preoccupation. Including a segment on money problems, along with news, interviews, cookery, fashion, beauty, health and personal items made it a woman's magazine on screen.

Before the show launched, I was given the task of creating a weekly 'paper' version of what was presented on the box for millions of viewers. I was led to believe that DD, my nickname for the man who had offered me the job, had signed contracts with ITV's *This Morning*. The people behind it – Dianne Nelmes, Rod Caird and David Liddiment – were very keen to get the project up and running, I was told.

* * *

There were just three of us employed by Broadsystem to create and produce *This Morning Magazine* (subline *'The TV weekly for women'*). I had two journalist helpers, a features editor/writer, and an Australian who had been working Fleet Street shifts for some time, who was chief sub/production.

They started immediately on short-term contracts and knew from the start the challenges we faced. We were confident that we'd find solutions and determined to do our best to create a new magazine. There were two major problems. The first, and most telling, was that we never knew what was going to be on the day's agenda of the TV show, so we were unable to prepare pages that would reflect the content and give vital information about stockists or suppliers or other details that would encourage advertisers to take space in the magazine.

Richard and Judy, plucked by Dianne Nelmes from the Granada newsroom (I later read), were reluctant to be held down to any demands that restricted their show. They wanted it to appear spontaneous, to be able to alter or change direction, for example, if someone unexpectedly arrived in town and could be interviewed live.

The second problem, linked to this, was production methods. Because of lead times for printing, we had to have subject matter in hand four weeks before the programmes aired. The practical spots, the regulars as we called them in magazines, naturally had their plans underway for the future – but why would any of the presenters give us their unique recipes, or thoughts on a subject, for free, to publish in *This Morning* Magazine which wasn't owned by the TV company? They had a contract with the show, but were self employed and expected payment for contributions to the magazine.

We devised a plan to try and 'flesh out' the basic schedule – provided, with little enthusiasm, by *This Morning* – with our own articles written by freelancers. I came unstuck with this as well. At the time the place to seek employees of any sort in the media was Monday's *Media Guardian* and my small ad for freelance contributors with women's magazine experience brought more than 8,000 replies. We didn't have time to read them! The Babe, assistant to DD, was our best bet.

At the start of this venture, our little group was set up on the same floor as all those working for the 'telephony company', Broadsystem, that was our employer as well. All we could normally hear around us were phones ringing, and every one that was answered was bringing in money. This was the first company to work entirely in phone marketing (I later learnt) and it was my introduction to what is at the end of those numbers you see in small personal ads, particularly in the tabloids. They were premium numbers at a rate per minute that was very profitable for the companies involved.

Try as we might, we couldn't ignore what was going on and it seemed to us on the eavesdropping side that we were hearing some very strange conversations which on occasions included odd sounds. Someone whispered that it was...phone sex. You can imagine how hard it was to concentrate on what we were supposed to be doing! The Babe, as we called her, especially seemed adept at altering her voice dramatically – though we couldn't hear what was being said on the other end.

Fortunately for us, she had a chance to rest her voice in 'TM' time. This was the sacred hour in the middle of every day when our employer went into a room adjoining his office – it was soundproofed and had a double mattress on the floor – and shut the door for Transcendental Meditation. Nothing was allowed to disturb him.

While he was thus occupied, the Babe sifted through the letters and CVs putting them into categories that we might be able to plumb. It revealed some very talented writers, a few of whom we were able to commission. I managed to bring in a few people I'd worked with on various magazines, none of whom I think would want me to mention their names. All did their best to give credence to the practical features: cookery, home, beauty and fashion. We used free pictures from sources such as PRs and publishers; photo agencies were a last resort.

From *Bella*, I knew the value of having a good crossword and word games that could be done when taking a coffee break, with tempting little prizes, and these we incorporated – thanks to IPC putting paid to one of its gems. The competitions department had been part of IPC for as long as I could remember and the people who worked in it provided puzzles, competition questions, crosswords and quizzes according to requests made by any magazine for readers of any age. They took pride in coming up with something different for everyone. When the end came, obviously a cost-cutting exercise, they put their clever selves onto the freelance market just as there was a huge explosion in mind games popularity.

After a while our small team moved into the basement where we had desks and phones and space for the freelancers to work. Choosing the editorial content was a hazardous process. If on the mostly nebulous schedule, for instance, there was an item about employment for women we would have a piece to set the subject in perspective: preparing a CV, written applications, interview tactics, sorting out childcare etc. But we had no foreknowledge of the angle that might be taken, or who the guests might be in relation to it. It might have been treated lightly or in depth, or might have been replaced by something else entirely.

We could never ensure our copy would get within cooee of what was on the screen. Each week's issue had to somehow represent the output of the five mornings, in essence at least. *This Morning* had strands which came from other TV regions such as Yorkshire, Tyne Tees, HTV and Border Television (all now part of the ITV network). With their cooperation sometimes we struck lucky and could feature the subject matter. Border's *Woolstrand*, for instance, gave a welcome fillip to dyed-in-the-wool and would-be knitters. That didn't happen often.

Health was one success, fronted by the popular medic Dr Chris Steele, from Manchester (now with an MBE, and still in residence on the show). Personal/relationship subjects worked for us too. They were dealt with by the empathetic and extremely professional northern novelist Denise Robertson whose own life story sounded like the stuff of fiction.

AGONY AND EMPATHY OF DENISE

Widowed twice, Denise Robertson brought up her own son with four stepsons and in 1997 married a childhood sweetheart, Bryan, who she hadn't seen for 43 years. She had her own website *DearDenise.com* but you need to read her autobiography *Agony? Don't Get Me Started* to appreciate the extraordinary sympathy and understanding she exuded, as her obituarists noted sadly in 2016. (Her book was published in 2006, after the death of one of her stepsons, from cancer, at 44, just after she received her MBE for service to 34 charities.)

I had to accept that the magazine's logo could not be the same as the TV programme's – though I didn't know until later it was because DD didn't have a contract. Our manipulation of it, done by a designer with desk-top publishing, never looked right. But that's all we had folks!

We managed to put together six issues, and the last three were mostly hagiographic – pages packed with everything bright and bubbly about Richard and Judy and their family that my feature writer could glean from spending time with them at the Liverpool studio. Backwards and forwards she went on the train – but at least it got her out of the office gloom.

This Morning continues as a TV programme but no magazine goes with it. Our one was never viable. Nothing really went right. Distribution, as appears obvious now from a distance, was never going to be easy. Just because millions tuned in every day, on couches all round the country, it was no guarantee they ever bought or even read magazines. It was the reverse of the Harvard 4P-plan which had made Bauer's magazines in the US a success.

All the companies I had worked for knew the ins and outs of publishing, this one had no experience at all (like Sir James Goldsmith who misjudged the market with *Now* magazine, 1979-81. At Bauer big bucks were spent on getting full-colour *Bella* to the readers each week (the Bauer mantra to editors is 'never say something was not accomplished because you didn't have enough money'), while the amount provided to produce *This Morning Magazine* meant that most of the pages were black and white, the paper quality extremely poor, resulting in a very limp product. Not a come-on for women buyers.

The whole project was ill conceived from the start. And my awareness antennae let me down. It never occurred to me that DD hadn't got the rights to publication secured. I should have asked to see the contract. I should have known a lot more about the TV show and its programme intentions, instead of presuming that journalists working on TV are just like those on magazines. In fact there is a big gulf, and I fell straight in.

To this day I do not know how DD could have expected to succeed. He couldn't have read the 1985 issue of *Folio*, an American magazine I came across on the web, which described the three basic rules for startups. 1: there must be a good size group of people who are interested enough in a specific field to buy a magazine and read about it. 2: there must be a continuing source of articles that are going to be of interest to those people. 3: first hand knowledge of a substantial body of suppliers who want to reach your readership group to sell them their products or services. The fourth, unwritten, rule was: unless you have experience in publishing you'd do better to buy another business.

We never got to first base on either 1 or 2. As for 3 and 4, DD knew little about publishing or processes of publishing. He seemed susceptible to bad advice, buying a computer system for desk-top publishing that was to link our office in Camden with that of the designer and production at Notting Hill, on the other side of London, but which never worked. Costs increased as copy and proofs had to be couriered between offices.

He was a devotee of Lord Bernstein, the legendary boss of Granada TV founded in 1954 in Manchester to provide independent television for the north of England. He believed that through him he had the inside running to the programme makers who would welcome this method of promoting *This Morning*.

He didn't get the go ahead until the fifth issue was

printed and already debts incurred were so great that he couldn't contemplate going on with it. He wanted a magazine produced out of thin air that looked as professional as *Woman* or *Woman's Own* and had a flavour of the big-selling dailies like *The Sun* and *Daily Express* with lots of numbers for the readers to call to add to Broadsystem's coffers. But one designer sitting at a computer in West London arranging type around pictures was never going to provide any pizzazz.

* * *

This was a sorry time in my life, but what I failed to do was soon to be the start of another revolution in publishing. In 1990 the BBC bought Redwood, producers of what are called contract magazines (created specifically for household-name companies like the AA, M&S, American Express, for instance), and formed BBC Worldwide, a commercial arm set up to maximise the value of the BBC's assets. This brought to the market big, glossy magazines allied to TV programmes.

Joy Davies, ex *Woman*, was the brains behind *BBC Good Food*, subsequently edited by another magazine journalist Mitzie Wilson. It reached a quarter century in 2014 with a monthly circulation of 1,357,000 and a website following of 13m people.

Gardeners' World was a great success, its editors/presenters becoming household names. *Homes & Antiques* was the inspiration of Jill Churchill, after she left *Family Circle,* succeeding on the back of *The Antiques Road Show*. (The long-running BBC TV show now has its own monthly magazine produced by Kelsey Media, specialists in life-style and practical publications.)

Much forward planning was essential but the money was there to pay the contributors who were the presenters. They found their readers from the start through their interests and hobbies. Complaints poured in from IPC and Emap whose similar magazines suffered: all they saw was endless free advertising on a channel supposedly not allowed to run ads or mention or show products. Other publishers said that the BBC had an unfair advantage and it took a long time to sort out.

The vital year was 2011 when Exponent Private Equity bought BBC Magazines, the UK's fourth largest magazine publisher, selling 82m copies a year, for £121m. Among 34 magazines now in the Exponent stable were *Radio Times, Olive, Gardens Illustrated, Top Gear, Lonely Planet* and *Good Food*, published under licence (the BBC retained control over several) by Immediate Media. Then, in 2017, a third very large German publishing company, Hubert Burda Media, paid an undisclosed sum for Immediate Media, and the UK magazine publishing world changed again.

* * *

The web allowed me to find out about the man I called DD (to me, he had a remarkable similarity to the cartoon character Daffy Duck). It was a revelation, for Stephen Kirk became something of a leading light in modern business. On his website, *BodyMindUnbounded*, he said that he struggled with the tension between his inner mind and cultural expectations. Discovering TM in the 1970s changed his future, giving him a "calling" (his word) to go into business: "This was a great surprise as I had no business experience (I was a computer systems analyst) and…had no interest in commerce."

First he set up Cable London, with cable franchises in five boroughs, then founded "an interactive TV company Broadsystem". Its Camden headquarters were almost next door to TV-AM where *Good Morning Britain* was launched in 1983 by broadcasters known as the Famous Five: David Frost, Robert Kee, Michael Parkinson, Angela Rippon and Anna Ford; it ran until 1992. [A programme of the same name continues today on ITV.]

Broadsystem pioneered premium rate telephony services for publishers and broadcasters – somewhere I saw this activity described as 'a licence to print money'. (Special phone numbers provide recorded or live information and charge a higher rate, allowing businesses to be funded by the calls, and are subject to regulation.)

Its main contract was with *The Daily Mirror* and Stephen Kirk tried to sell Broadsystem to its owner, Robert Maxwell, in 1989, but failed. In 1990 he sold it to News International (after "a personal chat with Rupert Murdoch"). In the decade that he worked for News Corporation, Skytalk, Sky TV's telephone service, started.

His journey to the top slowed, he says on his website, when he "began to believe the corporate myths about money and power", and in 1999 a diagnosis of colon cancer, and a successful operation, changed his future. Suddenly he had the determination "to devote my life to helping others". This was when he sold his stake in the Murdoch venture. It must have given him a useful kitty.

In keeping with modern times, he trained as a Master Neuro-Linguistic Programming (NLP) Practitioner and an executive coach with a passion "to help people transform into happier versions of their true selves". He does this in conjunction with Luiza Hardwick, his partner and second wife. His book *Enlightened Business*, written in 2009, is an invitation, he says, "to embrace business as a powerful tool to express who you really are, and to make the world a better place as a result." Its subtitle is 'making a living without selling your soul'.

He was a non executive director of Elisabeth Murdoch's TV production company Shine from 2003 to 2011 when it was sold to News Corporation, her father's international group. This was the year when phones, the hacking of them, caused a scandal that has preoccupied the UK for years (with claims still unsettled as I write).

The year before, I had been reminded of those constantly ringing phones at Broadsystem when phones and premium numbers featured in the disastrous voting system for popular television talent programmes on the BBC and Sky. Apologies had to be made and both broadcasters were required to repay voters the cost of the calls which had been made after the lines had closed.

Finding his website filled in many gaps. I could recall that he had a house in Hampstead Garden Suburb, one of Britain's most expensive addresses, had a wife and family, liked to support small theatres and when confronted with problems he didn't have answers for he would literally get under his large desk and hide. There was no mention of *This Morning Magazine.*

* * *

Things were very unpleasant in the last days. He saw me as a cause of the disaster and I was legally required to stay at that desk alone in the basement until the end of January 1989, sending back pictures we'd borrowed and archiving the magazine. I was emotionally drained but very glad, and deeply sad, to walk out of that building clutching only the kind letter Denise Robertson had sent wishing me well.

In light of what I found on *BodyMindUnbounded,* it wasn't so extraordinary that I too had to seek help to find a happier version of myself. What brought me back to life was an alternative therapy called ReBirthing, that aims to cleanse the body of negative blocks and beliefs. It combines gentle massage with a breathing technique that releases stored stress, pain and emotional trauma.

You might not notice that when stress strikes you lose the ability to breathe deeply, taking air right into the lungs and expanding them, so oxygen is carried to all the body cells. Your emotions prevent your body working to optimum capacity. The practitioner's home was near Wandsworth Common in London. At the first session I was almost knocked out by the effect, the way it made me cry. It took just two more sessions to bring a smile back to my face and a determination to start afresh, to recover from my appalling failure.

Though I felt better about myself and more optimistic,

I wasn't sure how it had all happened and I am indebted to Phillippa Perry, a psychotherapist (married to the cross-dressing artist Grayson Perry), for her explanation of what can be done if you find yourself in emotional difficulties. The brain, it seems, is plastic (ie, adaptable) and we can make new neural connections to change the chemistry and improve self-soothing, and self-regulation.

Some people who are in a downward spiral may need medication, others (like me) may need a new set of behaviours with four underlying and supportive structures:

1, a safe trusting reliable relationship (I felt I had this with my husband and family who had tried hard to help me during this time);

2, good stress from learning something new to enable the brain to make new connections (I decided to try and learn French properly);

3, develop your self-observational style (it took real and concentrated effort to notice my feelings and thoughts without judgment); and

4, get a fresh perspective on your life (I had to let go of the fixed ways I had of defining myself).

After the ReBirthing sessions, I had a mantra that I only had to repeat to myself in my mind to make me feel strong again and focused on the present. And I went back to playing tennis regularly so my body was getting a workover as well. But I didn't know whether I had, or wanted, a future in journalism.

One good thing came from my ghastly experience: it made me give up smoking forever. Suddenly the words used by Gillian Riley, the originator of a weekend course called 'Full Stop', which I attended while at *Woman*, made sense: the cigarette controls you. It took me some time to notice that whenever the phone rang, I'd pick it up with my left hand and light a cigarette with my right. I didn't seem capable of holding a conversation without a cigarette between my fingers. It was time for me to take control of my life. On December 29, 1988, I threw my fags and lighter in the bin and never smoked again.

Gillian's original counselling experience was with food addiction (with the same message, that it is the food that controls you) and her approach is most pertinent today with the troubling concern over obesity. Her methods are included in a book called *Full Stop* (which I would recommend to anyone needing to break deep-seated, and destructive, habits) and you can check out her user-friendly website *eatingless.com*

14

ABUNDANCE IN THE 80S

The second half of the 1980s was an extraordinary time, particularly in parts of the Soviet Union where fervour for political change was surfacing. In the UK, money was at the root. First were the get-rich-quick privatisations of state-owned gas and phones promoted by Prime Minister Margaret Thatcher. Then came the people's marches against the Poll Tax that Thatcher wanted to impose which were reminiscent of the anti-Vietnam protests in the 1960s (that I was part of). And in the world of magazines, it was vibrant, with many changes and launches (including *Bella*, *Best* and *Prima*, and *Working Woman*, the short-lived monthly).

In 1988 Emap expanded from the 'hobby' field to produce *More!*, a fortnightly supposedly focusing on fashion for the late teens and early 20s but which aimed to be feisty, forthright about sex, and a female alternative to a new 'lad mag' (*For Him* started in 1987 and became *FHM* in 1995). The Duchess of *Woman's Own* would surely have noted the presence of the 'dog's dick'.

The same year Terry Hornett, who'd sold his company Carlton to Reed in 1987 (titles included *Options*, *Looks*, *Country Homes & Interiors*, and *Woman's World*), launched *Riva*. It was the first "upmarket weekly for the post feminist woman" with Sally O'Sullivan as editor, and Rose Wild (ex *Woman*) as her deputy. It was post feminism too soon. It lasted for six issues.

Over 21, edited by Pat Roberts-Cairns, a former colleague at *First Lady*, came to an end that year (but Pat went on to edit *Good Housekeeping*, from 1996-98). Murdoch's News International produced *New Woman*, with Frankie McGowan (who started out on *Petticoat*) as editor, for 25-40 year olds. It was later bought by Emap and edited by Gill Hudson.

IPC launched *Marie Claire*, a French inspired monthly, with the refreshingly sparky Glenda Bailey at the helm. It was a bright combination of fashion and pertinently newsy in-depth features about women around the world. The Spanish sailed in with *Hello!*, a British version of its star-struck *Ola!*. Maggie Goodman (who'd launched the young women's monthly *Company* at NatMags in 1978) took up the challenge of introducing, in glorious colour, superior and well-heeled European gentry and unknown celebrities to awed, and receptive, Brits. Especially those frequenting hair salons.

In 1990 Sally Cartwright, who'd worked for both IPC and Harmsworth Publications, became publishing director and *Hello!* really took off. Producing a weekly magazine to the standards set by the Spanish was a huge task, solved by having two editors working on alternate issues. The two Maggies – Goodman, and Koumi, former editor of *19* magazine – were a great double act for years.

A company called GE Publishing, set up in 1986 as magazine packagers in a similar way to Carlton, in 1988 presented IPC with two new magazines to market: *Me* (designed to compete with the weeklies *Best* and *Bella*) and *Essentials* (a full-on challenge to the monthly *Prima*) which Gilly Cubitt edited from 1990 to 1994. Later she was editor of BBC's *Vegetarian Good Food* (closed 2000).

The G in GE was Liz Glaze who was responsible for the part work *Robert Carrier's Kitchen* published by Marshall Cavendish in the 1980s. Called the 'Peter Pan of Food', American-born Carrier was a chef, author and restaurateur and was well known in the UK for his TV appearances and articles in magazines, mostly *Good Housekeeping, Vogue* and the *Sunday Times Magazine*.

Like other influential foodie pundits at the time (Elizabeth David, Jane Grigson and Claudia Roden) he focused on developing the palate and discovering new tastes. His last years were spent in Morocco, then the south of France where he died in 2006, aged 82, with "his friend Liz Glaze by his side" said his *Daily Mirror* obituary.

* * *

In 1988 IPC Magazines paid £28m for International Thomson Publishing which brought *Family Circle* and *Living* into the mêlée at Kings Retch (as it was far from fondly known by those who worked there). The key, for IPC, was having pride of place in supermarkets so they would be able to place more of their products on the racks near the checkouts where shoppers queued.

However, round the corner from Reed's HQ a new publishing enterprise began which would affect their plans. Started by the husband and wife team Michael Wynn-Jones and Delia Smith (they met when working on the short-lived *Mirror Magazine*), *Sainsbury's Magazine* took pride of place near tills countrywide.

The irony of magazine publishing strikes again! When Thomson re-created and relaunched *Family Circle* in the 1980s, as quid pro quo for keeping its favoured position in Sainsbury's, the editorial staff contributed pages to help readers make the most of the supermarket. Mary Berry's sweet confections were a regular feature.

COOKERY'S FAVOURITE COVER GIRL

Mary Berry is today a household name, renowned for her television baking know-how. Her *Family Circle* specials – at Christmas and Easter – were popular for years. But ever-demanding pursuit of new ideas to include in the Sainsbury's section, different from what was in the rest of the magazine, became a burden. It may even have been this that changed the contract. Whatever the reason, celebrities replaced cakes on the covers. Then the final irony. Mary, who had been food editor on *Housewife* and *Ideal Home,* became a cover girl in her ninth decade (though not on *Family Circle* which closed in 2006 after 42 years). Mary's face on *The Lady, Good Housekeeping* and *You* magazine attracted readers who loved watching the TV show. She was made a Dame in the Queen's birthday honours in 2020.

Could anybody have foreseen that long ago how powerful and huge the supermarkets in the UK would become, how dominant in all areas of our life they would be? That they would sell magazines and newspapers, making life difficult for local newsagents and chains like W H Smith and Menzies? And produce their own magazines to give away to encourage loyalty.

The world of contract publishing captured the big stores: Tesco, Asda, Debenhams, M&S, John Lewis. All put their products in front of the shoppers in their own tailored publications – filled with advertising that aims to reach a particular group of buyers. A perfect package. As Thomson had set up years before.

In 1989 (according to Reed International's *Chapters from our history*), IPC reacted to emerging or ever-present competition by redesigning its 'big four titles': "*Woman* was given a practical emphasis to distinguish it from *Woman's Own* so that both would appeal to a younger woman. *Woman's Realm* [with Sue Garland – nee Reid, ex *Bella* – as editor] was restyled 'to attract a segment other than the more mature reader of *Woman's Weekly*.' The logo, design and typeface of *Woman's Journal* were changed to capture the older, more glamorous market."

The "older, more glamorous" market did not respond as the publishers hoped. It is a most difficult readership concept, yet *Journal* was the magazine that Laurie Purden loved most of all the ones she'd worked on. After 10 years, she chose to retire. And time was not on its side. Into her shoes stepped former editor of *19* Deirdre Vine (until 1997), followed by ex-*Cosmopolitan* editor Marcelle

D'Argy Smith (1998), then Elsa McAlonan (1999) who was there at the magazine's end in 2002.

* * *

The Government announced plans in 1989 to deregulate TV and radio listings, so broadcasters could sell information about their programmes to anyone for a price. Peter Davis, CEO at Reed, acted quickly, buying the popular *TV Times* from Independent Television Publications. For Richard Barber, who had left *Woman* to edit this magazine, it must have been a shock.

Finding himself back in the company of John Mellon (IPC chief executive from 1986) and Mike Matthew, he resigned, joining contract publisher Redwood. Here he set up and ran *Good Idea*, Woolworths' free magazine which shoppers really liked. [This high-street mainstay of the UK came to a disastrous end in 2009. In the 1990s Richard edited *OK!* magazine, changing it from a monthly to a weekly.]

Poised on the IPC carousel was Richard's old Carlton colleague Bridget Rowe who left *Woman's Own* for *TV Times*. She moved on, a few years later, to edit *The Sunday Mirror* and then *The People* – of her tenures, journalist Bill Hagerty wrote in the *New Statesman* in December 2000: "The only market she knew was so low it's a wonder she didn't strike oil". [Bridget died of Covid in January 2021, aged 70. Wikipedia says she was a friend of UKIP originator Nigel Farage.]

For the first time since they were launched in the 1930s, the biggest selling IPC weeklies were edited simultaneously by men: David Durman at *Woman* and Keith McNeill at *Woman's Own*. It didn't last; McNeill died in 1998 and was replaced by Terry Tavner, a woman (with a male-sounding name), formerly of *Chat*.

In the US, a glossy, perfect bound (as opposed to stapled) magazine called *Lear's* was causing a stir. First published in February 1988, it was named after its founder and editor Frances Lear who, in her late 60s, found herself with a handy $100m (from a divorce settlement), some of which she used to create a monthly publication for "women who weren't born yesterday".

Readers would be aged over 35 and interested in "women's and progressive issues". Smart, stylish and for grown-up females. It sounded terrific, but being different doesn't always get you anywhere with advertisers. Frances Lear objected to women "being defined by age rather than by sensibility and mindset". And she discovered a horrid truth (which I would also have to grapple with later): 'older' was a most damaging word because its perceived synonym was 'no sexuality'.

Then I heard about Ita Buttrose, my old Tweedledee of simultaneous pregnancy days. In 1979 she had been made OBE (Order of the British Empire) in the Queen's Birthday Honours (Australia makes its own recommendations), and in 1988 was put among the most august as an Officer of the Order of Australia (AO), in recognition of her accomplishments in journalism and charities.

Regarded as a trailblazer, twice she had been officially voted Australia's most admired or popular woman. She was chair of the National Advisory Committee on AIDS, and despite her lisp (a sibilant 's' problem) had her own radio show on Sydney's 2KY. She thought *Lear's* and what it stood for an idea worth trying.

Australia may be the world's biggest island, but the population is small (relatively speaking) and through the power of the press everyone knew Ita, what she looked like, who she was, how she sounded. Just like the Queen over here, wherever she went she was recognised. She was known as the "iconic Australia sheila" (not her words, but an admirer's) and so a magazine with her name on it would have no trouble being accepted. I read that she started it because she didn't want to go on working for others as she had done from the age of 15.

ITA MAKES HER NAME FAMOUS
For much of her career, Ita Buttrose was employed by
one or other of Australia's media magnates Kerry
Packer and Rupert Murdoch. She had burst through the
so-called glass ceiling with ease becoming one of the
first women directors of Australian Consolidated Press
(started by Sir Frank Packer) and publisher of its
women's division. She was the first woman to run a
major metropolitan newspaper (editor-in-chief of the
***Daily Telegraph* and *Sunday Telegraph* in Sydney) and the**
first Australian woman to be on the board of News Ltd
Australia. Now she would have a magazine with her
name on it.

She set up her own company, Capricorn Publishing (she and her daughter have this birthsign), bringing out the first issue of *Ita*, with herself plus dog on the cover, in 1989. I wrote immediately to congratulate her on the new venture, offering to send her, if she wished, a monthly update from London on whatever topics she felt would appeal to readers who weren't born yesterday. I explained that I was now freelance, hence the availability.

* * *

During the first half of 1989 I did a few short-term jobs (such as working on the subs' desk at the *Sunday Mirror Magazine* which Rose Wild had joined after the end of *Riva*) but I found myself enjoying being at home, living in the time I was in. I indulged in people watching, an essential habit for a journalist, and I'd never looked so closely before at my own high street, particularly on weekdays when I would normally have been working at a desk somewhere.

My eyes lit on the number of older people, mostly women with grey curly-permed heads, who walked badly, slowly, with sticks or leaning on a push-along shopper as though it were a zimmer frame. I'd see them mostly at Woolworths, lining up at the clear plastic boxes that held the sweets bought by weight. Was this comfort eating?

My garden was a refuge. I'd worked very long hours at *Bella* and *This Morning*, often with little sleep and despite Margaret Thatcher's belief that she (and ipso facto all of us) did very well on four or five hours a night, this is just not enough for the body to do its restorative work. I had to learn to relax again, to be in the company of family and friends without my mind being miles away.

When you have had a failure in your life the urge to go over and over things in your mind, 'endless rumination' as it is known, is neither fun nor healthy. I had to learn to differentiate between what I could control (and was worth pursuing), and what I couldn't (and had to be jettisoned). And I found gardening a wonderful therapy.

I also asked a neighbour (Sue, a bilingual secretary who worked at the French Embassy) if she'd give me lessons in the language I have always loved and in my mind can hear myself speaking easily. The reality is somewhat different, and I put this down to having been taught French for five years by an Australian who learnt his French from an Australian. My down-to-earth father (who died in 1986) never understood why anyone needed it (and it was beyond him why I studied Latin, which no one spoke).

Sue was patience personified as I worked from the children's grammar book used in French schools from the early years. I was a whizz at translating and understanding what she was saying, but often tongue-tied with my replies. Yet if things had been different I might have grown up speaking French (as would my father).

In Australia you can hear varied pronunciations of the many areas (in Tasmania and Western Australia particularly) named after the explorers who were looking for the new world at the same time as the British in the 18th and 19th centuries. Australia might have ended up as a French colony in 1788 had not a storm prevented Captain Laperouse from landing to plant the *drapeau tricolore*.

Somehow, the First Fleet commander Captain Arthur Phillip, with his cargo of convicts, avoided the weather to establish the first British colony on January 26 at Port Jackson on the east coast, north of Botany Bay (Botany and La Perouse are today suburbs of Sydney). But for that storm I might have been born in *Australie*.

One Monday in July I saw a small ad in *The Guardian* seeking an editor for a new project aimed at an older age group. I didn't consider myself grown-up enough yet to be a *Good Housekeeping* reader, but my 50th birthday was on the horizon and I was worried what this would mean in employment terms. I sent off a letter expressing interest and attaching my CV – the jobs I'd done, books I'd written or edited. I chose not to mention *This Morning*.

* * *

I was invited to attend an interview in Clerkenwell to meet Norman Wright and Heather Aylott. The *London A to Z* came up trumps with the unknown square in the unknown area near Farringdon. I climbed the stairs to a large room on the first floor that held a few desks. Surely it couldn't be another *Bella*, could it?

In this case, it wasn't the Germans but the French who had established an alliance with a large publishing company in the UK. Emap, based in Peterborough, was not as well known as the big players like IPC and National Magazines but growing steadily with many niche-market publications: 'hobby' magazines targeting specific readers who fish, cycle and garden, run, go caravanning, take photographs, follow films and the music scene, etc etc.

Emap started spreading its wings in 1987 with *For Him Magazine* (which became *FHM*), for the 'new lads' market. In 1988 came *More!*, a fortnightly for modern teenagers, and the monthly *New Woman* – its first entry into the women's, 30s-something market. In 1989 it launched *Empire*, a hugely successful movie magazine, and expanded its radio group. Broadcasting was energised with new, fresh stations with names such as Smooth, Melody and Heart.

Emap, as I was to discover, was an extraordinary media company. The initials stand for East Midlands Allied Press which owned 17 newspapers in the 1950s, the decade it branched out into 'magazines in newspaper format' as a way of keeping the printing presses active. Feeding the interests (ie, hobbies) of men was clever. First came *Angling Times* (in 1953), then *Trout and Salmon*, *Motorcycle News* and *Garden News*.

HOW WORDS MADE EMAP'S FORTUNE
Emap's advance as a publisher and place in the history of magazines really started in 1978 with the launch of a teen paper/magazine called *Smash Hits*, a fortnightly containing the lyrics of current hit songs. In 12 months the circulation went from 10,000 to 1,000,000. Incredible! It is hard to imagine today that so many wanted to read the words of the songs on the hit parade, the top 100, but that's what happened.

Robin Miller, who started as a cub reporter on *Motorcycle News*, ended up as company chairman. Emap's success was due to Miller's partnership with the very tall (6ft 7in in the old measure, the distance we were to keep between each other at the start of the coronavirus crisis) and soigné David Arculus. So said former journalist Colin Morrison, an Emap director from 1992-96, responsible for the b2b (business to business) division.

"Emap at its best was a bunch of brave, daring, agile teams nudged, influenced and encouraged by Miller and Arculus," wrote Morrison on *Flashes&Flames*, his online site (September 2011).

"Many of the magazines they produced are groundbreakers: *Just 17*, *Looks*, *Bliss*, *More!*, *FHM*, *Q*, *Mojo*, *Empire*, *Heat*, *Closer* and *Grazia* – though some came about after Miller and Arculus had left. But it was the culture they created, touchy-feely management, encouraging employees to be shareholders, that made Emap Britain's best media company." [Becoming a save-as-you-earn shareholder would make a difference to my life later.]

Norman Wright was Emap born and bred. His career started in his late teens on *Angling Times* and now he was the managing director of Choice Publications, a new division of Emap that would focus on people in the third age – *le troisième âge* which, I was to learn, was a French concept. Ex-journalist Heather Aylott was the publisher. She and her photographer husband had spent some time in the US where they worked at the notorious and popular *National Enquirer*, crossing paths with Dennis Neeld, the man who orchestrated *Bella*'s start in the UK.

Choice was already being produced under the aegis of the Pre-Retirement Association (PRA), a charity which aimed to prepare men and women for the years after paid work ended. Now a new future was planned for the magazine, along the lines of *Notre Temps* (Our Time), a monthly selling over a million (yes, 1m), produced by Bayard Presse in Paris. It sounded fascinating and I took away a few issues to report on, in terms of how its content would appeal here.

* * *

C ross Channel publishing had started in the 1980s and I needed to find out how the 'anglicisation' was tackled and who had been involved. *Elle*, a fortnightly, was the first to arrive, in 1985, with Sally Brampton, formerly of *The Observer* magazine and someone tipped by *Vogue* as going places, as editor. Its bright style influenced fashion and home magazines in the UK, particularly in the way readers shopped and happily bought goods with the magazine's name on them. Today *Elle* is the world's biggest selling fashion magazine with international editions and websites.

[Sally wrote one of the most remarkable and moving books I have ever read: *Shoot the damn dog: a memoir of depression*. She took her own life in 2016, aged 60.]

Also from France came *Marie Claire*, which was a phenomenon. In 2001, Glenda Bailey was appointed editor of the prestigious US fashion magazine *Harper's Bazaar* (succeeding Liz Tilberis who had died of ovarian cancer). Caroline Roux who had worked with her at the British *Marie Claire*, wrote about it in *The Guardian*.

"When *Marie Claire* was launched in 1988...it was a breath of fresh air...a magazine for women who read newspapers and a magazine launched in the 1980s for the 1990s. It was socially and politically aware." Excellent photographers, real women telling real stories, fashion "with interesting narratives" and no room for children – certainly a different formula.

Emap had established an alliance in Europe, with publishers Hachette Filipacchi, and launched *Red* in 1989, for women in their 'middle youth': ie, 30 to 39 year olds. It was different (and still is today), but its main contribution to the magazine world was the cover mount, an obsession that affected magazines for the next 20 years.

Psychologies, a Hachette Filipacchi publication which sells well in France, launched here in 2005. In charge was Maureen Rice, who had previously edited *19* magazine and *Options* (launched 1982, closed 1990 when Jo Foley was editor). Described as 'the thinking woman's glossy' it aimed to find readers who didn't want a magazine filled with celebrities and shopping. They would be "fully functioning adults", Rice was quoted as saying, not people with problems. She put female personalities on the cover and tried to make it clear that the content wasn't about neurotics or neuroses but self-understanding and empowerment. After four years, during which the circulation reached 140,000 then dropped back, New Zealander Louise Chunn took her place.

Louise worked on *Fashion Weekly* in the US before coming to London and joining Emap's new *Just 17*, which she eventually edited. Her career moves are most impressive: *Elle* (with Sally Brampton), *The Guardian* woman's page (after Brenda Polan left), *Vogue*, *ES* Magazine (for the London *Evening Standard*), *InStyle* (where she was deputy to Dee Nolan and became editor when she left), and then *Good Housekeeping*. Her tenure was short. Lindsay Nicholson had been editor-in-chief at *Prima* before being enticed to the top job at GH, which she held for years. She returned to the chair she'd vacated for Louise – and stayed there until 2017. She is an MBE and a winner of the Mark Boxer Lifetime Achievement Award.

After *Psychologies* (which was sold on to Kelsey Media) Louise started her own find-a-therapy website, *welldoing.org*, with "content devoted to self development, mental health and wellbeing". The need for it was based on her own experience of losing her job, redundancy and the anger and hurt which resulted.

TERRIBLE TRAGEDY ON THE THAMES

The *Marchioness* disaster on the River Thames in August 1989 was a ghastly shock. Alison McDonald, who was running the *Style* section of *The Sunday Times*, called me at home to tell me about the tragedy. The Thames ferry had been chosen for the birthday party of a young man deeply involved in the world of fashion and beauty. It went horribly wrong when the boat was hit by an 880 tonne dredger, *Bowbelle*, in the dark of a moonless night. What was to be a celebration turned to catastrophe: the *Marchioness* sank within minutes and 51 young people lost their lives. Because most of the party-goers were linked to *Bella* and other magazines, almost everyone knew someone who had died. The devastated parents formed the Marchioness Action Group which successfully campaigned for the introduction of lifeboats on the Thames, for new laws on being in charge of vessels under the influence of alcohol, and training for police family liaison officers.

I had no difficulty writing an enthusiastic report on the French magazines. The stories of the men and women across the Channel whose activities in older age made the Brits look couch bound entranced me. There was a feeling of inspiration ion all the pages whether it was food to be cooked or vitamins needed for health, or the latest information on medical procedures, music or books.

In the centre was a section, *Vos doigts,* with a range of topical topics such as money, investment, working as a volunteer, being a grandparent. The overall essence of the articles was that rights were closely tied to responsibilities, an approach I rather liked. And it was matter of fact, upbeat, didn't sound like preaching.

At the next meeting at Clerkenwell I met Hubert Chicou, the Bayard Presse director of the *Choice* venture. Thin as a rake and charming, Hubert spoke English well, looked directly at me when he spoke and listened carefully to what I said. His questions were about the subject matter in the magazines and its appropriateness here.

He told me about Bayard's background in educational and religious publishing, about *Notre Temps* being a staple in the lives of older people all over France. Norman gave me some copies of the existing *Choice* to take away and report on in the light of material from *Notre Temps* being available for our use.

A week later I handed over my report to Norman and Emap's Editorial Director Kevin Hand, the man who was in line to be chief executive and was propelling the company into the big time. It was he who could see great possibilities in a French connection. The meeting was very informal. We mostly stood around the table looking at the magazines spread out, talking about layout and design. Then Kevin, almost off hand, asked me "What do you think went wrong at *This Morning?*"

I felt myself blushing all over. I probably mumbled something like "a bad decision on my part" and can't really remember the rest of the interview. (Later I was to learn that at the time of issue four, Stephen Kirk had sought help from some magazine publishers hoping to find a partner. But the ship was already sinking and Kevin, at Emap, and Iris Burton, Editorial Director at IPC, could not be convinced it was worth saving.)

I thought 'That's it, I'll never hear from them again.' But to my amazement I did. And I was offered the job of editor-in chief-of what I consider the most exciting magazine of my career.

The only regret I had was that I had to write to Ita Buttrose and tell her that I couldn't now see my way clear to being a London correspondent for her eponymous magazine after all. She wished me well. [*Ita* and *Lear's* both came to an end in 1994.]

15

MAKING THE OLD THE NEW

My induction into the world of *Notre Temps* and *le troisième âge* took place over three days in October 1989. I flew to Paris and spent each day at the Bayard Presse building, in its own street, rue Bayard, near the ultra chic Avenue de Champs-Elysées. Aware of my lack of fluency in French (I did try!), Hubert arranged for a simultaneous translator to be by my side. Françoise helped me enthusiastically, asking my questions or giving my answers. I filled several notebooks as I listened to people explaining their roles in the magazine that had millions of readers.

Bayard is one of France's oldest publishing groups with three target markets: youth, seniors and religious. It is a private company owned by the Assumptionist religious order, adherents of the Roman Catholic Church, but Bayard Presse is independent and is run on a non-profit basis with profits ploughed back into the business. My up-to-date source on Bayard is encyclopedia.com from which I learnt about the daily newspaper *La Croix*. In the 1890s it "proudly declared itself the most anti-Jewish newspaper in France" but when the Assumptionist order was expelled at the start of the 20ᵗʰ century, and legislation was passed guaranteeing official separation of church and state, it moderated its views. In the 1990s it changed from an evening to a morning daily, sold by subscription.

Magazines are Bayard's prime focus – more than 200 are published worldwide with five million subscribers – among them ones for seniors in Belgium, the Netherlands, Spain and Canada, and publications for the young from three to 13. In France they sell via a type of 'at home party system' (like Tupperware used to) or at village fetes. This allows mothers to earn an income and also introduces young people to having magazines delivered regularly to them at home. And that's the secret of their success, that all ages like getting mail addressed to them. In the UK Bayard sells their children's magazines (*Chickadee*, *Owl*, *Chirp*, *Discovery*) via the web.

The company organises and runs trade fairs in Europe and publishes books to interest and inspire older people. One I have translates as *A Practical Guide to Memory – at all ages*. On the front is a besuited and smiling character, holding aloft a golden key, an image that sums up instantly the subject matter. Gabs, the illustrator, had found a way to be reassuring about a worrying subject.

Bayard takes its supporting role seriously. It produced a pamphlet called *SeniorScopie*, in which topics allied to older age are analysed or explained and the findings or projections backed by statistics. This goes to the media and advertising agencies, its purpose to trounce myths.

Notre Temps could prove that seniors, retired, old, aged people – whatever they were called – were a vital part of a community and should not be ignored or written off. Being on the verge of this new stage of vitality, it really appealed to me.

* * *

The relaunched *Choice* would be the January 1990 issue. I had under two months to find an editorial team and produce a magazine along *Notre Temps* lines that would establish us as the leading publication in the field. Then – as I've mentioned before – the magical osmosis in publishing occurred. There would be competition.

The Oldie was about to appear, with *Private Eye* originator Richard Ingrams in the editor's chair, as was *Modern Maturity*, along the lines of its American counterpart produced by the American Association of Retired Persons (AARP). There was also *Saga*, the magazine of the company that organised holidays for older-age groups, available on subscription.

[Following a management buyout and venture capital backing, *Saga* is big business: 500,000 subscribers plus an active website. Like all companies involved in travel, the 2020 coronavirus crisis will have had an effect but a rescue plan by its previous owner aims to give it new life.]

I had a lot to learn about retirement. In France and Belgium, I was told, it was almost an altruistic act (as more jobs would be available to be filled by younger people). And with time available retirees could reap rewards after years of hard work. The problem is that it is the people in work who are paying for those in retirement and when times are financially difficult governments require people to remain employed for more years before receiving state benefits. Raising retirement ages is not popular.

If people are living longer, are in better health and likely to spend as much time in retirement as they did at work, they need an income on which to survive. This is a challenge most societies face. Everyone needs to to understand how the system works, how what you pay in while you are working is used. It is not, as I read somewhere, a giant Ponzi scheme, a word that came to the fore when the ghastly shenanigans of an American called Bernie Madoff were revealed.

Madoff's outrageous investment fraud, called a pyramid scheme, involved paying existing investors from funds contributed by new investors rather than from profits derived from the funds' investment. It seems incredible that not only was the money paid into the scheme never invested by Madoff but that no one seemed to know this. The investors didn't ask because they thought they were on to a good thing and Madoff cleverly created phoney account statements that showed consistently good results even in turbulent times. (That should have been a warning!)

The original Ponzi, in the 1920s, enticed newcomers with the incredible promise of providing a 50% return in just 90 days. Investors flocked in, both the wealthy and the greedy – and all ignored two vital financial rules: 1. if it seems too good to be true it probably is, and 2. don't put all your eggs (eg, savings) in one basket.

When investors in Madoff's venture decided to bring

their accounts to an end and take their 'winnings', he didn't have the cash to pay them. He was a swindler and was sent to jail for 150 years though that didn't help those he harmed. Never forget those two financial rules.

* * *

The Berlin wall came down on November 9, 1989, and two days later, on my 50th birthday, those who would be part of the new *Choice* met in a room above the Cheshire Cheese, the oldest pub in London's Fleet Street, to hear the plans. I could tell the gathering – which included marketing, advertising and subscription staff who were based at the Emap HQ in Peterborough – about the French success and how we would try and emulate it. Readers would learn about people of their own age – what they were doing in the world around them, their roles in retirement, opportunities available. The first issue, dated January, had to be completed well before Christmas.

Armed with the philosophy of *Notre Temps* – to enable and empower by demystifying and encouraging – in my mind I could see how *Choice* could work. But we needed to find the right staff. Kevin Hand had brought Stanley Glazer into the Emap fold as an adviser on magazine design. Stan had made his reputation at *TV Times* (the old one, in the 1970s, with Peter Jackson as editor) and had worked with Jill Churchill to revitalise *Family Circle*.

He suggested I meet Malcolm Gipson who had been art-trained at *TV Times*, *Good Housekeeping* and *Home & Freezer Digest*. Malcolm, cheerful and good-natured, grasped instantly what the new *Choice* would be and after a meeting with Norman, accepted the job and set about creating spreads, using images from *Notre Temps*. And he found two illustrators who would produce the light relief on what could be considered dry or even solemn subjects.

Robert Bloomfield had a long career as a children's book illustrator. But he was now in the age group of our readers and happily came up with humorous drawings to enliven articles about pensions, tax traps or Serps (you might well ask! Explaining the State Earnings-Related Pension Scheme which ran from 1978 to 2002 was like translating from a foreign language.).

Martin Shovel brought life to the Pre-Retirement Association columns, at the back of the magazine as part of a contractual deal, with a character not unlike the one on *Notre Temps* publications. He studied philosophy at Sussex University, is an author, and taught English to foreign students using a cartoon-based approach.

I was delighted when Janet Horwood agreed to join us from *Woman* to be features editor. Having sharpened her French as an au pair in Paris before she went to university, she was brilliant when Hubert and others from *Notre Temps* came to visit.

As well as translating the articles which we adapted for *Choice* – the health ones in particular, which had positive images and saved us having to create them here – she came up with story after story featuring older people doing things of interest all over the country, and coordinated the efforts of the many freelancers writing for us. With her divorce from William Horwood well behind her, she was happy with John, a teacher. (Like the children's early reading series *Janet and John*, she said.)

The editorial team at *Choice* was small, talented and enthusiastic. Deputy editor/chief sub June Weatherall, a friend of Heather Aylott, had happily left her job on an East Anglian paper to get back into magazines. Rachel Symonds joined us as sub and contributor. We had freelance help from Simmy Richman (who became a columnist on the *Independent on Sunday*) and Heather brought her PA and friend Teresa Palmano as office manager.

I don't remember how we found Robert Cubbon, verging on 21 and a dedicated picture researcher, but I'm glad we did. Some of us must have seemed very old to him, like working with a lot of mothers and fathers. Usually he was courtesy itself but just once, when there was just too much to do and too many demands, he met one request with "I don't give a flying f...", an expression, which in the open-plan workspace, was clearly heard by all – and brought the house down. Those first months giving *Choice* new life literally ate time and having a good laugh was a real tonic.

Our first year was hectic, each issue coming together between our London office and the printer in Peterborough via the fax machine. Today faxes are hardly used but then they ran hot and at any time of day there would be someone standing by, either sending or receiving pages or putting in a new toner cartridge.

Malcolm drove up the M1 to Peterborough to pass the pages for press. In the second year we moved on to computers, another learning curve for us all, a marvellous innovation using small screen Apple Mac Classics. It was like inventing the wheel...

* * *

A friend who had no links with publishing told me about a writer called Allegra Taylor, Australian born but educated in America and Brazil. Anna was impressed by Allegra's earth-mother buoyancy and interest in what was then known as 'new age' ideas, including healing, of which she was a practitioner. Mostly she wrote about these and did interviews for monthly magazines such as *She* and *Annabel*.

Her book *Acquainted With the Night: A year on the frontiers of death* had just come out. It told of her work as a volunteer in a hospice and training to become part of London Lighthouse, a support network for people with AIDS. This – and HIV – was the little understood, terrifying illness that appeared in the 1980s and was propelled by myth. Her experience would be a good grounding for what happened 20 years later when she became a funeral celebrant, providing a holistic event for the bereaved.

Allegra, an attractive blonde with a deep infectious chuckle, had no difficulty providing interviews that brought new insight and gave a positive slant to ageing. We all learnt a lot about the people she introduced. First up was Peter Laslett, the Cambridge don who, with Michael Young, gave Britain the Open University (1960s) and the University of the Third Age (U3A, 1970s) which was based on a French idea. They were social innovators whose contributions lived on after they died (Laslett in 2001, at 85, and Young in 2002, aged 86 and leaving a five-year-old daughter. His son Toby Young is a journalist with controversial views, many at odds with his father's.).

With my interest in politics, I should have known about Lord Michael Young and his belief in a fair and equal society. So much of what is part of life today are organisations he created: the Consumers' Association (1956), now Which?; the Advisory Centre for Education; Institute of Community Studies; College of Health; U3A (in which retired people pass on their expertise in subjects such as music, art, languages, philosophy or physical fitness, to others in their age group); the National Extension College (to set higher standards in distance learning); the International Extension College (to spread distance learning to Africa and Asia); the Open College of the Arts; Commuter Study Clubs (to enable regular travellers to learn from each other on trains); Language Line (telephone interpretation service for doctors, police and non-English speakers they dealt with); the Family Covenant Association (non-religious welcome ceremonies for young children); the National Funerals College (to train civil funeral celebrants); Healthline (for telephone information on health matters, today superseded by NHS direct and various internet sites). Phew!

Allegra tracked down Alex Comfort, not long returned to the UK after years of living in the States. He was having success with his book –*The Joy of Sex (a gourmet guide to lovemaking)* – which I'd encountered at *First Lady* and is still available today. More importantly, he was the one who had founded the modern science of gerontology whose sole focus is ageing and its control. It was different from geriatrics which is the branch of medicine dealing with the problems and diseases of old age. He was 70 when he appeared in *Choice*, and died a decade later.

COMFORT'S RAGE AGAINST PREJUDICE
In the photo we published with Allegra's interview,
Alex Comfort was puffing away on a pipe. He looked
like a leprechaun. He had just revised his book *A Good
Age* in which he said that society's prejudices about
older life indoctrinate us and lead to the wrong
conclusions. He believed those prejudices were worth
fighting. Claire Rayner wrote his obituary for *The
Guardian* in 2000, describing him as a physician, poet,
novelist, anarchist and pacifist – and someone with a
very short temper as well as a breathtakingly wide
mind. Another hero for me.

Allegra spent a weekend learning about laughter as a
form of health therapy (now a popular yoga activity), and
searched out the eco warriors Edward Goldsmith, who
founded and edited *The Ecologist*, and brother of the flamboyant entrepreneur James, and James Lovelock with his
theories about the planet as a self regulating organism, or
Gaia (in 2020 he was 101!). She wanted to raise awareness
of the world we were passing on to our children and
grandchildren. [Today vitally important for everyone.]

Married at 17 to documentary maker Richard Taylor
(he won many awards and died in 2015), they brought up
six children, three of their own and three, including twins,
adopted from Africa. Having survived cancer once, it
seemed very bad luck when it was found in her other
breast. She sorted it out most matter of factly; she had a
second mastectomy and, as part of her recovery, set off
round the world on her own, visiting countries and
communities in which women and the role they played

were highly regarded. When she returned, five months later, her words and pictures of the women appeared in *Choice*. Her book, *Older Than Time*, had the subline '*a woman travels around the world in search of the wisdom that comes with age*'. It was an inspiring journey.

A freelancer who did occasional work for Faber & Faber put me in touch with Elizabeth Forsythe, a GP who had written very personal books about Alzheimer's disease and multiple sclerosis; she'd nursed her husband until he died from this most common form of dementia, and she had MS, though it was in remission.

In her opening article she wrote: "In the Western world, we are usually better at living the first half of life than the second...and medical services become less adequate at dealing with our bodies in maturity." She encouraged understanding of our own role in keeping well as we age.

It was a lucky day indeed when I made contact again with Jenny Glew, a former ActionWoman, who with Chris McLaughlin had set up a freelance group to supply magazines and newspapers with features on money and health. Jenny won the Argos Award for Magazine Consumer Journalist of the Year 1989 – and more lay ahead. Jenny and her husband John Fryer, the BBC's labour correspondent (a post that has been subsumed into home affairs), were Essex born and bred, and had two young daughters.

Jenny, still a few years from 50, had already experienced breast cancer, and when she found a second lump – by self checking – she opted for mastectomy after which she went on to Tamoxifen, then called a wonder drug.

This was in 1991, the year the government backed a

national screening programme (mammography) for women from 50 to 64, every three years (now increased to 71). What was sad was that her problems didn't go away; she developed symptoms of MS, the 'northern disease' as Scotswoman Elizabeth Forsythe called it. Elizabeth, Jenny and Allegra were among the most cheerful and remarkable women I have worked with, and they were integral to *Choice*'s success.

* * *

The prime focus of the magazine was retirement and pensions. In the UK, retirement occurred at different ages for men and women and also according to the type of work (firemen, doctors, teachers, for example, had earlier dates because their jobs are so demanding). What was done to help them at this new stage of life?

The Pre-Retirement Association (PRA) was set up by a man called Alastair Heron who was part of what became Age Concern (and later Age UK), to prepare people for retirement. Another charity, Help the Aged (invariably pronounced *a-jed*) also had a link to retirement planning and made its views known through the pages of *Yours*, a colour tabloid – it looked like a newspaper – which was part of Choice Publications. The PRA had space in our magazine to keep readers aware of its role.

Choice's prize element was Your Rights, the 12-page middle section printed on pale peach-coloured paper, which covered topics of vital importance to older people but pertinent to other ages. Jenny Glew edited it for the first year and was a contributor later as her health problems appeared. But we had a wide variety of writers, women and men, who brought their expertise to information about law, the NHS, pensions, capital gains and inheritance tax, banks and savings, the (then) annual Budget and its effect on the readers.

Planning issues was no problem: the subject list was never ending. From the start we knew we were breaking new ground. We had consumer journalists coming to us with ideas: Rebecca Smithers and Jill Papworth (both went on to join *The Guardian*), Helen Garlick, Sue Ward, Andrew Bibby, Jo Cooper (also ex-ActionWoman and *Best*, and eventual editor of the Your Rights pages) and Shirley Davenport. There were others as well, far too many to name, but all inspiring.

For two years in a row, 1990 and 1991, *Choice* won both the Argos Award for magazine consumer journalists (Jenny Glew and I were both named, just pipping Esther Rantzen's TV consumer programme) and was Bradford & Bingley's Personal Finance consumer magazine of the year in 1991. The times couldn't have been better for consumer journalism, and the world of finance.

We took readers through the finest points of privatization, community tax, personal pensions (which had been opened wide by Margaret Thatcher in 1989, creating problems that had not been foreseen), workplace pensions (such as final salary, and defined benefit schemes) and contributions, NICs, the iniquity of the married woman's 'stamp' and its effect on her pension, getting a pensions forecast, investing in shares and gilts – and even everyday banking so they knew exactly what to look for in their accounts. This was long before the internet, but it raised awareness of the importance of checking what went in and out every day, and whether it had been authorised.

* * *

Among our readers were many *Mirror* pensioners. One of them, Pamela Duveen, brought us a scoop about the company pension scheme and proprietor Robert Maxwell. This was the man who, when he bought the newspaper group from Reed International in 1984 – the year of the strike at IPC – undertook to preserve and protect all pension rights.

Pamela, who had managed the newspaper's reader service, retired in 1979 before Maxwell took over, then entered the field of pre-retirement education. She noticed her pension slip showed she had been paid by the Pergamon Pension Scheme (and later changed its name to Headington Group Pensions).

She joined the Association of Mirror Pensioners, set up to obtain a share of what was seen to be a large surplus in the pension fund's annual report. In early 1991 a legal action was pending, relating to lack of increases the pensioners thought they were entitled to. Then Maxwell floated half of the Mirror Group on the Stock Exchange, raising about £250m. Later, in November, came the news of his death at sea: whether it was suicide, an accident or murder it caused a sensation.

MAXWELL'S FINANCIAL LEGERDEMAIN
Robert Maxwell's death revealed a scandalous pension
problem and *Choice* told the story in the February 1992

issue, quite an achievement when you consider how long it took at that time to create and print a magazine (we still relied on the fax machine to get copy to the printer, and proofs back). The shocking revelation was that about £440m was missing from funds that were to provide pensions for employees of Mirror Group Newspapers and Maxwell Communications Corporation. Many of the 32,000 men and women who had worked for companies Maxwell bought and sold didn't even know he had been their boss until details of the pension theft emerged.

Maxwell had moved money around and changed the schemes' names so none of the pensioners felt completely secure and the fear that they would lose the biggest part of their income caused extreme distress. The pensioners campaigned for three years before there was a £100m government payout and an out-of-court settlement of £276m from investment banks, accountants and Maxwell's remaining media companies.

Big names like Coopers & Lybrand, Goldman Sachs and Lehman Brothers (whose filing for bankruptcy in 2008 was the largest in American history, an action that started years of austerity worldwide) all featured and it took 18 months of hard negotiation before it was agreed.

[Jo Foley, who'd left *Woman* in the mid 1980s to work for Robert Maxwell, wrote a newspaper article in 2107 in which she said she didn't have a private pension: "I'd spent years paying into a scheme but my pension pot disappeared over the side of a yacht with the media mogul for whom I worked at the time."]

The scandal opened up the subject of occupational pensions and eventuated in very much overdue reform of the role of the trustees. But the 'Bouncing Czech', as *Private Eye* called him, was extremely adept at financial jiggery-pokery. And, as the Occupational Pensions Advisory Service (OPAS) said, no amount of regulation would stop someone as wicked as he obviously was.

[OPAS became The Pensions Advisory Service (TPAS) through which volunteer advisers give free and independent advice on defined contribution pensions as part of the new pension rules from April 2015.]

But it is still not completely safe as the BHS pension scandal in 2015 showed; vigilance is needed to safeguard funds and members' pension rights. It took four years before a satisfactory conclusion was found for the thousands of former employees of BHS affected by the pension deficit of more than £570m. Sir Philip Green eventually paid £363m into the fund and Dominic Chappell who bought BHS for £1 from Green was ordered to pay £9.5m. Chappell also stood trial over tax fraud allegations of £500,000 and was gaoled for six years.

After the BHS debacle, the parliamentary investigation into the case described the hole as "the unacceptable face of capitalism". It said the owners had systematically plundered the company. Green was not stripped of his knighthood which he received, under Prime Minister Tony Blair, for services to the retail industry.

At the time of writing the devastating effects of Covid were appearing in the retail sector with the future of Debenhams and Green's Arcadia Group in grave doubt. Arcadia has 13,000 staff (from Topshop, Burton, Dorothy

Perkins, Wallis, Evans and Miss Selfridge) and a £350 million pension black hole.

KEEP A WATCH ON YOUR PENSION
Pamela Duveen's experience, which she described in a letter to *Choice*, may be pertinent to many today: the only pre-retirement counselling she received was an interview with the pension person in the personnel department (now usually called Human Resources) which was followed some time later by a letter setting out her financial entitlement. "This was not sufficient to arm me with the know-how to understand the changing fortunes of my pension fund, or my rights, if any, under pension legislation." Pamela died in 2011, in her 90s, and her obituary was published in *The Guardian*. Her message was clear: all retired people need to understand what's being paid and when, and to keep a close watch on it every year.

Choice readers, up until the relaunch, mostly came through the Pre-Retirement Association which celebrated 25 years of existence with these words: "Britain was in the grip of a baby boom and the Beatles in 1964 when the PRA started using education to widen the horizons of people in the years before they retired."

They ran two-day courses (with the help of employers, civic authorities and trade unions who paid the costs) to cover subjects such as finance, pensions, housing, diet, physical and mental health. Or holiday courses were offered: a week in spring and autumn, and three-day breaks, at Pontins Holiday centre in south Devon.

The financial specialists were provided by Prudential, the company that Peter Davis from Reed International would join: he appeared in their TV ads, as 'the man from the Pru', the door-to-door 'penny insurance collector' known to working class people saving for a rainy day.

Another source of subscribers to the magazine were pension funds. *Choice* could be tailored to company retirees by adding eight or 12 pages to the centre of each issue. So, for instance, the *Choice* delivered each month to a pensioner of Allied-Lyons, the huge food and drink conglomerate (which became Diageo), had a section with news and views of the company they worked for. This was a type of contract publishing.

Choice, before the new investment, was more a newsletter in style than a magazine but it had a strong following, particularly among those who received it free. And a lot of them did not take kindly to the new look and approach. They did not care that it was now 100 pages packed with colour, had interesting articles and challenging mind games. (Eddie Waltham, my puzzle-champion from *Bella*, adapted Bayard's word maze and anagram, and provided a clueless crossword as well.) We also had a page on Bridge, a pastime particularly popular with the more mature.

Some of the early letters to the editor were not only outspoken but often quite rude (they did stop after a while, thank goodness). Fuelled by both naïve optimism and enthusiasm, I thought that readers would welcome change, but the reality was that it would take some time to get across the positive philosophy of *Notre Temps* and to banish set-in-their-ways views, particularly about ageing.

In an ideal world, who would be a *Choice* reader? Male and female, educated, interested in others, independent and open minded with a broad outlook and wide horizons. If they weren't already playing a sport or exercising, our articles month after month would surely inspire them to stay fit and be healthier longer.

The irresistible spur was bringing in the amazing Diana Moran, the Green Goddess, who had faced physical and personal problems and emerged with a smile – how could anyone reject her positive approach in making the right moves for wellbeing? [In 2019 her book called *Sod Sitting, Get Moving* carried the same message as new *Choice* did. Aged 80, she returned to BBC breakfast TV with a keep-fit programme during the coronavirus crisis. And re-appeared in *Choice* magazine.]

M y chance to promote the rejuvenated *Choice* was nearly scuppered by an interview I did with Jenni Murray on Radio 4's Woman's Hour. Don't you think that's rather patronising, she said (or words to that effect); why would older people want such a magazine?

I really was taken aback by the sharpness of her tone and did my best to explain that *Choice* would be filled with thoughtful features that had readers' interests at heart, that focused on them, their health, wealth and their present or possible lifestyle, their contributions to the world around them. I could see by her face that she wasn't sympathetic and I could not understand why she intimated that providing information was patronising. I couldn't think of a humorous way to deflect her.

When the broadcaster, 10 years younger than me and by then a Dame, reached the age group *Choice* focuses on, she was in the news because she chose to have a gastric band fitted to counteract her inability to lose weight. When she reached 70 (and her 33-year career at the BBC came to an end), she published *Fat Cow, Fat Chance* about her lifelong attempts to keep her weight at a healthy level. Fat-shaming should be classed as hate speech, she stated.

Obesity is a problem worldwide and desperately needs to be tackled. When I met her, she must have felt there was no need to read a magazine designed for her age or to take well-meaning advice. To stay in good form as the years go by requires a conscious decision about being the best we can be and no one else can do it for us.

According to *Notre Temps*, the interests and inclinations of those in the third age are wide and varied, though perhaps not as much as those in the second (the age of work and parenting) and first (the age of childhood and education). When retirement comes you can look back to those activities that attracted you and rediscover them with a new zest. No argument, I thought. But I was to find that not everyone wants to know about other people in their age group or receive inspirational information (except, maybe, on finance).

The seventh series of the TV show *The Apprentice*, with Sir Alan Sugar in a Machiavelli role, set the young aspiring entrepreneurs the task of creating from scratch new magazines to present to advertising people who make the decisions about what ads appear where. One group came up with *"Covered"* for 'thinking, business orientated lads'. It wasn't much different from others (particularly *Front*, the short-lived Sally O'Sullivan magazine of 1998) – but it got ad support.

The second group's magazine was for the over 60s. Called *"HIP Replacement"* (subline *'out with the old, in with the new'* – the sort of wry humour *The Oldie* specialised in). Only the young who have no concept of their own ageing could think this title a come-on to those in the age group. It was okay as a one-off, but ongoing?

The only research the group did, in a bowling club, was laughable but highlighted the difficulties anyone wanting to understand older people finds: those in it are impossible to categorise, possibly even to please. [Group meetings shown on TV before the Brexit Referendum in 2016 were very similar.] The men joked about it all, a typical male response when not sure about something, and the lone woman did not want to read anything that contained a knitting pattern. This rang a big bell because I knew about *Yours*.

* * *

Those who were instrumental in creating Bayard Presse's senior network had difficulty with *Choice's* sister publication *Yours* which was so unlike anything in France that its readers could have come from Mars.

Choice – like the others in the group – was for the 'doers' (those who prized independence and wanted to make their own decisions based on the best information and experience). *Yours* was for the 'would be done bys' (who expected to be looked after as they aged and were happy to have decisions made for them). But *Yours* would be the magazine to go places, and far faster than *Choice*.

The editor at this time was Neil Patrick, a former newspaper journalist who had worked with Emap, and Norman Wright too, for many years. He created the mix of domesticity, nostalgia and humour that appealed to older readers, essentially women, many of whom might never have had a skilled job, had little money to spare and were probably caring for another person even though they might not be in good health themselves.

There was low-cost uncomplicated cookery and a knitting pattern (often a toy or garment for a grandchild), heroic stories about illness and the war, a get-in-touch page that featured reunions and missing people, gardening and a column by old-time variety comedian Roy Hudd OBE who looked far older than he was (he died in 2020) and had exactly the right words for his audience. The sentimentality was anathema to the French.

All of this came to the fore at the first conference of Bayard's senior publications that Norman, Neil and I attended – and Neil stole the show. He was an am-dram man (who enjoyed a good pub sing-song and a pint or two) and during his presentation painted a picture of adorable, grey-haired old people, mostly women, who were the backbone of the country.

All of us – French, Belgian, Spanish, Canadians and Brits, from the different Bayard publications – were caught by surprise and responded with laughter. Later, Bayard's *Le Bel Age*, published in Canada, was an attempt at the over-70s market, but it was closed in 1999. No other countries tried to emulate *Yours*, and I don't think what happened to it could have been predicted (though Norman was always a great fan).

After Neil retired, Emap invested in *Yours*, improving the paper, colour and design, and turning it into a traditional women's magazine, with older celebrities on the cover and unashamedly promoting the notion that getting older was a good club to join. The circulation sky-rocketed and *Yours* was suddenly one of the top 10 monthlies.

BAUER HAD EYES FOR *YOURS*

The acquisition of *Yours* was possibly what made Bauer bid for Emap magazines and radio stations when they came up for sale in 2007, paying £1.14b for the group. As part of Bauer Consumer Media, *Yours* was relaunched as a fortnightly in 2014, keeps its price low, has spin offs featuring food and fiction, jokes and puzzles, and has a website that highlights dieting and dating, retirement and financial services, celebrity gossip and news and views for 'women in their prime'. It has its own fashion awards and you can even download a knitting pattern.

The new *Choice* of 1990 had at its back an advertising agency called Harari Page to promote the idea that the over 50s were the 'new' youth (in marketing terms, that is). They produced a book of postcards showing ageing hippy-style images representing the 1960s generation in their 50s. Their presentation to possible advertisers made points such as "over 40% of the country will soon be over 50", that "everyone from brand managers and product designers to copywriters and media buyers will need to understand what it's like to be over 50".

But magazine publishing is not altruistic; its fuel is making money. It came down to how to get this affluent group – who had a high disposable income, owned their own homes outright, controlled 70% of the total savings in Britain and every year inherited over £10b – to spend their money. "We need to know what motivates, what frightens, what reassures and what opens the cheque books of our elders. We'll need to know how to talk to them instead of at them. We'll need to do this...because they are also becoming the richest group in Britain."

The trouble was that the *Choice* readers in the early 1990s were not of the generation born from 1939 onwards – though from 1945 may also be a baseline – who had the rebellious attitudes and *joie de vivre* of that unusual decade (and I am one of them). Our readers were more likely to be over 60, more aligned to before World War 2 than after and probably had just one job all their working lives. If they saved it was for a rainy day or a once in a lifetime trip (most likely to Australia or New Zealand or a cruise around the world – as so tellingly revealed in the coronavirus pandemic).

They saw no need to spend on improving the comfort or look of their houses, on changing furnishings or furniture, preferring to cling on to old beds, sagging mattresses and low-level, old-fashioned sofas that made their mobility worse. They wouldn't spend money on employing an electrician to alter the lighting so they could see better, or getting rid of floor coverings that could easily cause a fall. They were not of a generation that went to the gym, or exercised for pleasure (golf aside, in the case of the men).

In 2012 there was a letter in the *Weekend Financial Times*, from a 75 year old who'd been on the first leg of a world cruise. "Many of the elderly passengers were on their way round the world at a cost, for a couple, of between £50,000 and £90,000, and I met several who were on their third or fourth such voyage." He had a message for them: "step up to the plate" to support grandchildren or great grandchildren who were struggling to pay university fees or find the deposit for a house.

Could any of these older, loaded, lot been *Choice* readers? Their money, however they came by it, puts them into the bankers' bonus category: people who have no need for guidance on spending it. But they may be greedy, like those tempted by Madoff, willingly believing the convincing twaddle that they are 'lucky' and can double or triple their nest egg.

* * *

One of the worst sides of the last and present century are the scammers who cleverly part people from their money and keep the Serious Fraud Office busy. I have personal experience of such a tragic situation: a relative who, in his late 80s and living alone after the death of his much older wife, was targeted by very smart operators over six years and handed them over £1m for dubious shares. He fell hook, line and sinker for 'boiler-room scams' run by fake stockbrokers, only one of whom was caught.

His name must have got on what I can only call the 'list of mugs', attracting clairvoyants and lottery sellers, competition groups and pill merchants who offered incredible returns for a small investment. In just one year he sent off cheques adding up to £25,000 (little amounts, £10, £15, £20, for 'registration'). His 'winnings': £2! Every week over several years a hundred or so letters arrived, piling up in cardboard boxes in every room. This intelligent former businessman who'd owned his own company was obsessed with the idea he'd win a million (as a clairvoyant had told him) and seemed completely unaware of how much wealth he'd lost.

Eventually the intervention of his stepson – going to the Court of Protection to invoke an Enduring Power of Attorney, stopping the mail and telephone, and reporting the situation to the Serious Fraud Office – saved him. In his 90s and physically frail, he was moved to a care home for his own safety.

THE ROUTE TO GETTING HOOKED

When the stepson cleared his house he found a box of *Reader's Digest* circulars relating to special offers of records or books. On each his stepfather had marked, in red, the amount he'd sent for the 'special numbers' allocated for 'a guaranteed award' – the dates started in the mid-1970s so he was hooked early. The papers showed that the *Digest* ran its competitions through "Strike Lucky Games Ltd/Express Awards" with a PO box number in Ross-on-Wye. One rule that the Serious Fraud Office always states is: never send money to a post box number.

You might be surprised to know that the editorial side of the magazines I knew rarely had any say in what is advertised on the pages, or what is accepted as an insert, usually at a special rate – the circulars, booklets etc stuffed inside an issue and fall out the moment you open it. It is among these that tricky operators may lurk, offering scratch cards and prizes – for which you have to call a premium number. Publishers have a duty of care to their readers: not to promulgate material that could cause harm. If you object to receiving it you can bin it, or better still complain to the Advertising Standards Authority.

One underlying rule of *Choice*'s Your Rights section was to raise awareness about a lot of things that should carry the warning 'buyer beware' or 'invest only what you can afford to lose'. Some very good contributors had a nose for financial stories so we frequently covered topics rarely seen in other publications then.

We became deeply involved in reporting scandals such as the unregulated home equity schemes where strapped-for-cash homeowners over a certain age could raise money from selling a share of their house, a situation which was eventually made less dangerous by the establishment of SHIP (safe home income plans). Providers had to sign up to their rules, to ensure financial regulation of a system which had caused people to lose their homes. However, even with this in place, such plans could not be considered fail-safe. When someone's offering to lend you money you have to ask yourself what's in it for them…

Then there was the iniquitous situation of retirees choosing to live in stationary mobile homes in parks or in sheltered housing on estates designated for the over 55s.

The owners of the land held all the cards and wielded quite Draconian power in the charges they made and decisions about who could and couldn't buy.

What our features mostly uncovered was a lack of robust regulation that protected investors, especially those in retirement. We hoped politicians would take notice – which is why, when Prime Minister John Major turned 50, I sent him our best wishes, several copies of *Choice* and offered a subscription (he didn't take it up).

* * *

Politically and financially 1991 was not a good year. (The early years of each decade from the 1970s were similarly afflicted.) For *Choice* it was a winner. We received the top award from Bradford & Bingley for our persistently strong coverage of personal finance matters.

At London's Savoy Hotel, Alistair Darling (MP for Edinburgh south west and not nearly as well known as he was to become) did the presentation. He was made Chief Secretary to the Treasury when Labour won the 1997 election, and in 2007 became Chancellor of the Exchequer. His first challenge came in 2008: the Global Financial Crisis (GFC) after Lehman Brothers collapsed was paralysing the world.

Bradford & Bingley, whose origins in West Yorkshire go back to 1851, during my time at *Choice* was a leading building society with the admirable intention of fostering better understanding of financial matters. It demutualised in 2000 and became a bank which, by 2006, was valued at

£3.2bn. What happened next was quite unexpected, taking the shareholders by surprise.

In 2008 B&B, the bank, was so badly affected by the GFC and the unforeseen sub prime mortgage disaster in the US in which it was involved, that it announced huge job losses and its share price fell to a record low. The government, in the guise of Prime Minister Gordon Brown and Chancellor Darling, moved fast to nationalise the mortgage half (due to insolvency) and sold the other half, the savings side, to Abbey National, by this time owned by the Spanish group Santander, for £612m.

Then came the Northern Rock debacle – which even to this day has not been satisfactorily explained. The sale of half of it to Richard Branson of the Virgin conglomerate put it into a new category of financial history. The former building society turned bank was also nationalised and like B&B became part of the government owned UK Financial Investments Ltd.

The most vociferous opponents were the irate shareholders of both banks who received no recompense – though their shares probably cost them nothing and came to them because they had an account with £100 in it when the building societies demutualised (a popular investment at the time, in hope of a windfall).

The fighting groups they formed could only be bravado. Doubtless they were sad that two fine establishments, set up to make life better for the people of the northern mill towns, could not do the same for themselves. But they forgot the 'buyer beware' rule.

16

APPEALING TO VESTED INTERESTS

As far as I was concerned, *Choice* was a general magazine with articles applicable to both men and women who had retired or were nearing the age when they expected to leave their jobs. Actually any adult with a vested interest in work, family and life in retirement would have found the content informative.

Notre Temps introduced us to the way people lived in parts of the EU. Their well-illustrated reports on areas of France gave an insight into local seniors (well groomed, not glamorous) talking about everyday life (family, hobbies), activities (keep fit, dancing, social clubs), amenities (hospitals, doctors, libraries) and benefits (travel, reduced price eating or hairdressing).

Graphs detailed the cost of living, seniors as a percentage of the population, their roles in the communities – grandparenting, volunteering etc. Perhaps if we had had the same sort of data about areas of the UK the vote for Brexit in 2016 might not have been such a surprise.

We translated a few features about pensioners in several countries, a satisfying way of learning about Spain (where the retired are called *jubilados,* which sounds celebratory), Greece, Portugal and Italy – though all are today facing overwhelming hardship. A *Notre Temps* team had come to the UK to investigate life here and the jolly picture they published in France coincided with pensioners around Britain on the march for improved benefits. Our realities were different.

Leslie Kenton suddenly reappeared. Again, it was uncanny as I had been struggling with what to do about 'beauty' in a magazine for older people, its presence supposedly more likely to attract advertising. Like her, perhaps even influenced by her, I believed that health and looks, so-called body image, were part and parcel of each other. After years of working on women's magazines I had concluded that 'beauty' was a difficult concept to get across (the eye of the beholder etc?). Not being able to meet some accepted standard was often at the root of a woman's lack of confidence.

Showing ways to put on makeup or style hair appeal to the young who like to experiment or look like everyone else. More relevant for older women would be how to care for skin, hair, body and nails – all of which are on display. A lot might depend on your genes but you can improve your overall appearance. If you want to. And it can be costly: the cosmetic industry led the charge of the light brigade.

Leslie was still the high priestess, the guru of health, and her life in glorious isolation in Wales with a very much younger man had been featured in the press. In

1991 she was actively promoting a new product called Imedeen, an 'anti-ageing natural supplement' for the skin developed by a Swedish biochemist – still on sale today.

When I went to Sweden in the early 1980s, on the press trip that launched Flora, the first low-fat spread, I learnt that much investigation was going on in the interests of anti-ageing; both Imedeen and Vivida, another supplement, were the result. In the 1990s the Danish Pharma Nord came up with a range of dietary supplements which included Co-enzyme Q10 (ubiquinone), a vitamin-like substance found naturally in the body but whose levels decrease with age and illness.

This was the first time I'd come across the term antioxidant and I was impressed that trials showed it inhibited the development of periodontal disease, a curse of the over 50s resulting in painful, bleeding gums and loss of teeth. It was something that affected me.

Medical research was also indicating a connection between the gums and heart disease, of huge importance to older people. About the same time there was a major breakthrough in the treatment of stomach ulcers. Two doctors in Perth, Western Australia, discovered these were caused by *helicobacter pylori*, bacteria, which could be eliminated with antibiotics. Could this bacteria have entered the digestive system via the teeth?

Leslie was now actively promoting a new drink made from aloe vera, the jelly-like substance inside leaves of a fleshy Caribbean cactus which is known to soothe burnt skin. The liquid, described as a complementary therapy, was taken to alleviate back pain, knee pain and even irritable bowel syndrome. And she had written her first novel, *Ludwig*, based on Beethoven. She was rarely out of the public eye and 2010 was a real show-stopper: she produced her "memoir of obsession, tragedy and grace" called *Love Affair*. In it she revealed that her internationally-known jazz leader father Stan Kenton had regularly raped her. She then moved to New Zealand and into the obesity business.

WEIGHT BECOMES BIG BUSINESS
A video on Leslie Kenton's website showed an experiment she ran in New Zealand with a group of overweight people. The regime was possibly the basis of Cura Romana, a protocol 'for the body and soul' launched in 2011 in the UK. It garnered two complaints to the Advertising Standards Authority (ASA) which were upheld: that the ad promoted an unlicensed medical product, and that the dietary and weight loss claims were not compatible with good medical and nutritional practice. When fat really is much more than a feminist issue, "Welcome to the miracle of Cura Romana" would be a come-on for a very overweight person. It had two parts: "a natural Essence Spray, and a highly specific dietary protocol". It was implied that the spray contained 'human chorionic gonadotrophin (hCG)' "which lets your body burn only inessential fat stores. It will spare muscle tissue, restore the natural shape of your body and can leave you looking and feeling better than ever." The ASA said it believed hCG was not authorised or registered for use in the UK and

was an unlicensed medicine. Leslie's response to the ASA said the spray was physically nothing more than pure water and 25% ethanol. It "was not a medicinal product or a homeopathic formula, but was a vibrational essence that had itself been energized by several non-material vibrational essences including well known gem essences". [This is the sort of gobbledygook that gives science a bad name.] The ad was found to have breached the code and "must not appear again in its current form". Her website *lesliekenton.com* says you can order hCG and that no one should enter the weightloss program carelessly. "It is not like any other in the world," it says. Leslie died unexpectedly in New Zealand in 2016. Her fourth child, Aaron, now runs the company.

* * *

At *Choice* we received a lot of mail, often from people who turned their hand to writing and photography in retirement (both, of course, are therapeutic), and hoped to be published. It took me back to my role as poetry editor at *Woman's Own*, and the difficulty of saying no. We just didn't have enough pages.

In the first year we found an ageing American hippie, Irv Thomas, complete with iron-grey ponytail, who became a contributor, an on-the-move philosopher with a playful tone. I received a lovely article from a woman called Edith Courtney about finding love and new happiness in retirement. She was founder and first secretary of the Swansea Writers' Circle and a published author (*A Mouse Ran Up My Nightie, Fares Please,* and *My Feet Are Killing Me*), all biographical and very funny.

What tickled me though was a note included from her (new) husband who asked if I was the Wendy James of *The Complete Cook,* from which he had taught himself to cook when he'd been widowed! My first fan. That was my "Yes, there is a Santa Claus" moment.

Naturally we ran their story, and another by ITN's former science editor and *TV Times* writer Peter Fairley. He told how he had nursed his wife through her final illness and never thought he would marry again. Never say never is the message here, for he did, and the story was told by his new wife, Helen, describing herself as a spinster of this parish until she became Mrs Fairley in her 60s. They did not have many years together for Peter died of cancer in 1998, aged 67.

Even after all this time you can see him still on screen: on YouTube there's a short clip of him on the 1960s children's series *Timeslip* saying "Today's sci-fi is so often tomorrow's science fact." His daughter Josephine Fairley is an award-winning beauty and environmental journalist and entrepreneur: she and her husband Craig Sams gave the world Green & Black's organic chocolate.

The EU designated 1993 as the year of older people, providing an opportunity to focus on possibilities and options in the *troisième âge.* I don't think many people noticed or were interested (like much that was good about the EU, unfortunately). But *Choice* was and we attended a conference in Brussels organised by *Notre Temps,* taking with us for a weekend several *Choice* readers who were winners in a competition we ran. A very young Danny Fielder, feature writer and subeditor, was fluent in French and an excellent go-between. He, like all the editorial staff, approved the magazine's positive philosophy.

In our Clerkenwell office, we bonded over once-a-month lunches in the boardroom. The picnic-style array, mostly vegetarian, was prepared by the lovely Teresa in our small kitchen. Sometimes Norman would be there, or some of the marketing people from Peterborough, or any contributors who were visiting.

At this time *Choice* was the only Emap magazine in London and we weren't even sure whether other parts of Emap knew about us. The best barometer of our rating in the company was the annual awards, a shindig which Kevin Hand saw as the best way of bringing together the wide variety that was Emap.

[I liked Kevin, a dedicated Francophile, who learnt the language via a three months' 'saturation' course, similar to that provided for Foreign Office personnel taking up posts in foreign countries. He was soon confidant enough to chair meetings in French.]

Mostly I think the event was a bonus for the advertising and marketing employees who were under pressure to meet increasingly demanding targets every year. Extremely short skirts and deep cleavages predominated and excess alcohol and very loud music fuelled the exuberance. Usually held at a venue around Peterborough, for us it was an outing for a chosen few on the staff, a trip north by train and an overnight stay at a hotel. It was skilfully organised: the table you sat at indicated whether you were in the good or bad books. The first couple of years we weren't far from the stage which meant we had been recommended and not disparaged by the judges.

Once we carried off the award for most improved magazine – handed over by guest of honour Derek Jameson, ex newspaper editor and personality with his own BBC Radio 2 show, who sounded and looked much as he did at my interview in 1966. [He died, aged 82, in 2012.] In 1993, however, the table allotted to *Choice*, at the event's venue, Alexandra Palace in north London, was nearer the exit than the action.

It became clear that *Choice* wasn't doing in the UK what *Notre Temps* does in France – their readership was so large the magazine could lobby the government on their behalf! We thought we had a lively and interesting publication but the higher ups didn't agree. There was a gap between the vibrant activities on the pages and the ads which focused on the very old and immobile. The basic fact was we needed more people who paid money to buy the magazine.

Kevin Hand reactivated Stan the Man, much older than all of us and therefore supposedly in the reader group, who closely scrutinised several issues. He was quite blunt about not finding subjects of interest to him. He was critical of our covers: mostly healthy, positive looking anonymous people. Then at the end of 1993 my decision to put Maya Angelou there brought opprobrium.

Even Hubert Chicou, generally considered in his comments, could not understand why an American black woman should feature in a British magazine. This accomplished author, poet, singer, actress, dancer, civil rights activist deserved to be applauded, having been chosen, at the age of 64, to read her poem (*On the Pulse of the Morning*) at President Bill Clinton's inauguration.

MAYA'S LEGACY TO THE WORLD
I thought Maya Angelou's struggles and achievements could not fail to interest *Choice* readers, that they would appreciate that age had not stopped her being productive or being appreciated. In hindsight, I doubt they did. Perhaps they only saw a stranger, a black woman whose age was irrelevant. But she was magnificent and many around the world mourned her death in 2014. I hope her book *I Know Why the Caged Bird Sings* will introduce generation after generation to the effects of cultural and sexual discrimination. We all need heroines and heroes who try to make a difference.

[It is interesting that a young black woman, an American poet and activist called Amanda Gorman made a huge impact at President Joe Biden's inauguration, an echo of Maya's presence over 25 years earlier. They both made the cover of *Time* magazine.]

Malcolm Gipson, as art director, was under pressure to interpret the criticisms that were coming from all sides and to find a new look for the spreads. Our features were challenged: newsy stories about active older men and women should be dropped, and traditional service articles added: cookery, maybe fashion, maybe beauty, much more travel, celebrities instead of ordinary people.

Exercise and alternative health spreads – of which we were proud as no other magazine was as enlightened then – brought a wry "so what?" from our somewhat over-weight scrutineer. (Stanley Glazer was of the non-active school of ageing.) It was very trying.

Our budget was cut. We no longer had a receptionist, we had to do our own correspondence. And the editorial staff was down to bare bones. Even so, in 1994 *Choice* won the Bradford & Bingley General Consumer Magazine of the Year for "its bright format, snappy writing style and good lay-out" on the personal finance pages. It wasn't enough. Just weeks later Norman and Hubert decided to close the London office and move *Choice* to Emap towers in Peterborough. It was crunch time. I chose not to go.

Neil Patrick, helped by June Weatherall, ran both *Yours* and *Choice* while Norman searched for a new editor-in-chief and I organised the Your Rights section as a free-lance commission from my home in London.

Janet Horwood remained features editor, commuting from Kent to Peterborough (and later went to *Woman's Weekly* as Health Editor). Danny Fielder stayed with Emap, working on magazines here and in France; along the way he changed his name to Dan Brotzel and published several well-received books. Rachel Symonds took redundancy and started a new life in Kent. Claire Hoffman went to Save the Children then moved to the Bill and Melinda Gates anti-malaria charity. Teresa Palmano joined *BBC Music* magazine which had been the brainchild of Heather Aylott, the new *Choice's* first publisher; later, at *Eve,* she honed her marketing skills.

Malcolm Gipson went from redundancy to assistant

then art editor of the phenomenal all-colour *Hello!*, taking layout artist Phil Philpott with him (he later took Malcolm's place). After six months editing Your Rights, and after Sue Dobson (former editor of *Woman & Home*, who specialised in travel writing) became editor-in-chief in Peterborough, the award-winning section was taken back in house with Jo Cooper as its editor. My involvement with *Choice* came to an end.

CHOICE MOVES WITH THE TIMES

Choice left the Emap umbrella in 1999. Norman Wright publishes the magazine under the aegis of Bayard Presse UK and is also the editor-in-chief. *Choice* can be bought in some newsagents, is sold on subscription in paper form or to read on the web. It has a lively, traditional mix (including celebrities, much travel, readers' reunions and poems) and, moving with the times, is on Facebook and Twitter. Neil Patrick's a contributor: writing about life in retirement with a lot of harking back, in memory-prompting style, which was popular in *Yours*.

* * *

The older market is still there. At newsagents you can find *The Oldie*, *People's Friend*, *Woman's Weekly*, *Woman & Home*, and if you subscribe to the travel firm *Saga* you get a copy of their magazine which features thoughtful articles by known over-50s people (like Jeremy Paxman, Dame Jenni Murray, Alan Johnson is the agony uncle, and Paul Lewis of BBC Radio 4 Money Box covers

Money Matters). Online are *50PLUS* magazine, *Retirement Today*, and *Silver Surfers*. As ever, there are critics. On one of the sites about magazines for older people I read: "What a boring list! We're not all shuffling round in slippers, searching for a funeral plan and doing puzzles. We were the trendsetters in the 70s, 80s and 90s but we're not dead yet."

Perhaps she's joined Extinction Rebellion, an action group that aims to raise awareness of the awful problems we have caused on the planet. Members believe the time is right to prevent further damage in the interests of our children and grandchildren – as Allegra Taylor made clear to the readers of *Choice* in the early 1990s.

Raising awareness is what magazines do well if editors are committed to doing so. I've said elsewhere that publishers are not altruistic but there is an exception: *The Big Issue*, started in 1991 by long-time friends John Bird and Gordon Roddick (of The Body Shop) as a response to the increasing numbers of homeless people. It is a weekly magazine that is sold on the street by homeless or near homeless people.

By becoming vendors they earn some money and can also be helped by the Big Issue Foundation, the charitable arm, which offers advice and support on housing, health, wellbeing and welfare, personal finance and addiction.The coronavirus crisis affected high streets dramatically and vendors had no one to sell to. Instead, the magazine was sold through shops (and by subscription and app), and the sales income was dedicated to tiding the vendors over until the 'new normal' began.

I enjoy reading it. It is a magazine fuelled by social

consciousness, is cheerfully laid out and full of wide-ranging features of interest to all ages. John Bird, editor-in-chief, is forthright about the crisis the country faces: "We do not want to live in a society that is busted by austerity again." I'm behind him all the way – he is one of the voices in the House of Lords worth listening to.

17

AFTERTHOUGHTS

As my pension pot was in Emap's hands, and having learnt the lesson of the *Daily Mirror* retirees – the Duveen factor, as I called it – I kept my eye on the company's fortunes. I had joined the innovative employees' share scheme; each year my stake grew and on retirement at 60 it could be converted to cash to boost my pension.

Emap's shares in the last years of the 1990s were volatile. The company made the news in 1998 when it purchased Petersen, an American publishing group, paying – said city analysts – an unjustifiably huge amount. The next year the French-British partnership hit the rocks when Emap bought *Pleine Vie* – Full Life, for women over 50, published in France – *Notre Temps'* main competitor. After financial losses at Bayard, longtime president Bernard Porte, the driving force behind the company's international expansion, was removed from his post. This, plus the Petersen debacle, led to a massive loss and a crisis in 2001 when Kevin Hand quit his job.

Before too long he was appointed CEO of Hachette Filipacchi UK, in charge of (among many other publications) *Elle*, *Elle Deco* and *Red* (which he'd obtained for Hachette from Emap when the French partnership was dissolved), and *Psychologies*. In 2011 he was special adviser to Hearst Magazines UK, created by the merger of Hachette UK and the National Magazine Company.

According to *Marketing Week*, the combined audience after the merger comprised about 16m print readers and 20m unique users online – among them would have been readers of *Company*, which was ailing when Anna Jones took over as boss in 2014. Knowing of its strong social presence on Twitter, Instagram, Facebook and YouTube, she provided *Company*'s tablet-savvy 16 to 24 year olds with their own world online and 4m of them respond every month. That's almost the same number of magazines that *Woman* and *Woman's Own* used to sell each week more than half a century ago.

Kevin was chair of Hachette Filipacchi UK as well as the Professional Publishers' Association (formerly the Periodical Publishers Association) and also a director of IPSO, the UK's post-phone-hacking watchdog, when he died suddenly in 2016, after a short illness, aged 64. The *Flashes&Flames* website described him as 'a leader in the heyday of magazines'. That was the 20th century.

* * *

The new millennium saw a surge of activity in the magazine market. Probably the most significant was National Magazine Company (NatMags) buying the

German UK group Gruner+Jahr. Managing Director Terry Mansfield said it was a great match. For the first time it would be publishing a weekly, *Best*, and the leading monthly *Good Housekeeping* would sit beside *Prima* and *Red* on the newsagents' and supermarket shelves.

Two new magazines for women appeared. In 2000, Marcelle D'Argy Smith wrote in *The Guardian* that *Aura* aimed to close "the gap in the women's market" for those over 40 "still interested in sex, life, fashion, beauty and intelligent reading matter". It was for "women who had outgrown *Cosmo* and *Marie Claire*" but the *Good House-keeping* image wouldn't "complement their kitten-heeled mules and Agent Provocateur bra".

Aura's editorial director was Eve Pollard, one of the four partners in Parkhill Publishing. Editor Deirdre Vine (editor of *Woman's Journal* after Laurie Purden retired) chose Hollywood actor Susan Sarandon for the cover of the first issue in April: "draped across the floor, arms flung back, hair extensions tumbling, legs in the air, wearing a feather boa, fishnet tights and high heels. This was, perhaps, the first time an adult, intelligent woman had been portrayed on a cover looking really sexy," D'Argy Smith wrote.

Among *Aura*'s contributors were many renowned grown-up women: Germaine Greer, Fay Weldon, Leslie Kenton, Cherie Booth, Erica Jong, Chrissy Iley, Kathy Lette, Edwina Currie and Vanessa Feltz. Paula Yates, the troubled ex-wife of Bob Geldof, was the agony aunt but tragically died from a heroin overdose within months.

As the August issue went on sale, the staff was told the company was running out of cash and a buyer was being sought for *Aura* and sister magazine *Wedding Day* (launched 1999). D'Argy Smith's account made *Aura*'s short life sound quite awful for the staff, freelancers and famous contributors. It was summed up as a far too ambitious business plan devised by people who knew nothing about magazines, with a management team from newspaper backgrounds. Publisher, editor, advertisement and circulation directors all resigned. As D'Argy Smith put it: "It was Ab Fab meets Fawlty Towers."

Brian Braithwaite, former director of National Magazines, wrote forthrightly in *The Press Book* (Peter Owen, 2009): "The world of women's magazines is not for underfinanced minnows." Eve Pollard told the trade press: "The barriers to entry for small independent publishers of upmarket, glossy magazines, is formidable."

[Eve's glittering career started from being a tea girl at *Honey* under Audrey Slaughter and led to editing two Fleet Street Sundays, the *Mirror* and *Express*; today she is honorary president of a prestigious group called Women in Journalism. Married to Sir Nick Lloyd, former editor of the *Daily Express*, her daughter from her first marriage is TV presenter Claudia Winkelman. She received an OBE for services to journalism in 2008.]

As *Aura* faded away, *Eve* appeared, a monthly aimed at the same audience and published by BBC Worldwide. Editor Gill Hudson joined *Eve* from *Maxim* (best-selling magazine for men launched in 1995 by Dennis Publishing and now, as *Maxim Digital*, is the largest young men's lifestyle brand in America reaching 4m a month). *Eve* launched its website with chat rooms seeking readers' opinions on female problems, film and book reviews. Gill was quoted as saying she didn't want to treat readers as a merchandising opportunity. But everyone else did.

Red and *Woman's Journal* were credited with starting the trend and, by 2004, all sorts of publications added covermounts – umbrellas, flip flops, sequinned sunhat, sun glasses, underwear, CDs, novels, gardening tools, even free software – so newsagents' shelves looked like gift shops. *Eve* was popular and a good read but as it had no direct link to BBC TV programmes it had to be sold. Bought by Haymarket (owned by Michael Heseltine) it found new impetus and did well until the global financial crisis near annihilated advertising revenue. Its end in 2008 devastated the small but dedicated staff among whom was Teresa Palmano, my co-worker at *Choice*.

* * *

Gill Hudson has an outstanding magazine CV: *New Woman* (which owners Bauer closed, also in 2008), *Company, Maxim, Eve, Radio Times,* and *Reader's Digest* UK just before the company went into administration. [Earlier, in 2008, Sarah Sands (formerly of *The Telegraph*, then editor of the London *Evening Standard,* followed by BBC Radio 4's *Today* programme which she left in September 2020) had tried to give the *Digest* (a favourite of dentists' waiting rooms) a sharper, contemporary feel but it didn't halt the circulation decline.]

Gill, after 10 years at BBC Magazines, knew the *Digest* needed investment to revive its fortunes (new subline: *small, but perfectly informed*). A management buyout and support from Better Capital (set up to put money in distressed companies) enabled her to get the new look and the columnists she wanted. In 2011 her efforts were rewarded when she was named Consumer Editor of the Year at the Periodical Publishers' Association awards, and won the British Society of Magazine Editors' Mark Boxer Award for her contribution to UK magazine publishing.

[Mark Boxer who died in 1988, aged 57, of a brain tumour, was founding editor of *The Sunday Times* Colour Supplement in 1962, was a cartoonist, and at the time of his death editorial director of Condé Nast Publications. He was married to Anna Ford, television journalist.]

It was fascinating to read that Gill had changed the 72-year-old magazine's focus to "a new generation of switched-on and self improving over 45s…who are media savvy, often still have children at home and are driven by the desire for knowledge and self improvement".

That sounded very familiar to me! I wondered if they were the children of the readers of *Womancraft* (which I edited in the 1970s) and *The Complete Cook* (1970s/1980s) or other information-expanding part works of yesteryear.

Sadly, the fortunes of the *Digest* soared then sank. The generation game was over. In February 2014 Better Capital wrote off £23m in investment over four years, saying "it's not worth the time and effort it now takes to run", and sold it for a nominal sum to Mike Luckwell, a 'media veteran' who had the idea of making it the magazine for 'go-ahead over 60s' (where have I heard that before? Hope certainly springs eternal in magazine publishing.). It survives online, selling by subscription.

In the 21st century older women are active online on the community sites Mumsnet and Gransnet where opinions are unrestrained, and subjects wide and varied. And traditional magazines like *The People's Friend* and *Yours* have an appreciative following. In 2019 newsagents saw a new arrival: *Platinum,* a glossy monthly from DC Thomson, Dundee, aimed at women over 55. At its launch the editor, Ali Kirker, said: "Women over 50 feel younger than ever today, but they also feel misrepresented by the media. They want to see things that inform and reflect their lives...*Platinum* will share the(ir) health obsession...challenge them to be bold and adventurous, inspire them to live life on full power."

How *Platinum* will fare in Covid crisis times remains to be seen. There were big drops in circulations in 2020, according to the web's *Mediatel.* Gardening and leisure publications were less affected than the women's market.

* * *

I retired at the millennium (thankfully before the Emap share price wavered) just as the web was coming into its own, bringing my working life in magazines and related publications to an end. But much was happening in the publishing world, the most dramatic being the desertion of Kings Reach, the smoked glass and aluminium buildings near Waterloo in London where so many magazines were created.

In 2001 the former IPC/Reed Elsevier – renamed IPC Media after the management buyout by Cinven – was gobbled up by Time Inc (the publishing subsidiary of Time Warner in the US) which paid £1.15b for the company. All the magazines moved to a new building on the South Bank of the Thames. "Don't take anything with you," the staff were told, "you'll have everything you need waiting for you." But more occurred later.

A publishing group in Bath called Future Plc, specialising in modern hobby magazines (featuring technology, gaming, photography and music), had tried to buy IPC Media but lost to Time Warner. According to the website *Flashes&Flames*, Future (which started in 1985) was then making a loss. But it kept its eyes on the prize.

In 2014 Time Warner became Time Inc UK, and in 2018 it was sold to a private equity firm, Epiris, and renamed TI Media. Its CEO Marcus Rich, ex Emap, over five years closed 10 magazines among them *Look*, *Now*, *Uncut*, *SoapLife*, *Marie Claire UK* and *InStyle* – all originally from the Ministry of Magazines.

Out of the blue, in 2019, Future pounced, paying £140m in cash for TI Media's (remaining) 40 magazines. This audacious act made it Europe's largest magazine group with revenue of more than £400m, twice the size of its closest UK rival, *Flashes&Flames* declared.

When you think of all the German, French and American wealth that flowed into British magazine publishing in the 20th century, it seemed astonishing that a UK company led the way in the 21st century. The deal, said *Flashes&Flames*, marked the end of a publisher which dominated UK magazines for more than 50 years.

But more was to come. Just as I thought my reminiscences were reaching an end, it all changed again. In November 2020, Future took over the comparison website GoCompare (GoCo) paying £594m in a cash and shares deal. Future's CEO Zillah Byng-Thorne, had sat on the Board of GoCo since 2017 and could see the way ahead. Future has been a winner in the pandemic as interest in hobbies and crafts increased during lockdown. It has the future sorted.

The second surprise occurred in Australia. Here German publishing giant Bauer dramatically bowed out of magazine publishing – "after wrecking the industry", according to mumbrella.com.au. "Good riddance," declared the website. The coronavirus crisis played a part. In July eight of the country's most famous magazines, suspended since April, were closed by the company : *Harper's Bazaar, Elle* and *InStyle*; *Men's Health, Women's Health* and *Good Health*; and *NW* and *OK*, wrote Tim Burrowes on *Mumbrella*). Some were published under licence from Hearst in the US.

Burrowes painted a sad picture of Bauer's "disastrous eight years" which began with the purchase in 2012 of "close to bankruptcy Nine Entertainment Co" owned by James Packer. "Soon the company known as Australian Consolidated Press, then ACP Magazines, before it absorbed Emap Australia and Pacific Magazines along the way, will change its name once more." In September 2020 Bauer's buyer, private equity firm Mercury Capital, rebranded the group as Are Media.

The jewel in the crown, *Australian Women's Weekly*, is still there, and despite the name is published monthly. In New Zealand, Bauer walked away from its entire stable of 11 magazines (including *NZ Woman's Weekly*, a weekly, published since the 1930s) and 237 staff. The NZ government offered to assist Bauer with subsidies but this was refused. Some were restarted by Are Media.

Burrowes was critical of the Hamburg-based company, led by Yvonne Bauer, which assumed it could replicate successful European business models. He referred to poor local management, citing "the notorious stint of CEO David Goodchild who continued to run H Bauer Publishing in the UK from the side of his desk too."

Bauer Australia had six CEOs in eight years, including Colin Morrison, ex-Emap and owner of the *Flash-es&Flames* website. Magazines closed during this time were *Cleo* (see Chapter 4), *Cosmopolitan*, *Top Gear*, *Zoo*, *Grazia*, *BBC Good Food* and *FHM*.

* * *

Collapsing circulations and losses lead to calamitous endings and the most vulnerable are often in the struggling women's lifestyle sector. In the UK 2004 was particularly bad: Emap closed *The Face*, *J17* (Just 17), and *Here's Health*. In 2013 *Zest* was closed by Hearst, *More!* by Bauer and *Easy Living's* print version by Condé Nast.

You can see why no one who becomes an editor can think of it as a job for life. In my time closures, illness and death removed some editors from their posts while others were jettisoned in dramatic 'night of the long knives' style. But what does being in the top job mean to the person?

David Durman, when he was editor-in-chief of IPC's Women's Group and launching *Now*, a new celebrities-and-sex magazine in 1996, told an interviewer that he'd edited *Woman* for six and a half years (he took over from Richard Barber who'd moved to *TV Times*). This was possibly 18 months too long according to the formula of

Jenny Greene who had experienced working in newspapers before joining a magazine.

A VIEW OF LIFE AT THE TOP

One of the magazines TI Media kept (and is now in the Future stable) was the long-lasting weekly *Country Life*. Jenny Greene, who had been beauty editor at *Woman's Own* under Jane Reed in the 1970s, edited this "quintessentially English magazine" (description on its website) with its mix of horses, architecture, art, personalities and society, from 1986 to 1992. Just before she retired, Jenny gave her views about how editors work: they spend the first year improving their magazines, the second getting rid of people who are in the way, the third coasting, the fourth looking for another job, and the fifth panicking because they haven't got one. A bit tongue in cheek perhaps – five years sounds a long time in today's world!

I read a different view of life at the top by Peggy Makins (*The Evelyn Home Story*, 1975) who was employed aged 21 as a subeditor by the first editor of *Woman*. "Miss Stuart Macrae was a dynamic Titian-haired lady, elegant, knowledgeable about food and drink, sophisticated and completely versed in traditional women's mag fare," she wrote. But "the men who engaged her couldn't bear to let her have her head". Too many times she had to remove a commissioned feature, to "substitute something more intellectual or educational which a bossy male felt ought to be served up to women readers for their own good." One of those males was John Dunbar, who I never met.

Poor Miss Macrae became a scapegoat for *Woman's* failure to surge ahead and Mary Grieve, a Glasgow journalist, was given the job of resuscitating the new magazine. Which she did very well indeed, for 22 years. MMG, as she was known, "was allowed to imprint her very definite personality on every page," wrote Peggy Makins.

One of the first innovations was a personal problems feature with the byline Evelyn Home, an 'aunties' page as it was called, which Peggy was in charge of until she retired nearly 40 years later. The Evelyn Home policy, according to Peggy, was a mix of the Ten Commandments, the Sermon on the Mount, and a working knowledge of the law in case you committed pornography [sic] or libel. [Anna Raeburn was her successor at *Woman*, writing under her own name as did another 'aunt' Virginia Ironside who was there when I was in the 1980s.]

If I'd known about Mary Grieve (she received an OBE in 1998, the year she died) I might not have thought I'd taken a step back in journalism when I started at *Woman's Own* in 1966. Then I regarded myself as a newspaper journalist. I was a rebel, against the Vietnam war, full of socialist ideals of equality (as was Mary Grieve, I learnt from her book *Millions Made My Story*, written after she retired). I didn't have a career progression plan and joined a magazine simply because I needed a job. It turned out to be a good move.

I was aware that publications produced for women had a long history and that the general intentions were to be of help and inspiration to their readers. For most the domestic/service element remained paramount – because that's what the advertisers wanted. This was revenue the publishers counted on. But readers' inclinations are the unknown quantity. They might not be satisfied with what went before and don't want the magazine their mothers read. Perhaps it is the successful editor who gives them what they think they want!

When the Germans and Spanish showed how to be popular with their short, targeted pieces and abundant pictures, *Woman's Own* and *Woman* then transformed themselves to look busy and colourful. Other magazines appeared with commanding names like *Pick Me Up!, Real, Reveal, Look, Closer* and *Now* – focused on celebrities. It is hard to find anything more than captions to read, some longer than others but how you could look and what you could wear are still a big part of the mix. Because that's all that women think about dontcha know!

Jane Bruton, who for 10 years edited Emap's very successful fashion-based *Grazia* before becoming deputy editor of *The Daily Telegraph*, revealed in an interview in *The Independent* in 2005 how she found her future. She said it was meeting Jo Foley, former editor of *Woman*, on a press trip to the Caribbean in 1993, that gave her the courage "to break out of honeymoon reporting for *Wedding and Home*". [Translation: writing up idyllic places for newly marrieds to stay.]

From her, she said, she learnt that "pictures must come first and you should be able to tell a story in 100 words". As you might not get even that many in the snippet-style editorial of today's weeklies and fortnightlies it seems to have been a universally shared epiphany.

* * *

How do others see the purpose of publications produced just for women? Cynthia White's conclusions in *Women's Magazines 1693–1968* included extracts from critical articles in the (male oriented) *Economist, New Statesman* and *Spectator* in the early 1960s which raise points pertinent to the next four decades:

"While they [give] women plenty of mainly sound advice on how to dress, eat, housekeep, have their babies and even make love, they have never attempted to tell them what to do with their minds."

"One would have thought that...a little social conscience might have been introduced into them, or at least an awareness of new things...for instance the new voices and new attitudes that have invaded the theatre."

"It seems to be assumed that the woman reader is not interested in savings, insurance, investments, stocks and shares. There is nothing about finance in her papers. There is nothing, either, about mortgages or leases, or the law of the landlord and tenant...There is nothing about jobs, careers or equal pay. Nor do the controversies about education penetrate her papers...I can find no reference to day nurseries, comprehensives, or university places."

The writers, all male, would have been lucky to find subjects like these in their own magazines. If I look back at the different ones I worked on, all the points were covered as time went by in many publications. By reading widely, women would find information to tackle problems of everyday living brought about by more and more wives and mothers joining the work force, working and housing conditions, childcare, ill health, disability, discrimination, marriage break-up and single parenthood. Finding solutions and encouraging resilience are part of the new 'woke' age of the worldwide web, feminism and multiculturalism. A 'magazine' is after all, in another context, a holder of ammunition.

* * *

As for me, when reading Cynthia White's book, my eye caught one particular quote (from a *New Statesman* article, April 24 1962) which struck an ominously personal note: "Woman had a social conscience once, when it was first launched – the social conscience of the late John Dunbar, then Editorial Director of Odhams and once a member of the I.L.P. [Independent Labour Party, disbanded in 1932].

"In 1937 Dunbar thought the magazine should deal with social problems as well as flower arrangements and fancy menus to tempt young husbands. Its sales dropped to a third. Not until Dunbar accepted the facts of life as they appertain to women's weeklies and freed it of its social conscience did its circulation rise. It is a lesson no one on women's magazines forgets."

I must have missed that issue of the *New Statesman* which I would have read in Australia when magazines never impinged on my journalistic plans. I'd like to have known about Mr Dunbar and his social conscience earlier. Was he wrong to want to focus on problems in society at the time? Were there other reasons why the sales dropped? Were the readers just not interested? Perhaps the subjects were not presented in an enticing way. Cynthia White's conclusion that removing its social conscience helped the circulation to rise could just be wrong. It might have been that Mary Grieve had the magic touch, providing material that readers wanted (and not being overpowered by Mr Dunbar).

There's no doubt that the magazines of the 20th century did inform and educate. And the specialists, in all sorts of areas, had an irrepressible ability to come up with inspiring contributions. My heroes are the consumer journalists who are like tigers in their pursuit of information to benefit readers and protect them from misunderstandings and downright obfuscation.

At *Choice* I discovered a passionate belief in enablement – providing ammunition so readers themselves could make changes they thought necessary to improve matters, better their lives and keep in good form and spirit. (The obverse of this, of course, is: you can take a horse to water, but you can't make it drink.) In this I was enabled by the talented people who worked for and contributed to the magazine.

With my old Dad's favourite dictum in my mind (Do unto others as you would have others do unto you), only now do I realise that underlying the *joie de vivre* I wanted to create in the pages, showing the wide and varied, positive, ways people in the third age lived, was something of Mr Dunbar's social conscience. I couldn't see any reason to make prejudices about ageing even more ingrained and divisive in society. Men and women in retirement can continue to achieve, enhance their communities, expand their experiences, live life to the full. That's the message that came across from the French and I embraced it.

* * *

The awful irony of longevity is that you don't know for how long you'll have good health and the coronavirus pandemic certainly gave a new, and tragic, slant to old age. In the US, ageing provided new marketing opportunities for Fox News, the American station much approved by Donald Trump that has made Rupert Murdoch and News Corporation powerful and outstandingly wealthy.

Tim Dickinson, writing in *Rolling Stone* magazine, looked at how Fox News became successful with the over 65s (the median age of the station's viewers): "Ads cater to the immobile, the infirm and the incontinent, with appeals to join class action hip-replacement lawsuits, commercials for products such as Colon Flow, and testimonials for the services of Liberator Medical: 'Liberator gave me back the freedom I haven't had since I started using catheters'." So graphic.

NEEDS ARE LIFE-LONG
It's worthwhile remembering what gerontologist Dr Alex Comfort said in his book *Good Age*: "As an old person you will need four things: dignity, money, proper medical services and useful work. They are exactly the things you always needed". With increased longevity already revealing major problems, it is to be hoped that the coming generations, and politicians in particular, will take the opportunity to reassess older life in this way.

While stairlifts and physical aids for older people were par for the course in *Choice* I really did think that the editorial – first hand, honed information about living well in the third age – was more illuminating. Was I naïve? Possibly. Was it the Australian in me that fell hook, line and sinker for the *Notre Temps* philosophy which is not to rail against but to relish the time you're in? To find the right tools for the battle against ageing and not accepting that debilitating illness is inevitable?

At retirement, I had a plan at the ready, learnt from one of the PRA's course directors, a charming man called Cecil Kellehar who had his 80th birthday when contributing to *Choice*. Always full of the joys of spring, after years in management and advising on retirement, he did a creative writing course and turned out poetry, skits and musical plays for children. [He died in 2005 aged 90.]

His three-pronged strategy is suitable for us all: someone to love, something to do, something to look forward to (which took a back seat in the pandemic unfortunately). It sums up involvement with family and friends, with your community, and planning ahead.

Of all the subjects that magazines have included, one has survived very well indeed: mind games! The puzzles sector occupies young and old, in newspapers, magazines, books and there's even a 'puzzling channel' on cable and satellite TV that is pay-to-play. According to Puzzler Media Ltd, leaders in this market, it started way back in 1973 when, as British European Associated Publishers (BEAP), they launched the revolutionary *Home & Freezer Digest* with Jill Churchill at the tiller.

The company grew like Topsy, and once they had the

European distribution rights to Sudoku, the fiendish non-words based puzzle, there was no stopping them – their first export market was Australia and New Zealand where they do very well despite all that's happening in publishing out there. The future, however, will be digital.

My grandchildren have grown up in the user-friendly age of technology and it is more natural to them than writing with a pen (unless it is the sort that can be used on a tablet). Canny publishers know this (an example is the success of *Teen Vogue* which does appear to have captured the spirit of youth). Their magazines are guided by the 'kagoy factor', an acronym for 'kids are getting older younger'. The oldies in my young days called this 'growing up too fast for your own good' – implying a lack of maturity – but back then we really did know little.

Girls were not as educated or informed as they are today and adults, probably because they didn't know the answers themselves, never discussed with us the emotional and physical effects of our changing hormones. It may have been painful learning on the go, even into adulthood, but I was fortunate in not having the number of accessible quagmires that are freely available now.

*   *   *

And I am glad that I became a journalist for my career opened the world to me. In following the fortunes of magazine publishing, I can trace my own: training as a reporter on free weekly papers owned by the Packer family in Sydney, then to New Zealand and later the UK where I worked for the big companies: IPC,

NatMags, Emap and Bauer. The circle was completed with Bauer taking over Australian Consolidated Press and Emap, both in the UK and the countries Down Under where my career began.

Overall, I would describe myself as a 'practical' journalist in that many of the publications I worked on gave instructions whether for knitting or cooking or gardening or keeping tabs on your pension and savings. Always my impetus – as it must be for all journalists – was curiosity allied to communication: explaining the who, how, when, where and why of any subject.

What took place during 2020 – the pandemic, the US Presidential Election and Brexit – all had the same things in common: confusing messages and falsehoods. It was all very well fact checking after the event, but the lies were hard to kill. When journalists challenged them, up went the cry 'fake news'! Eradicating them may be impossible.

Journalists take no oath but generally the aim is not to do any harm and to report honestly and fairly. Conflict can come when the publications that employ them have distinct biases that are instrumental in making facts and experts enemies rather than guides to understanding. For instance, the campaigns that produced Brexit and Trump revealed what are called 'ideological bubbles', where people expose themselves only to the views of those who think the same as they do.

Worryingly, these views may be based on 'agnotology', a word coined in 1995 by an historian at Stanford University in the US, to cover the study of how ignorance is deliberately produced! He was investigating the tobacco industry and came across "Cancer by the Carton", an article by the BBC's North America correspondent Alistair Cooke in *Reader's Digest* in 1952 which stated that scientists were publishing solid evidence of a link between smoking and cancer.

These indisputable facts from indisputable sources, however, were countered by the powerful tobacco lobby; it was many years before most countries accepted that smoking kills and that something had to be done about it. The modern equivalent is the anti-vaxxers in the coronavirus pandemic, the climate-crisis deniers, pollution creators, palm oil producers, and the soft drink industry and sugar and sweetener producers who are doing most to protect their products from being linked to worldwide health issues: overweight problems and the devastating increase in diabetes.

SAD DEVELOPMENTS
The ideological bubbles and dissemination of agnotology are among the saddest developments of my lifetime and all media is affected. Print versions of some highly respected newspapers are already in financial strife and it would be an added disaster if people stopped believing what is printed in them. (The obverse of that is: or believe what is printed in them, in the case of the provocative tabloids.)

My journalism training was very different from those who today learn via universities' media courses. But the world of communication has reached a very critical stage and those students must remember that whether they are read, or listened to, or watched, they are key to translating information for all. Their aim should be clarity, not bias, to be even handed. And to ensure that agnotology never gets the upper hand. It must never become the 'new normal'.

Even if I didn't know about John Dunbar and what happened to *Woman* magazine in 1937, nothing would have made me give up my social conscience. (I don't think you could be drawn to journalism if you didn't have one!) Caring about what happens to others will make a huge difference to the future of our children, grandchildren and the planet (and I really admire Greta Thunberg – another hero). My own comforting mantra is one to share: what Louis 'Satchmo' Armstrong sang in 1967:

> *"I hear babies cry, I watch them grow*
> *They'll learn much more than I'll ever know."*

I'm sure they'll find the ammunition to keep our wonderful world safe. As Greta says, it's the only one we've got.

ACKNOWLEDGMENTS

In the text I have given sources that I have referred to with regard to people and publications. The online Magforum was very useful as was Wikipedia, a great research site which relies on public contributions to survive and which I am happy to support financially. My thanks to Laurie Purden, Brenda Polan, Jose Northey, Gilly Cubitt, Angela Antrobus, Lorrie Spooner, Sarah Harrison, Petsa Kaffens and Dan Brotzel for their memories, Angelina Kalahari for her incisive self-publishing advice, my husband Ian Dear for his stalwart assistance, and Alan Reinl for his patience and unfailing support.

My book is a memoir, not a monograph about publishing, but I found a good perspective on what women read, and why, in *"They Opened Up a Whole New World"*: Feminine Modernity and the Feminine Imagination in Women's Magazines, 1919-1939, by Fiona Anne Seaton Hackney (thesis in partial fulfilment for the degree of Doctor of Philosophy, Goldsmith's College 2010).

SELECT INDEX OF PEOPLE

Complete Cook contributors: Clare Ferguson, Sheena Davis, Lorna Walker, Maria Bird, Elaine Bastable, Joyce Hughes, Carole Handslip, Jennifer Kay, Hilary Foster, Cathy Gallop

Womancraft contributors: Sylvia Madden, Shelagh Hollingsworth, Frances Rogers, Felicity Murray, Valerie Barrett, Christine Parsons, Caroline McDonald-Haig

Choice Your Rights contributors: Rebecca Smithers, Jill Papworth, Helen Garlick, Sue Ward, Andrew Bibby, Jo Cooper, Shirley Davenport

Printed in Great Britain
by Amazon